REVIEW 14

REVIEW

Volume   14   1992

Edited by

James O. Hoge
*Virginia Polytechnic Institute
and State University*

James L. W. West III
The Pennsylvania State University

University Press of Virginia

Charlottesville

THE UNIVERSITY PRESS OF VIRGINIA
Copyright © 1992 by the Rector and Visitors
of the University of Virginia

First published 1992

ISSN 1090-3233
ISBN 0-8139-1410-8

Printed in the United States of America

The editorial assistants for volume 14 of REVIEW are
LaVerne Kennevan Maginnis and Flora C. Buckalew,
both of The Pennsylvania State University.

PENN STATE   Virginia Tech

Funding for *Review* is provided by the generous gifts of Mr. and Mrs. Charles O. Gordon, Jr., Mr. and Mrs. Adger S. Johnson, and Mr. and Mrs. R. W. Mullins, Jr., to the Virginia Tech Foundation, and by a grant from the College of the Liberal Arts, The Pennsylvania State University.

Contents

Enlarging the Text   1
    by D. C. Greetham
       Review of Dave Oliphant and Robin Bradford, eds., *New Directions in Textual Studies*

Conrad, Ford, and the Eternity of Good Letters   35
    by George Core
       Review of Alan Judd, *Ford Madox Ford; The Collected Letters of Joseph Conrad, Volume 4, 1908–1911*, eds. Frederick R. Karl and Laurence Davies; Jeffrey Meyers, *Joseph Conrad: A Biography*

Singing the Blues: The Voices of Eighteenth-Century Bluestockings and Later Literary Women   45
    by Janet Ray Edwards
       Review of Sylvia Harcstark Myers, *The Bluestocking Circle: Women, Friendship, and the Life of the Mind in Eighteenth-Century England*; Judy Simons, *Diaries and Journals of Literary Women from Fanny Burney to Virginia Woolf*

Not So Idle Tears: Re-Reading the Renaissance Funeral Elegy   57
    by Ronald Strickland
       Review of Dennis Kay, *Melodious Tears: The English Funeral Elegy from Spenser to Milton*

Professionalism and Women Writers in Victorian America   73
    by Susan Albertine
       Review of Susan Coultrap-McQuin, *Doing Literary Business: American Women Writers in the Nineteenth Century*

Of Making Many Books on Chaucer   87
  by D. S. Brewer
    Review of Peter Brown and Andrew Butcher, *The Age of Saturn: Literature and History in* The Canterbury Tales; Katherine Heinrichs, *The Myths of Love: Classical Lovers in Medieval Literature;* Erik Hertog, *Chaucer's Fabliaux as Analogues;* Charles A. Owen, Jr., *The Manuscripts of* The Canterbury Tales; Lee Patterson, *Chaucer and the Subject of History;* Sabine Volk-Birke, *Chaucer and Medieval Preaching Rhetoric for Listeners in Sermons and Poetry;* Katharine M. Wilson and Elizabeth M. Makowski, *Wykked Wyues and the Woes of Marriage: Misogamous Literature from Juvenal to Chaucer*

Vital Signs: Humanist Scholarship, Literary Theory,
and the Body of Knowledge   101
  by L. M. Findlay
    Review of Alvin Kernan, *The Death of Literature*

Coleridge and the Retreat from Democracy   115
  by Norman Fruman
    Review of John Morrow, *Coleridge's Political Thought: Property, Morality, and the Limits of Traditional Discourse*

The Refeminization of Dickinson   135
  by Bruce Michelson
    Review of Judy Jo Small, *Positive as Sound: Emily Dickinson's Rhyme;* Joanne Feit Diehl, *Women Poets and the American Sublime;* Mary Loeffelholz, *Dickinson and the Boundaries of Feminist Theory*

The Body and the Body Politic in Lawrence   143
  by Virginia Hyde
    Review of James C. Cowan, *D. H. Lawrence and the Trembling Balance;* Tony Pinkney, *D. H. Lawrence and Modernism*

Contents   ix

E Pluribus Unum   155
  by Ilan Stavans
    Review of Earl E. Fitz, *Rediscovering the New World: Inter-American Literature in a Comparative Context*

Wallace Stevens: Toward an Erotics of Place   173
  by Milton J. Bates
    Review of Barbara M. Fisher, *Wallace Stevens: The Intensest Rendezvous;* Margaret Dickie, *Lyric Contingencies: Emily Dickinson and Wallace Stevens*

The Cambridge Conrad   183
  by James M. Haule
    Review of Joseph Conrad, *The Secret Agent: A Simple Tale,* eds. Bruce Harkness and S. W. Reid

Science Fiction in the Nineteenth Century   191
  by John R. Pfeiffer
    Review of Mary Shelley, *The Mary Shelley Reader,* eds. Betty T. Bennett and Charles E. Robinson; Anthony Trollope, *The Fixed Period,* ed. R. H. Super; Andrew Martin, *The Mask of the Prophet, The Extraordinary Fictions of Jules Verne;* Lyman Tower Sargent, *British and American Utopian Literature, 1516–1985;* Everett F. Bleiler, with the assistance of Richard J. Bleiler, *Science-Fiction, The Early Years*

Edith Wharton's Network   205
  by Elizabeth Ammons
    Review of Candace Waid, *Edith Wharton's Letters from the Underworld: Fictions of Women and Writing;* Susan Goodman, *Edith Wharton's Women: Friends and Rivals*

The Magic Hand of Chance: Keats's Poetry in Facsimile   213
  by Susan J. Wolfson
    Review of *John Keats: Poetry Manuscripts at Harvard, A Facsimile Edition,* ed. Jack Stillinger, with an Essay on the Manuscripts by Helen Vendler

A Defense of Thomas More against Modern Revisionism   225
  by Philip C. Dust
    Review of Louis L. Martz, *Thomas More: The Search for the Inner Man*

True Fairy Tales   231
  by Alan Richardson
    Review of Jeanie Watson, *Risking Enchantment: Coleridge's Symbolic World of Faery*

The Body-Soul Topos in English Literature:
The Evolution of a Literary Motif   239
  by Mona Logarbo
    Review of Rosalie Osmond, *Mutual Accusation: Seventeenth-Century Body and Soul Dialogues in their Literary and Theological Context*

A New Dreiser Biography—For Our Time   259
  by Frederick C. Stern
    Review of Richard Lingeman, *Theodore Dreiser: At the Gates of the City, 1871–1907;* Richard Lingeman, *Theodore Dreiser: An American Journey, 1908–1945*

Byron in Context   271
  by Malcolm Kelsall
    Review of Peter W. Graham, *"Don Juan" and Regency England*

Varieties of Blasphemy: Feminism and the Brontës   281
  by Peter Allan Dale
    Review of Irene Tayler, *Holy Ghosts: The Male Muses of Emily and Charlotte Brontë*

Contributors   305

Editorial Board

Felicia Bonaparte
City College, CUNY

George Bornstein
University of Michigan

Anthony J. Colaianne
Virginia Polytechnic Institute and State University

Paul Connolly
Bard College Center

Geoffrey Day
Winchester College

Alan Filreis
University of Pennsylvania

T. H. Howard-Hill
University of South Carolina

D. C. Greetham
CUNY Graduate Center

James R. Kincaid
University of Southern California

Pierre Michel
Université de Liège

Peter L. Shillingsburg
Mississippi State University

G. Thomas Tanselle
John Simon Guggenheim Memorial Foundation

Stanley Weintraub
The Pennsylvania State University

Enlarging the Text

D. C. Greetham

Dave Oliphant and Robin Bradford, eds. *New Directions in Textual Studies*. Introduction by Larry Carver. Austin: Harry Ransom Humanities Research Center/University of Texas at Austin, 1990. 187 pp.

There was a telling moment during the 1989 conference of which this volume is the proceedings. During the question period following D. F. McKenzie's paper on "Speech-Manuscript-Print" a member of the audience asked the speaker to comment on what might be the traditional intentionalist view of the social issues raised in the paper. Given his non-intentionalist stance, McKenzie quite properly demurred about taking the question and asked the audience at large to respond. Silence. This silence, the unwillingness of anyone in the audience to act as public spokesman for traditional intentionalism, says much about the gathering itself, much about the proceedings, and much about the Kuhnian "paradigm shift" that one of the contributors, Hans Walter Gabler, draws attention to (p. 154)—a shift from an author-centred textual criticism whose main purpose was the recovery of what the writer had actually written or intended to write to a social or reception-based model emphasizing the significance of the transmission of the text and its role as physical artifact, bearing meaning in what Jerome McGann has called "bibliographical codes" (the physical means of presenting a text) as well as in the more familiar "linguistic codes" (the verbal text itself), long the focus of most textual studies. It is not, of course, that traditional intentionalist textual critics have not considered the evidence of the physical artifact, for the growth—indeed the dominance—of analytical bibliography earlier this century was premised on the influence of the technology of print on the form and content of the text. But while recognizing that readers' responses can be influenced by such features as type design and layout, intentionalist critics like G. Thomas Tanselle have frequently drawn a cordon around this bibliographical "meaning," declaring that "if one is reconstructing texts intended by their authors, one generally need not preserve these features of documents, for they are not, except in unusual cases, part of the intended texts."[1]

Tanselle was not present at the Texas conference and is not, therefore, included in the proceedings. This is unfortunate but perhaps inevitable, given the charged language of Larry Carver's introduction, for after what has by now become the familiar rhetorical topos of the "separation of editing from literary criticism" (a *planctus* contradicted by the contents of the volume and by much else written in the last few years), Carver proceeds to a brief analysis of the supposed orthodoxy of the formalist texts produced under the auspices of the New Criticism (although he does not articulate how such formalism was, perhaps ironically, co-terminous with intentionalism). Whether such orthodoxy was ever as entrenched as Carver maintains is open to some doubt, and the position can only be sustained at all if one restricts the coverage to Anglo-American textual scholarship, ignoring what was going on in European textual circles; but if the orthodoxy of the uneasy marriage between formalism and intentionalism is now over, what has, and what will, take its place? The Texas volume is an attempt to answer this question—hence the plural "Directions" in its title. But its pluralist credentials are not as tenable as its editors might have hoped.

Take the matter of the bibliographical codes. Tanselle's *Rationale*, just quoted from, is an austere artifact. It bears only the intended text of its author, and even abstains from the heavy documentation often associated with Tanselle's work. It has no illustrations, no notes, and no visual devices inviting the reader's eye to make interpretations of its bibliographical codes. This is all quite proper in a linguistic text-based critic. But *New Directions* is quite another sort of book: it has almost fifty very handsome

Enlarging the Text

illustrations, most of them drawn from the rich holdings of the Harry Ransom Research Center and thus intended to document and advertise those riches, and all of this is complemented by numerous fanciful illustrations in Randall McLeod's essay on Harington's Ariosto. But the illustrations in the volume are not *merely* illustrative, for in most cases the authors depend upon the visual component to make their arguments—indeed, McLeod makes much of the reader's willing participation in the visual games (e.g., puns) which would be unintelligible and unnoticeable in a non-visual medium. In only the last two essays, by Gabler and Anne Middleton, does one feel that the illustrations, delightful though they may be, are primarily decorative and do not add much to the argument. But in even these cases, the authors specifically discuss the significance of the spatial and the visual, with Gabler defending the inclusive synoptic method of textual display and Middleton provocatively discussing the "marginal" status of annotation.

What is going on here, and is it all just an accident of the conference's fortunate location? I think not, and I would use McGann's terms to explain it. Despite Carver's insistence on the plural directions embodied in the book, the bibliographical codes in their very existence demonstrate one of the persistent themes of the essays—that texts achieve meaning not only in their linguistic codes, as the intentionalists would have it, but in their social, cultural, and visual function as bearers of coded significance. As the following analysis of the essays will make clear, there are several themes, several predispositions prevalent in the book: that texts are visual, that texts have accumulated meaning in their transmission as artifacts, that texts are socially as well as authorially constructed, and that the main focus of textual critics should not necessarily be on editing, or at least not on editing as conceived by the traditional eclecticists. It is even possible to observe an "anti-editing" school at work in the essays, even an "anti-reading" (where McLeod, for example, declares that he has been trying not to *read* Harington's Ariosto in order to *see* it better). Thus, despite Carver's attempt in the introduction to enlist McKenzie as an intentionalist (describing an essay primarily concerned with the social validity of the three media—speech, manuscript, and print—and documenting persuasively the gradually increasing absence of the author from one medium to the next) the Texas volume does not effectively cover all the "directions" that textual criticism might take. In its concentration on the social it is remarkably similar to the collection (*Textual Criticism and Literary Interpretation*) edited by Jerome McGann in 1985 which is, like the present volume, the proceedings of a conference. Like the McGann book, it is a fascinating, provocative, and always enlightening demonstration of the implications of a textual theory, but unlike the earlier volume it seems mercifully free of misprints and other evidence for post-authorial meaning.

It is appropriate that McGann, as the primary theorist for this and the earlier collection, should begin both conference and proceedings. His essay "How To Read a Book" is in large part a now-familiar exposition of the principle that texts are to be read for their physical as well as their linguistic content, applied in this case to such disparate "texts" as Pound's *Cantos* and "Reagan's Farewell," the latter a formal, indeed ritualized TV "event" in which meaning could not reside in words, for none could be heard above the noise of the departing chieftain's helicopter as the mock "news conference" became a game of non-communication. McGann sees in this oft-repeated charade the fourth estate's complicity in the construction of a non-linguistic meaning, but while one can appreciate the humour of the self-serving play at failed linguistic codes, the ritual itself is only a version of the many social acts to which an agreed meaning has been attached, from handshakes to coronations. It does not tell us much about books, unless we concede that books are simply events in the great social text of the new historicists, an admission specifically rejected by defenders of bibliographical intentionalism. McGann is thus on more secure ground in his discussion of his other text, the Pound *Cantos,* but even here he does not fully overcome the suspicion that the *Cantos* are an extreme case, different in intent and form from what we might normally designate a book-text. McGann makes much of the phenomenological rather than linguistic content of the Chinese ideograms, functioning as visual "figures of stability" in Pound's layout, a "gestalt for organizing the way the eye will scan the page" (p. 22). Indeed, but is it not the very fact that the typical Western reader will not be able to give a linguistic content to the ideograms that allows Pound this semiotic luxury? An English-speaking Chinese reader would presumably respond quite otherwise to the display, and as a mediaevalist, I'm reminded of the runic letters embedded in Caedmon's poems to spell out his name, in a display that would have been recognized both linguistically and visually by his audience, and I'm also reminded of a conversation with Hugh Kenner some years ago in which he talked of the peculiar visual and linguistic problems of producing an Italian translation of the *Cantos,* in which the Italian quotations in the original text would have to become—what?—English (to mark off their "difference" from the Italian context) or Italian (to be faithful to Pound's "quotation," which was in any case often a mis-quotation)?

McGann's discussion of Pound is thus a fascinating tour de force of critical exposition, but I am left with some doubts: are the theoretical implications he tries to draw from this rather peculiar case really as far-reaching as he would have us suppose? For example, the very large claim that "all poetry, even in its most traditional forms, asks the reader to decipher the text in spatial as well as linear forms" (p. 25) does not withstand scrutiny. To begin with, much "traditional" poetry is oral not literary and has no immediately spatial component at all, beyond the dramatic re-enactment, which is in any case linear because it occurs more in time than in space. This fact does not presumably render such poetry less "poetic." And the bibliographical codes of much early verse in manuscript will not support McGann's contention: the *Beowulf* poetic manuscript, like many Old English and classical-language manuscripts, renders the text as continuous prose, so that it is not the eye but the ear which produces the sense of form; and the ear can do this only linearly, for it must accustom itself to the dominant alliterative sound in a sequence of phonic "events" before it can perceive the shape of the verse. The phenomenology of such a poetics, and the bibliographical codes in which it is represented, are far removed from McGann's visual, spatial metaphor.

I will concede that the examples I have drawn are "special" cases, but no more "special" than Pound or Reagan. I will concede that in literate and print cultures we are trained to expect a correlation between spatial phenomena and meaning (even genre). Thus, before Charlton Hinman demonstrated that the broken, free-form verse lines of certain outer leaves of the First Folio *Timon of Athens* depended upon errors in casting off copy[2] (and that the lines were in fact prose) it was doubtless possible for critics to "read" these lines spatially, as poetry, but incorrectly so. I am also persuaded, by the work of such textual scholars as James McLaverty[3] and David Vander Meulen,[4] that discriminating authors like Pope exerted a control over the spatial phenomena of their works (for example, by Pope issuing his translations of Homer in different formats for different audiences, and playing upon the layout of the contemporary scholarly edition as part of the satire in the *Dunciad*). I am similarly persuaded by McGann's work on Byron, on Arnold, on Blake[5] (and on Pound) that authors and readers can invest texts with visual codes, codes that can change as the intended or perceived meanings of the poems change. These are valuable insights, but they are not the single key to unlocking meaning. The weakness of McGann's argument is not in the perceptive, illuminating, and always provocative analysis of the texts he selects, but in the assumed presence of those he does not, in the invocation of the word *all*. Paradoxically, while McGann is the major theorist of this and other volumes, he is, I believe, a finer and more discriminating practical critic than he is a theorist, as his careful and enlightening critique of Pound demonstrates.

Given McGann's generally hostile view of the typical eclectic critical edition, it is perhaps surprising to learn that it is this sort of edition which best exemplifies the other main argument in his essay—that since language itself is a "constructive acquisition" (p. 28), it should not be treated as if it were natural, and thus that a style of reading which embodies this constructed quality best represents the act of acquisition and making of meaning, whereby a text is an "enactment" (p. 27) rather than a received and fixed narrative. McGann designates this constructed, re-enacted reading as "radial" rather than linear, and he finds the typical critical edition as an ideal site for such reading because it tends to forbid linear progression by its drawing the eye of the reader to other, competing codes beyond those of the text proper. The apparatus, textual notes, glossary, index, list of line-end hyphens—all of this scholarly paraphernalia prevents or interrupts the sort of direct, linear reading we bring to the comparatively simple decoding of, say, popular fiction.

Well, perhaps, but even here there are degrees of "radiation." McGann tends to treat the genre of scholarly edition as if it were a uniform, accepted, spatial format, and insofar as such editions look like the parody in the *Dunciad,* then we can accept the spatial, radial metaphor. But there is surely an irony in the fact that the dominant scholarly, critical editions of the last few decades (and particularly those produced under CEAA/CSE auspices) have in their visual, spatial presentation attempted to occlude or even deny radial reading. Thus, the clear-text edition favoured by the Greg-Bowers dispensation (against which McGann has fought so strenuously) does not look like the *Dunciad;* on the contrary, its very deliberate spatial hierarchy encourages the reader to stay in the clear-text pages of the "text itself" and to turn to the "paraphernalia" only in dire need, for the rejected readings of textual apparatus and other marks of scholarly diligence are buried, almost always in smaller print as a mark of their inferior status, at the back of the book. Far from this sort of scholarly edition's *encouraging* of radial reading, as McGann claims, its very spatial hierarchy tries to prevent it, substituting faith in editorial judgement for direct readerly control and construction of meaning. (For a recent project, it took me several hours to reconstruct the second-edition readings from the apparatus of the Northwestern-Newberry edition of Melville's *Typee,* and even in some inclusive-text rather than clear-text editions, like the Kane-Donaldson *Piers Plowman,* it is impossible, from the text-page evidence, to reconstruct a complete tabulation of variants—and this failure has been one of the criticisms levelled against the editorial sleight of hand committed by such editions.)

None of this is to say that the evidence of critical editions cannot be used by a reader in the sort of radial reading that McGann envisages. I share Jo Ann Boydston's enthusiasm for apparatus[6] and would hope that radial reading is what we might all strive for. But to turn McGann's language on its head, I doubt that radial reading is as "natural" to the critical edition as he supposes, and I would claim that typical critical editions of both clear and inclusive modes may fail, sometimes quite deliberately, in their promise of an expansive, non-linear reading. The radial reading of a critical edition, particularly a clear-text eclectic edition, has to be just as "constructed" as is any reading of any text, and I note that Boydston, despite her enthusiasm for apparatus, had sadly to note that the riches of such scholarly research seemed to be largely ignored, for she could find not a single example of any critical work based on the vast and comprehensive apparatus of the thirty-nine volumes of her Dewey edition.[7] This paucity is not as noticeable in my own field, where the apparatus of Kane-Donaldson's edition has been used by such critics as David Fowler[8] and Charlotte Brewer[9] to demonstrate the inadequacies (and even the fraudulence, in the eyes of such critics) of the editors' reporting of variants. But the Kane-Donaldson is an inclusive text, unlike the CEAA/CSE editions, and therein may lie the difference. The problem with McGann's paradoxically naturalistic argument is that it ignores the function of hierarchy and privilege in typography, layout, and bibliographical position, a strange omission in a critic whose basic textual philosophy depends on an acknowledgment of such features.

Thus, McGann's claims notwithstanding, it may be that, despite our scholarly hopes for radiation, a critical edition of the clear-text model is quite as "self-absorbed" (to use McGann's phrase) as a Harlequin bodice-ripper. This distinction between the self-absorbed, a limited reading-field discouraging a reader's construction of text, and the radial and expansive reading-field McGann associates with critical editions is an important one and in its articulation in this essay sounds very much like Barthes's distinction between the *lisible* "readerly" text (the closed field) and the *scriptible* "writerly" (open field), and I would have liked to see McGann use his customary critical intelligence to draw further on the distinction in these Barthesian terms. The problem, however, is that Barthes himself plays on the difference, for in his best-known "radial" reading of a text—*S/Z*'s chopping up of Balzac's *Sarrasine* into independent *lexias* or reading units, and his reading of them against the linear "grain" of the Balzac novel[10]—he demonstrates that he can take an apparently naturalistic, clearly narrative closed text, far removed from the opentext play of such works as *Tristram Shandy* or *Ulysses,* and subject it to the *scriptible,* radial approach. In other words, the distinction is, like McGann's, finally a matter of the reader/critic's determination of the genre and style of the work: there is nothing intrinsic or "natural" to text or work. It is, I believe, McGann's failure to observe the Barthesian implications of his neat dichotomy, and his paradoxical invocation of the "natural" in his comments on *all* poetry, that together undermine the validity of his perceptions in this essay. On the one hand, he does not go far enough in exploring the characteristics he notes, and on the other he goes too far in his claims for his theory.

None of these criticisms should, however, suggest that this introductory manifesto to the Texas volume is inadequate or misguided. As ever, McGann gives us a fascinating series of insightful readings of problematic texts, and extends the reach of textual theory in so doing. All textual critics will be forever grateful to him for the way he has stirred up the textual world in the last decade, and this essay is a distinguished addition to an already distinguished roster. My cavils are only to point to areas that yet need attention for his work to achieve its fuller implementation.

I have spent some time analyzing McGann's introductory essay because, as I suggested earlier, its principles and assumptions underlie much of what is to follow. This does not make the likes of McKenzie, Warren, Gabler, and Willison into mere acolytes of McGann, for each has constructed a specific field, a specific type of textual enterprise, that has advanced textual study during the last few years. But as a group the remaining essays in this volume can be seen as exemplifying various demurrals to intentionalism and eclecticism, and can thus be treated as further commentary on the debate initiated by McGann in this volume.

Michael Warren's essay "The Theatricalization of Text: Beckett, Jonson, Shakespeare" follows the argument we might expect from the editor/constructor/producer/historian of the "complete" *King Lear*,[11] that long a-borning project to lay before the reader the fragments of text, in their original typography, that constitute all the competing states of the play. This edition, unlike Stephen Booth's edition of the Sonnets[12] (in which the facing pages of modern and original typography dramatize what McGann calls the "historical gap" [p. 30]), sacrifices such drama for the authenticity of the contemporary, in which the editor becomes an arranger and designer, attempting thereby to efface the mediating role in what Donaldson has properly called an "editorial death-wish,"[13] and is an instance of what I have already noted as an anti-editing school among the participants of the conference. Warren's *King Lear*, which was still not available at the time of the Texas conference, has now appeared, unfortunately at the prohibitive cost of $230, which vitiates its original purpose as a student's "do-it-yourself" kit for making the play called *King Lear;* but such are the realities of scholarly publishing. The kit form obviously emphasizes what Warren calls in his essay the "provisionality of all text" (p. 57, citing the Oxford Shakespeare, and specifically the two texts of *Lear* in that edition, as his evidence), although Warren might also have noted that the largesse of the Oxford editors does not extend to providing the provisionality of other disputed texts: there is only one *Hamlet* in Oxford, not two, or three, and the Oxford editors have not, therefore, uniformly surrendered the traditional prerogatives of literary text-makers in all cases.

From this principle of provisionality Warren draws very large conclusions, amongst which is the generalization that "the nature of theater and the nature of editing produce contrary impulses" (p. 58), whereby he identifies editing not only as a literary as opposed to a performing or oral medium but also as a genre demanding "certainty." Such a model of editing might be that determinative one often assumed by literary critics in their disdain for the Dryasdusts of traditional philology, but does Warren include his own editorial work on *Lear* in this model, the synoptic method of Gabler's Joyce, or the other (genetic, textological) alternatives to clear-text eclecticism? Well, no, he doesn't, for the rest of his essay is a paean to the "need to transcend the limitations of the ideal text format" (p. 58) and an endorsement of such advances as electronic hypertext, to break with "the platonic ideal text" (p. 59). Any demurrals? Not in this company.

And yet there are problems in the formulation of this wish-list. Warren claims that editing is (or has been) largely a "function of book production, the materiality of bookness" (p. 59), and that this consciously literary function has obscured the theatricality of performed texts. He does admit, as he has to, that some dramatic texts were always "potentially literary" (p. 40), citing Jonson as the obvious example—Shaw would be another—and noting that in his alterations to the quarto texts of *Every Man In His Humour* and *Every Man Out of His Humour* for the folio collected *Works* Jonson was in effect attempting to "suppress" the quarto texts, so great were his "aspirations to the classic and the lapidary" (p. 46). None of this is news or a particularly radical rethinking of the history of dramatic texts, but Warren's compounding of the formula so that editing becomes only material, and improperly so, whereas drama or performance is resiliently insubstantial and uncertain, misrepresents the dual history of theatricality and text. As a first quibble, I might note the obvious: a text-page can be a good deal more hospitable to variance than can a stage. As my colleague Steven Urkowitz has often reminded me, a play director must know who is speaking what lines to whom and cannot afford the luxury of multiple or parallel texts. To invoke McGann's principle of radial reading here: I can imagine the simultaneous, spatial, radial, contradictory, and variant literary *reading* of a play text, but find it very hard to visualize a similarly unfixed simultaneous and variant and insubstantial *performance* of a play: stage left devoted to the quarto *Lear* and stage right to the folio, just like the parallel texts of Warren's edition? I'm being deliberately simple-minded in this misinterpretation of Warren's position, of course, but the earnestness of his rejection of book over theatricality and his endorsement of the inevitable fixity of the former over the fluidity of the latter needs further questioning.

To take an example from his favourite play, *King Lear,* what would Warren do with the performance history of that play during the eighteenth century, with its happy ending (Lear living on to a respected old age and Cordelia married off to Edgar), a performance history at odds with the textual, editorial history of the play during the same period, in which *Lear* retained its tragic, if insupportable ending, albeit in a conflated textual state? And an example I have cited elsewhere from music: the last word in the edited score of Berg's opera *Lulu* is Geschwitz's dying *Ewigkeit* "eternity," followed only by the notated "sigh" of her death. However, in the first (and apparently all subsequent) productions of the full three-act version, Geschwitz sings the non-authorial word *Verflucht* "Cursed" to this notated sigh, a word derived not from Berg but from Berg's source Wedekind, and a word which changes the entire meaning of the lesbian relationship and even the genre of the opera. The "theatrical" version in both these cases is indeed insubstantial and resolutely non-bookish, but it is not prima facie evidence for the inferiority of an "edition" compared to theatrical performance. I am aware that Warren would probably respond by asserting that his electronic text could take care of such variance, and I welcome the hospitality of the medium, but I am still somewhat disturbed by the inferred hierarchy in his formulation that would downplay the significance of the literary edition.

Moreover, the motto that Warren accepts for his style of anti-editing—"Nothing to be done," from Beckett's *Godot*—seems again to take refuge in Donaldson's editorial death-wish, as if electronic editing were a purely passive activity, one in which texts and variants come and go in a vague, almost hallucinatory state. As John Miles Foley demonstrated some years ago in his computer program HEURO for the editing of Yugoslav oral epics,[14] electronic editing is if anything more invasive, more productive, more dictatorial than is conventional book-editing. It may not produce single editions of single texts, but it does not mean that there is *nothing* to be done—quite the contrary.

Despite his own valuable work in making materiality available, Warren finds the concrete form of books objectionable. To Randall McLeod, however, it is this very materiality and concreteness that is to be celebrated. Like McGann, McLeod attends most assiduously to bibliographical codes, but unlike McGann he rejects, or tries to avoid attending to, the linguistic codes: "I can't I I I I can't simultanusly read I can't *read* a book I can't *READ* a book and **LOOK** at it at the same time" (p. 61). And his essay, indeed much of McLeod's career to date, has been spent looking rather than reading, perceiving the meanings of typeface and design rather than the meaning of the linguistic "text" proper.

Not only does he comment on the physical rather than the linguistic features of text and book, he actually produces these meanings in his own texts, and this essay is a particularly rich and evocative (or irritating and disruptive, depending on your taste) example of vintage McLeod. He seizes the advantage offered by the visual hospitality of his Texas editors, and includes, not just illustrations of several pages from the Harington Ariosto pertinent to his discussion, but also a continual visual gloss on his text: thus a reference to the Oxford edition of Harington produces an illustration of an ox in a ford, with the caption "OX FORD" (exemplifying the "textual gap" opening in the Oxford edition), balanced by a later illustration of a Norwegian fjord (without fauna), bearing the caption "OX FJORD no bull." But the visual component is not just a commentary, not just the raw materials on which a bibliographical argument is based, it is also the very raison d'être of McLeod's style. Thus, the title of the essay "from Tranceformations in the Text of 'Orlando Furioso,'" in addition to emphasizing that the published essay is only a part of the address given at the conference, makes a visual pun (Tranceformations) that could not be appreciated in another medium (and certainly not in the oral medium of the conference). His text is full of visual plays like "I recoiled Lyndon Johnson's cruel joke," "the Brothers wouldintone," and "I seemed always to mi shear"—the last of which is almost impossible to pronounce with any surety and makes sense only as a visual dislocation. In his use of typographic display and pun, his dense system of allusion, and his stream of consciousness style, McLeod is the paradigmatic modernist textual critic. In fact, his prose can often read like a belated version of Joyce or Woolf.

My logoeccentric educ—well, no sooner do I pick up a book (this was my *earliest* training, you understand) than I fall into
which I now have a name for: "The Missionary Position of Reading." *Sit in chair back very straight hands above board feet on floor.* Both *hands above board. Light falls onto page over left shoulder* (just as it does when I am in the other proper posiBut I *never ever* am to *write* in my book.) *Open front cover eye begins tracking rightwords from upper left along horizontal of the—* "typefaith," I seemed always to mi shear. "Parallel to the Earth's Horizon," the Brothers wouldintone. "Book as *Geo*metry, for God gave man two Books, but they are One." *Title, By, Author's name, Publisher's, ISBN, Copy*right down to the "End" and the "." of "The End.". Period. [p. 61]

What is going on here, and does textual scholarship really benefit from or need such display? While McLeod may be no Joyce, his prose is nonetheless meaning-ful. Thus, the quasi-biblical phrase "God gave man two Books, but they are One" presumably refers to the famous McLeod collator, whereby two images from two different copies of the same edition are optically superimposed to reveal discrepancies—illustrated (upside down, of course) on page 62. Two books "become" one. And, just as the physical form of the Texas volume as a whole makes a rhetorical point about its argument, so McLeod's visual style, his typographic and illustrative jokes, emphasizes his message: that books must not be read as if they were just texts, they must be *seen* as artifacts as well. The problem for the reader is that not only does the often dense bibliographical argument have to be followed carefully in order not to miss McLeod's artful demonstrations, but the bibliographer's own prose and display also have to be de-coded. It can be frustrating, but it can also be rewarding, as one does to McLeod what he is doing to Harington.

And this, I believe, is the point of it all. Just as Geoffrey Hartman (in *Criticism in the Wilderness*) and other post-structuralists have insisted that criticism is not different in nature from the literature that is its ostensible subject, all of it being subsumed under *écriture,* so McLeod is claiming for his brand of textual criticism—and perhaps for all—that our criticism *is* also literature, not merely a commentary on it: the two are infolded on each other. Sometimes this is literally so, as when McLeod first alludes to Proust ("At first I did very well in the Combray school. I was training to be a textual editor" [p. 62]), and then, a couple of

Enlarging the Text

pages later, folds overlapping (and therefore "unreadable") strips of Proust's text into his own—presumably deriving the Proust from the Modern Library edition, a part of whose logo appears upside down in the gutter of an earlier page, with *possibly* an extract from the dustjacket of *Swann's Way* (the text is so fragmented, like a frail piece of the Dead Sea scrolls, that its content cannot be fully determined—and that is the point).

The modernist mode of McLeod's writing is specifically acknowledged when he cites Joyce as a latter-day Harington: "it all seems familiar now because I've watched Harington froglic in the same tradition, invoking the downright heness of the male, by playing with his letters. Who says Joyce is an innovator? Redefine the Renaissance, and she's a tradictionalist" (p. 64). And that is what McLeod is out to do—to redefine the Renaissance and its texts, to show authors, compositors and readers playing with their letters, just as now he plays with his. He must act as visual translator over the great chronological divide, for "Renaissance books use different visual codes than ours. And not just neutrally different codes, but pointedly different, because we arrived at our codes by undoing theirs!" (p. 76).

It's an enormous task, to make us unlearn our spatial habits and observe those of a distant culture and understand their semiotic systems, and on the way to this understanding we will, according to McLeod, have to jettison our editorial pretensions. In this insistence, he is similar to Warren and his suspicion of critical editing. The essay is full of announcements of the impropriety and imminent demise of editing ("Editing means you have to take charge of the text" [p. 67], "photography has killed editing. Period. (*Someone* has to tell the editors)" [p. 72], "Indeed, what rationale can there be for editing? Indeed, what rationale can there be for editing?" [p. 76, repetition, *sic*], "*Someone* has to tell the editors that *critical* editions suck" [p. 76], "Once we know how the text is struggling to be itself, who will remain enchanted with the single-minded fix of modern editions?" [p. 84]). Like Warren, he is thereby displaying a very limited view of the aims, procedures, and results of modern editing, and identifying the various revisionary, fragmentalist, genetic, and textological schools of editing with the clear-text eclecticism of the Greg-Bowers dispensation, a mischaracterization of the present pluralism.

I have spent some time discussing McLeod's manner, as if his essay had no content. In part, this is because his message resides equally in both, but I should acknowledge that under? behind? within? the idiosyncratic style there is a well-documented and convincing study of such technical issues as "driving out" in the Elizabethan printing house, stop-press alterations to type in Harington, and pen-and-ink alteration on expensive-paper copies. McLeod clearly knows his stuff, and he argues forcefully from his bibliographical evidence. But that style? Very much a question of *chacun à son goût*.

D. F. McKenzie's "Speech-Manuscript-Print" continues the theme of the significance of printed form in determining meaning, but brings a psychological concern to the study—a concern that we still have. Thus, while he locates his argument in the seventeenth and eighteenth centuries, when much formerly oral or manuscript transmission began to turn to print, McKenzie notes that in the late twentieth century we feel "reverse anxiety as we shift from pen and paper to our PC screens—the fear that, by the flick of a switch, or the touch of a key, our words in this new form may once more prove as evanescent as . . . speech" (p. 88, ellipsis McKenzie's). Most scholars, indeed most present-day writers of any sort, have already accumulated cautionary tales of the loss or mutilation of text in electronic transmission, and Warren's promotion of the electronic edition over the conventional printed form has already reminded the reader that print may be only a passing phase in the storage and presentation of data; thus McKenzie's appeal to anxiety at this critical moment in the change of medium is well taken. But it is the continuum as well as the change which he wishes to emphasize in his essay, noting that "we did not stop speaking when we learned to write, nor writing when we learned to print, nor reading, writing, or printing when we entered 'the electronic age'" (p. 87).

The historical ecumenicity, the observance of similarities in transmission problems no matter what the medium, is perhaps only a temporary concession, for McKenzie is primarily concerned with noting the gaps, the disparities, and, yes, the anxieties in the transfer. Thus seventeenth-century lawyers express anxieties over the law being *fixed* in print rather than argued orally or disseminated through a thriving scribal industry, Fran-

Enlarging the Text

cis Bacon resists the reduction of common law to statute law, government agencies depend on handwritten rather than printed records, Donne writes for, and has deep reverence for, a manuscript rather than print culture, and Daniel laments print's unrevisability. All this is the familiar litany against the singularity posited by the printed book, and especially against the canonical singularity of the "great books," those works of literature which have been the traditional focus not only of critical attention, but also of editorial diligence. Note, for example, how McKenzie cites his examples from both literary and non-literary genres, and finds no ontological distinction between them.

Thus, against the anxiety-ridden pronouncements of Daniel, McKenzie opposes what he calls the "ephemerality" of print, which he links directly to his larger new historicist agenda: "One book is never more than a thesis, or an antithesis, in an endless dialectic" (p. 100). This view, of the contextualized book as a cultural artifact and of literature as just one among many competing modes of transmission, is at one with the program for the Cambridge History of the Book in Britain, of which McKenzie is an editor, and with which two other contributors to the Texas collection (Willison and Hellinga) are also involved. The Cambridge History, in its early modern coverage, takes the STCs as its basic database rather than a fixed canon of great works, and this "text" is large enough both to emphasize the "endless dialectic" McKenzie sees in print and to forbid the hierarchical structure of literature and the Romantic endorsement of the all-powerful Author by (for example) demonstrating that much "writing" in the seventeenth century was determinedly and properly anonymous—by design rather than through constraints of censorship. Such an enlargement of "text" has been held by some to promote anarchy over order and a post-structuralist indifference where, quite literally, "*Il n'y a pas dehors de texte.*"

But while McKenzie's "endless dialectic" should, I believe, be viewed within this agenda, his concern in the latter part of the current essay is with the intertextuality of the components of the speech-script-print continuum, even with the co-option of one by another. Thus printers may seek "to limit the difference of print by devising ways to suggest its affinities with speaking and writing" (p. 101), through such means as the printed dialogue, address, or letter. And typography may also be used to suggest levels or types of discourse, as when the parishioner in a 1617 dialogue on the Bible uses "demotic" roman type as against the pastor's "formal authority" of black letter. In a comment which McLeod and McGann would doubtless endorse, McKenzie notes that "printing is far superior to speech in the spaced presentation of forms that cannot be read aloud" (p. 104).

McKenzie's case is well-documented but he fails to demonstrate that the spatial, intertextual codes he describes are in any way specific to the anxieties he has recorded in the earlier part of the essay. Would his position be better or worse if he had noted that the roman type chosen by Sweynheym and Pannartz at Subiaco (1465) and Rome (1467)—as against the black letter of Gutenberg or Fust and Schoeffer—was similarly a semiotic statement appropriate to the time and place, as was Caxton's use and then importation into England of a Burgundian bastard type for his vernacular publications? What would he do with the evidence of the "hierarchy of scripts" during the Carolingian renaissance, when a form of roman square capitals might be used for the title, rustics for rubrics, uncials for incipit, and Caroline minuscule for the body-text? How would he have dealt with the pointed insular vernacular glosses in the round hand Vulgate text of the Lindisfarne Gospels? What would he have made of the "anxieties" of Cardinal Giuliano della Rovere, who had Wendelin of Speier's 1472 printed edition of Appian's *Civil Wars* recopied back into script, since print did not seem to make it a "real" book? And how would he treat the intertextuality (and the anxiety) of the forty-two-line Bible itself, with its three hundred sorts, most of which were necessary only to make the first printed book look like a manuscript?

I am not suggesting that McKenzie's canvass should have been very much larger than it is already, but rather that the conditions he notes as being exemplary of a particularly critical period in transmissional history can be replicated at various points in the western history of the book. If there is some quality of transmission specific to the seventeenth and early eighteenth century in his account, some specific anxiety which had not been encountered before, this does not come over in his account.

Given their close association on the Cambridge History, it is no

Enlarging the Text

surprise to discover that Ian Willison ("Editorial Theory and Practice and the History of the Book") echoes McKenzie's enlargement of the text to non-book, and non-literary media. Willison's text includes not only "newspapers, maps, music" but also "the various modes of orality," the *histoire totale* to be "presented in the context of the cultural-political history of the English-speaking world" and to involve a concern with the "history of reading and of libraries as well" (p. 111). These are very large aims, and one wishes the contributors to the Cambridge project both scholarly rigour and longevity in undertaking such an enormous plan. That the agenda for the project is based upon a repudiation of the traditionally technical concerns of Anglo-American analytical bibliography in favour of the cultural history promoted by the French *l'histoire du livre* is openly acknowledged by Willison, though his ideological placing of his enterprise seems to require a mediating role between the two extremes of "potential inwardness" in analytical bibliography and the "imperious historico-sociological *élan* of the *Annalistes*." While one cannot but commend Willison's formulation of a cultural and bibliographical synthesis, a middle ground for competing ideologies, it is disturbingly ingenuous of him to claim that these national distinctions are somehow "natural" or endemic to the peculiar circumstances of text-production in each culture. Thus, he asserts that it was because there was no "editorial problem in Corneille" that social rather than technical research dominates French textual work and that it is the "complicity between author and book trade" in France (as opposed to what McKenzie notes as British "disjunction" between author and trade) which have cumulatively caused and validated the rival schools.

On the first question, the lack of editorial "problems," Willison is simply ignoring those features of the transmission of French literature which do not fit his simplistic characterization: the facts are otherwise. From Bédier's quarrel with Lachmannian stemmatics in the early twentieth century[15] to the current Franco-German infatuation with genetic editing, there have been as many editorial "problems" in French literature as in Anglo-American.[16] It is true that there are differences to be noted, for there is no English equivalent to the centralizing authority of the Imprimerie Royale (unless it be in the various exclusive rights to publish holy scripture and the Edward VI Prayer Book given to such printers as Richard Grafton and Edward Whitchurch). And, with the possible exception of the CEAA and CSE, there is no Anglophone equivalent to the CNRS. Moreover, there is to this day (as Richard Serra discovered when he attempted to prevent the U.S. government from destroying his "Tilted Arc")[17] a significant difference between Anglo-American law of copyright, which can be sold and therefore alienated, and French *Droit d'auteur,* which recognizes an author's continued moral—as opposed to property—rights in the artifact.[18] But to leap from these differences to the assertion that it is the lack of editorial "problems" in French literature that can explain the Annalistes school betrays a peculiar disregard for the evidence.

Thus, Willison's five-part analysis of the British book-trade from mediaeval to modern, while heavily dependent on McKenzie and while containing many valuable insights, must be read and evaluated with some care. For example, the first principle of the "ubiquitousness" of the codex which (following McKenzie) Willison attributes to printing (pp. 116–17) is true in a less limited sense than both critics would have it. As Willison (again following McKenzie) remarks in his second principle, "the technological and entrepreneurial dynamic meant that print took off in terms not so much of the book, as of what eventually expanded into newspaper publishing and reading" (p. 117). So it was not specifically the codex which achieved ubiquitousness, but the broadsheet, the pamphlet, and the non-book. Indeed, the codex had (through its association with and adoption by Christianity in the third and fourth centuries) achieved a ubiquitousness which made it the dominant form until the political and later the electronic revolutions of the modern era. Willison and McKenzie are right to draw attention to the "synoptic potential" of the codex—for unlike the roll, a codex can use internal citation and reference with ease, making it an ideal vehicle for the sectarian feuding of early-mediaeval patristics and late-mediaeval and early Renaissance political and religious debate—but Willison's second principle of ubiquity contradicts his first, unless heavily qualified by an acknowledgement of the inherent bibliographical synopticism of the codex, a synopticism long recognized and employed in the pre-print period.

In general, Willison's treatment of the national peculiarities of the book trade raises more problems than it solves—and this may be all quite proper as an introduction to a vast project still in the planning stage. Just a few examples: in citing the transmission of *Piers Plowman* as evidence of the British "disjunct" McKenzie has noted between author and book trade (and aligning the idealism of Kane-Donaldson in their attempt to overcome the perceived corruptions of scribal transmission against Pearsall's open hospitality to the creative engagement of the scribal role in constructing the texts of Chaucer), does Willison mean to suggest that the mediaeval English book trade is fundamentally different from Continental models? Yes, *Piers* is a notoriously *scriptible* work, inviting scribal intervention, but so is much mediaeval (and classical and biblical) literature elsewhere: try a Kane-Donaldson idealism on the *Divine Comedy*, on Boccaccio's three conflated versions of the *Decameron*, on the *Chanson de Roland*. On the other hand, not all variance is a product of book-trade corruptions, as the two authorially released versions of the Prologue to Chaucer's *Legend of Good Women* demonstrate.

During the so-called common-reader period of Willison's analysis (from 1688 to the mid-nineteenth century), while noting the collaborative relationship between author and publisher, Willison's schema does not acknowledge, or have a place for, the sort of tight control over the circumstances of publication and the fine detail of typography and page layout practised by Pope or Blake, where the disjunct between author and book-trade is virtually imperceptible.

Finally, the section on film and television is unconvincing, both in its selection of examples and in its general argument. To rest a two-paragraph analysis of television on Dennis Potter and his insistence that "writers, and not directors, are the king" betrays either a total misunderstanding of the corporate authorial structures of both commercial and public television or the most ingenuous of wishful thinking, as does Willison's repeating of the charge that "Television . . . still awaits its Dickens." Potter is the aberration in television, not the norm against which crass commercial corruptions of authoriality can be measured, and the very nature of the corporate medium does not "await" its Dickens, it specifically forbids the emergence of the novelistic manner. The recent failed forays of David Lynch and John Sayles into television should be sufficient evidence of that (and, one should note, even in these cases, the "authors" were responsible for only the first couple of programs and occasional others, the bulk of the work being rotated among a group of contributors writing parodistically "in the style of" the author). Potter at least has the savvy to regard this non-authorial situation as "endemic" to television, but Willison is apparently more hopeful.

The discussion of film, though limited to the work of Greene, Selznick, Welles, and Reed on *The Third Man*, is more persuasive, although unbalanced as an account of the type. The access to production documents in the Texas archives no doubt dictated the selection of this film, and the competing roles of writer, director, and producer are shown in detailed operation, but there is no attempt to acknowledge competing models (either the complete studio vehicle, in which writer, actor, and director are simply assigned to the project, or the *auteur* model of the *nouvelle vague*, Fellini, Bergman, Allen, or—again—Sayles or Lynch). By moving "vindication" (for example, of the ending of *The Third Man*) to "public reception," Willison seems to be endorsing the very commercialism he finds so problematical in television, and there is obviously much to be thought through before a convincing theory or history of either medium can be successfully incorporated into the final volume of the Cambridge project.

Lotte Hellinga's "Editing Texts in the First Fifteen Years of Printing" confronts an embarrassment—that since the fifteenth century is not generally regarded as a period of great literary merit, printers rather than authors "get the heroic parts" (p. 127), but that incunabula are frequently disdained by textual critics because of their supposed unreliability. Of course, there are exceptions to this principle (before the discovery of the Winchester manuscript, Caxton's *Morte Darthur* was the only witness to Malory, and even after the recognition of the manuscript is still regarded as a very important *independent* authority), but Hellinga's two points are well taken, as is her attempt to

Enlarging the Text 23

overcome the predisposition of print historians (e.g., Kenney and Eisenstein) to regard print transmission as basically unilinear, unlike the proliferating, contaminating, and conflating tendencies of script transmission. Again, there are important exceptions, as the recognition of the non-linear print history of *Hamlet* and *Lear* demonstrates, but Hellinga's caveat is again well-taken.

While acknowledging that stabilization was an important feature of the Vulgate in the early print period, Hellinga wants to emphasize the transitional and complex nature of much incunabular printing, dealing, for example, with the three independent print traditions of Jerome's letters prepared in Rome, Strassburg, and Mainz (1468, 1469, and 1470, respectively). Each of such different traditions would attempt both to establish the authority and correctness of the text and to present the text as something new, and therefore different from its predecessors. Such an intent is not, of course, limited to the incunabular period, for in the sixteenth and seventeenth centuries, texts would often be published with a claim that the work was "newly augmented and improved," especially if an earlier printing were pirated or otherwise unauthorized.

Concentrating on the desire for correctness, Hellinga emphasizes the careful proofreading and correcting of the Jerome and other incunabular texts, but while the examples she cites are well-documented, it would be difficult to extrapolate from these a demonstrably coherent and uniform attitude to proofing and correctness on the part of early printers. Where evidence is more complete—in the sixteenth and seventeenth centuries—it would be hazardous to suggest such a devotion to the principles of correctness. The mixed states of leaves of the Shakespeare First Folio and the consequent fact that no two copies are therefore identical is only the most famous example of a somewhat more cavalier attitude to the release of uncorrected proofs (often together with corrected) than that observed by Hellinga. Indeed, one might argue that paradoxically the very survival of the *manuscript* (i.e., proofing) corrections to printed texts that Hellinga uses to illustrate her essay is evidence both of the desire for correctness and yet (as in the case of the Shakespeare) of a willingness to release for publication type-pages not reset to incorporate the corrections noted in manuscript. Hellinga argues that such carefully proofread texts are "the result of long, hard labors not to be spoiled by careless resetting" (p. 145) and that a second setting would incorporate the corrections in the text, but that still leaves us with the paradox already noted.

It is when Hellinga attempts to translate this principle of correction into a textual theory that her essay runs into real problems. In claiming that the incunabular corrector was "in his function of editor ... assum[ing] the place of his author" and that this principle of "textual emendation is contrary to every modern principle of textual criticism" (p. 148), Hellinga is perhaps displaying the parochialism of the strict documentary mediaevalist. As the rest of us know from the conflicts between literary editors of the Tanselle school and the editors of many American documentary editions,[19] such principles of emendation are by no means "contrary" to *all* modern textual criticism. Moreover, the frequent normalization of Old English texts to "classical" West Saxon forms (and even some Middle English texts, most notoriously those by Chaucer) in standard scholarly editions suggests that the phenomenological transference Hellinga finds so unusual in her incunabular editors is quite acceptable even among mediaevalists, as Middleton demonstrates in her account of *Piers Plowman* editing later in this volume.

For this reason, Hellinga's appeal (along with similar appeals by other contributors) for "a more general understanding of particular forms of text in a specific cultural environment" (p. 149) needs itself to question whether the specifics noted in the cultural environment of incunabular printing and editing are quite as aberrational as she seems to suppose. The documentary evidence she provides is provocative and helpful to the charting of "editorial" techniques in a still too-little-known period, but the general principles that Hellinga draws from the documentation should be treated with some caution.

Hans Walter Gabler has perforce spent much of the last few years defending his edition of Joyce's *Ulysses* against the several criticisms of John Kidd and others. In his essay for this volume, "Textual Studies and Criticism," the focus of this defence turns away from the text of Joyce to the methodology, and specifically the synoptic apparatus, employed in the edition. Situating the synoptic display in an account of the history of "integral apparatus" and within the "dialectical coexistence . . . of the synchrony and diachrony of texts" (p. 162), Gabler acknowledges, as Louis Hay and other geneticists[20] have done elsewhere, the structuralist ethos of such an apparatus, and while not overtly admitting the consequent inherent contradiction of an edition bearing both synoptic apparatus and intentionalist reading text, Gabler does at least recognize that the reading text can be "deemed a concession to the general reader" (p. 162) and therefore could be dispensed with if one were to accept what he calls the "relentless purity" of such an approach, identified here with Gunter Martens's "Textdynamik und Edition." Obviously, Gabler's own Joyce edition does not aim for such purity, since it does contain a facing-page reading text, but it is curious that he should claim that he has never seen an edition in which this purity is realized, for the (notorious) example of the Harvard Emerson, or the Cornell Wordsworth, would offer such a demonstration.

Gabler's concentration on apparatus is perhaps inevitable, but his argument is contained within a much larger agenda, none other than a brief against the apparent divorce between textual scholarship and literary criticism. Using Zeller's distinction between *Befund* (an actual reading) and *Deutung* (interpretation of such a reading) as paradigmatic of the divorce (p. 164), Gabler cites the *Textual Companion* to the *Oxford Shakespeare* as a refreshing instance of the current "integrate[d] critical discourse" (p. 163), where the commentary abandons the formal apparatus lists of conventional scholarly editions "in favor of an amply verbalized discourse achieving an easy transition between text-critical and literary critical argument" (p. 164), a disposition which Gabler hopes will lead to the recognition of a New Commentary movement.

But how new would such a movement really be? Gabler is right to suggest that in some scholarly editions the reductionist tendency to distill emendations and other aspects of apparatus into unarticulated lists can have a deleterious effect on the "discourse" of textual scholarship. But even the most rigidly formalized of the CEAA/CSE editions using such lists at least allowed for the possibility of fuller discourse in the textual notes. Moreover, Gabler's history has to ignore the enormous tradition of biblical, classical, and much mediaeval textual scholarship if it is to certify the integrated criticism of the Oxford Shakespeare as something new and revolutionary. From the Alexandrians and the Byzantian scholiasts (e.g., Eustathius of Thessalonica's variorum commentary on Homer, where the first line of the *Iliad* occupies ten pages of dense literary/textual commentary) through Lorenzo Valla's *Adnotationes in Novum Testamentum* (published by Erasmus in 1505) and his *Emendationes sex librorum Titi Livi*, to Erasmus himself and on to Skeat, Housman, Manly/Rickert and many others, the rhetorical history of textual scholarship has been concerned precisely with the sort of "commentary" which Gabler now finds so new. The Oxford *Textual Companion* would be better considered the vernacular fulfilment of the commentary tradition, rather than a modern aberration from that tradition.

One understands Gabler's desire to overcome the division between pure philological, documentary research and literary interpretation (for his synoptic method of display demands such an argument), but this is not securely achieved by ignoring the mainstream of "classical" textual scholarship and using as one's negative evidence the (unnamed) "conventional . . . modern editions" against which his view of apparatus is aimed. Furthermore, while it is true that there have been proponents of New Bibliography and analytical bibliography who have emphasized the technical aspects of textual scholarship against the interpretative (one thinks of Greg's occasional pronouncements on the mere "shapes" and "marks" of a text, having no meaning in themselves[21]), it is equally true that all the major recent figures practising in contemporary bibliography (Bowers and Tanselle specifically) have continually insisted that textual study is an inherently *critical* and therefore interpretative, activity. It is the ignorance of the literary critics which has been largely responsible for the perceived divorce, and as McGann has pointed out, in embracing such ignorance, they ceded to textualists a territory thought well lost.[22] The invasion of the *critical* empery by a wide

Enlarging the Text

range of textual scholars has in part reversed the situation, but it is still largely true that most literary critics, even those for whom problems in text and textuality are central to their dispensation, have not yet felt it necessary to investigate the current revisionist atmosphere of textual scholarship and thus still believe it to have the definitive pretensions and scientific method they have themselves abandoned.

Insofar as essays like Gabler's can counter such misinformed prejudice, then our discourse with the critics may eventually become truly "integrated." Thus, when Gabler notes that contemporary editors, particularly those operating under "versioning" auspices, are "not the author's executor, but the historian[s] of the text" (p. 159), he is effectively drawing the Kuhnian paradigm shift in textual studies into the current critical climate. I note with approval that it is he, not McKenzie, who specifically cites the ramifications of Derridean absence (p. 154) in the inevitably distanced activities of textual scholars, although the Derridean concept would have been particularly illuminating to McKenzie's case. Gabler is thus serving his agenda well, and his comments on commentary are appropriate to the current state of textual and critical indeterminism, but it is a pity he feels it necessary to rewrite so much editorial history in order to further his claims.

It is again the problems of commentary which motivate the concluding essay in the collection, Anne Middleton's "Life in the Margins, or, What's an Annotator to Do?" Middleton answers her own question in the strongest possible terms, by deconstructing the expected master/slave relationship of text and annotation to place the annotation and annotator at the ontological centre of text-construction and interpretation, citing Ralph Hanna's characterization of annotation as a form of aggression and suggesting that it becomes "guerrilla warfare" since it depends for its success on "living in another's space" by "doing cultural work using somebody else's materials and time" (p. 169). Through such raids on the "properties" of the text, annotation "theorizes the entire text to which it is nominally in service, while in no single place is it forced out from underground to acknowledge this dimension of its enterprise, which it presents on each occasion as merely an ordinary practical activity, a modest attestation that a working public utility is indeed working as it should for the general benefit" (p. 169). Annotation is thus a potentially seditious activity, and it could undermine the very text it ostensibly seeks to elucidate in this power-play for control of meaning. This is especially true of annotation of the Kane-Donaldson *Piers Plowman* on which Middleton is engaged, for, as she quite properly notes, the editors of the Athlone edition approach the poem as if it were a "classical" text, and attempt to restore a putative cohesive original form and meaning to the totality of the work, rejecting its role as a "national scripture" (in McGann's phrase), its bearing "distinct layers or iterations of authorial production and intentionality, interlaced almost impenetrably with several kinds of and states of scribal practice and habit" (p. 168). The inevitable product of the guerrilla "scattered raids upon local meaning" of traditional annotation would be a dispersal of the authority vested in the restored text by Kane-Donaldson, and would thus problematize the very creative discipline brought to the editing. Middleton has no easy answer to this paradox, but as my few quotations from within a couple of pages of her essay already suggest, her interrogation of the theory of annotation is a rich, lively, and consistently rewarding intellectual tour de force in an area of textual scholarship which has so far received scant theoretical attention. While her concerns are obviously produced by the peculiar circumstances of the *Piers Plowman* text(s) and the Athlone edition of these texts, her account of annotation as a challenge in both mediating the "otherness" of a text and in producing a rival construction of meaning is required reading for anybody working on annotation in any field or period, for Middleton brings to her discussion a range of procedural and artifactual options which should be considered before any tentative annotation is embarked upon. Moreover, her argument is dizzyingly provocative throughout, and brings to the volume a degree of intellectual sophistication only intermittently present elsewhere.

So dense is this argument that I have space here only to touch upon some of the other challenges she issues in the essay. For example, in addition to the liability of dispersed elucidation already mentioned, she notes that the "phrasal grammar" (rather than clausal) of annotation can become an anti-narrative (pp. 169–70), that it can therefore allegorize the text, producing a "vertical density," a system of reference to a putative life-world outside the work, versus the "horizontal strands" of narrative development. This procedure can "obliterate rather than support broader understanding of the work as a production" (p. 170). She notes that annotation is both necessitated by and embodies "interpretive reticence," in that it displays "what went without saying" and that thus "to its contemporaries, [the work] had no gaps or lacunae: it was, in other words, deeply and totally legible in its own time" (pp. 170–71). I find this assertion provocative in the extreme, for while total legibility is always potential, it is rarely achieved, and may be deliberately avoided, especially by mediaeval authors. Boccaccio's rigorous defence (in the *Life of Dante* and the *Genealogy of the Pagan Gods*) of poetic obscurity as a productive and emancipating activity of both comprehension and misinterpretation was based on the highest and most impenetrably illegible of all texts—holy scripture—which had been made *difficult* (i.e., filled with "gaps and lacunae") precisely in order to render its function as text, as a "woven" authority needing unweaving, the more plausible. Langland (and his audience) cannot have been unaware of the typological fullness which lay in the doctrine of both divine and secular "signatures," and these signatures were not to be patent or translucent. As Boccaccio puts it, the function of a poet is to write, and not to "rip up and lay bare the meaning which lies hidden in his inventions."[23] Thus poetry worthy of the name virtually demands annotation, to its contemporaries almost as much as to later centuries. I recognize that some mediaeval authors were acutely aware of the problem of misinterpretation, even at the very local level: when Chaucer writes his own annotation on the reference to "Dana" in the *Knight's Tale,* insisting that it is Daphne not Diana whom he is citing, and when Trevisa (or his scribes) scatters his neologistic prose with the phrase "that is to seye" to gloss and contextualize his own coinages, they are both playing with the notion of the "difficult" reading needing a "vertical" elucidation, by incorporating the annotation into the "horizontal" narrative of their composition. But such cases do not, I think, fully substantiate Middleton's account of the rationale for traditional annotation of mediaeval vernacular texts.

One of the problems in the density of Middleton's argument is that she can often only sketch the distinctions she regards as significant. Thus, when talking of the "three blurry snapshots" (a wonderfully evocative phrase) that characterize the three "versions" of *Piers Plowman,* she attempts to suggest that these three snapshots are not the "work" but only variant aspects of its "text." She goes on to ask whether the annotator can "say anything about the *text* that will conduce to understanding of the *work*? Is it useful, or fatal, to this or any other effort at annotation to admit such a distinction into our project?" (p. 174). As most practising textual critics are aware, the answer to this question as it has been expounded by Tanselle in his *Rationale* and many other places would be a resounding "Yes," absolutely necessary to an understanding of the both text and work. And yet the only authority cited by Middleton is Foucault's "What Is an Author?" and that only inferentially. Foucault's position is particularly relevant both to Tanselle's argument and to Barthes's essay "From Work to Text," which proposes exactly the *opposite* dialectic. One of the pertinent passages in Foucault deals specifically with the problem of editing and the publication of "works," as both Middleton and Tanselle have defined the issue: "Even when an individual has been accepted as an author, we must still ask whether everything that he wrote, said, or left behind is part of his work. The problem is both theoretical and technical. When undertaking the publication of Nietzsche's works, for example, where should one stop? Surely everything must be published, but what is 'everything'? . . . How can one define a work amid the millions of traces left by someone after his death? A theory of the work does not exist, and the empirical task of those who naively undertake the editing of works often suffers in the absence of such a theory."[24] Tanselle and (even with her disclaimer, Middleton) *do* have such a theory of the work and its relation to text, and employ this concept as an attempted answer to Foucault's challenge of "everything" and to the evaluation of "traces," and it is to my mind

Enlarging the Text

unfortunate that Middleton did not have space to articulate her practical and conceptual response to these important issues. And, as I have already suggested, it is doubly unfortunate since Foucault's essay is itself a response to the even more dangerous challenge presented by Barthes. For example, Barthes's insistence that "work" "refers to the image of an organism which grows by vital expansion" whereas the proper metaphor for "text" is "that of the network . . . it is as a result of a combinatory systematic"[25] has particular relevance to much of Middleton's essay, with its concern with the New-Critical dogma of the organicist text. Moreover, when Barthes declares that "Once the Author is removed, the claim to decipher a text becomes quite futile,"[26] he is questioning the very raison d'être under which Middleton's account of annotation (deciphering a text) operates. Similarly, his assertion that "To give a text an Author is to impose a limit on that text, to furnish it with a final signified, to close the writing"[27] is a direct comment on one of Middleton's major concerns—the "dispersal" of meaning versus the imposition of classical form and meaning through the Athlone editors' appeal to the orginary moment(s) of inscription.

I cite these theoretical contexts not as criticism of what Middleton actually has to say about the problem of annotation but because the theme and manner of her essay depend upon such theoretical contextualization. I feel her argument would have been stronger had it been placed in the larger discourse, particularly since she allusively but incompletely refers to the Foucault essay as corroborating evidence.

But what we do have in this essay is a powerful and constructive analysis of annotation as a major textual enterprise. It is a fitting close to a volume which has offered similar provocations throughout. As I have suggested, some of the assertions at other points in the book could bear further reflection and a more balanced contemplation of historical and cultural evidence, but the reader interested in obtaining a wide-ranging display of the thinking of several of our major textual critics will find the book continually stimulating. The University of Texas, as befits its recent status as a repository of textual riches, is to be commended both for mounting the conference itself and for producing this handsome and instructive volume.

Notes

1. G. Thomas Tanselle, *A Rationale of Textual Criticism* (Philadelphia: Univ. of Pennsylvania Press), p. 92.
2. William Shakespeare, *The First Folio of Shakespeare*, ed. Charlton Hinman (New York: Norton, 1968), p. xvii.
3. James McLaverty, "The Mode of Existence of Literary Works of Art: The Case of the *Dunciad* Variorum," *Studies in Bibliography*, 37 (1984), 82–105.
4. David L. Vander Meulen, "'The Dunciad in Four Books' and the Bibliography of Pope," *Papers of the Bibliographical Society of America*, 83 (September 1989), 293–310.
5. See for example, Jerome McGann, "What Is Critical Editing?" *TEXT*, 5 (1991), 31–46.
6. Jo Ann Boydston, "In Praise of Apparatus." *TEXT*, 5 (1991), 1–14.
7. Boydston, p. 9.
8. David C. Fowler, "A New Edition of the B Text of *Piers Plowman*," *Yearbook of English Studies*, 7 (1977), 23–42.
9. Charlotte Brewer, "The Textual Principles of Kane's A Text," *Yearbook of Langland Studies*, 3 (1989), 67–90, and "Authorial Vs. Scribal Writing in *Piers Plowman*," *Medieval Literature: Texts and Interpretation*, ed. Tim William Machan (Binghamton: Medieval and Renaissance Texts and Studies, 1991) pp. 59–90.
10. Roland Barthes, *S/Z*, trans. Richard Miller (New York: Noonday, 1974).
11. Michael Warren, ed. *The Complete "King Lear"* (Berkeley: Univ. of California Press, 1989).
12. Stephen Booth, ed., *Shakespeare's Sonnets* (New Haven: Yale Univ. Press, 1977). Repr. with corrections, 1980.
13. E. Talbot Donaldson, "The Psychology of Editors of Middle English Texts," *Speaking of Chaucer* (New York: Norton, 1972), p. 105.
14. John Miles Foley, "Editing Oral Epic Texts: Theory and Practice," *TEXT*, 1 (1984), 75–94.
15. Joseph Bédier, "La Tradition manuscrite du *lai du l'Ombre:* réflexions sur l'art d'éditer les anciens textes," *Romania*, 54 (1928), 161–96, 321–56. Repr. as pamphlet, 1970.
16. See, for example, the problem of suppressed intention in Molière's *Dom Juan,* multiple intentions in La Bruyère's *Les Caractères,* the question of early versus late intentions and the consequent problem of selection of copy-text in Corneille, Racine, and Ronsard, and the eclecticism of Périer's conflated edition of Pascal's *Pensées* versus the differing "versionist" authority in the "première copie" and "seconde copie" manuscripts—to say nothing of the current edi-

torial wrangles over the Proust edition. For Willison to claim that there are no editorial problems in Corneille and the rest of French literature betrays nothing short of a wilful blindness to the textual history of that literature. For details of this and other national literatures, see the relevant chapters of *Scholarly Editing: A Guide to Research*, ed. D. C. Greetham (New York: MLA, forthcoming).

17. Richard Serra, "Art and Censorship," *Critical Inquiry*, 17 (Spring 1991), 574–81.

18. See, for example, David Saunders and Ian Hunter, "Lessons from the 'Literatory': How to Historicise Authorship," *Critical Inquiry*, 17 (Spring 1991), 479–509.

19. See G. Thomas Tanselle, "The Editing of Historical Documents," *Studies in Bibliography*, 31 (1978), 1–56; Don L. Cook, "The Short, Happy Thesis of G. Thomas Tanselle," *Newsletter of the Association for Documentary Editing*, 3.1 (1981), 1–4, and Robert Taylor, "Editorial Practices—An Historian's View," *Ibid.*, 4–8.

20. Louis Hay, "Genetic Editing, Past and Present—A Few Reflections of a User," *TEXT*, 3 (1987), 117–34. For a bibliography of genetic editing, see Graham Falconer and David H. Sanderson, "Bibliographie des Études Génétiques littéraires," *Texte*, 7 (1988), 287–352, and for a survey of European genetic editing, see Bodo Plachta, "Scholarly Editing of German Literature," *Scholarly Editing: A Guide to Research*, ed. D. C. Greetham (New York: MLA, forthcoming).

21. See, for example, "I start then with the postulate that what the bibliographer is concerned with is pieces of paper or parchment covered with certain written or printed signs. With these signs he is concerned merely as arbitrary marks; their meaning is no business of his" (W. W. Greg, "Bibliography—An Apologia," *Library*, 4th Series, 13 (1932), 121–122).

22. Jerome McGann, "The Monks and the Giants: Textual and Bibliographical Studies and the Interpretation of Literary Works," in *Textual Criticism and Literary Interpretation* (Chicago: Univ. of Chicago Press, 1985), p. 181. For a recent account of the attempts of McGann and others to overcome the gap, see Michael Groden, "Contemporary Textual and Literary Theory," in *Representing Modernist Texts: Editing as Interpretation*, ed. George Bornstein (Ann Arbor: Univ. of Michigan Press, 1991), pp. 259–86. See also the collection of essays by many of the current practitioners of textual theory (including Gabler) in *Devils and Angels*, ed. Philip Cohen (Charlottesville: Univ. Press of Virginia, 1991).

23. *Medieval Literary Criticism*, ed. O. B. Hardison, Jr., Alex Preminger, Kevin Kerrane, and Leon Golden. (New York: Ungar, 1974), p. 191.

24. Michel Foucault, "What Is an Author?" *The Foucault Reader*, ed. Paul Pabinow (New York: Pantheon, 1984): pp. 103–4.

25. Roland Barthes, "From Work to Text," *Image, Music, Text*, trans. Stephen Heath (New York: Hill and Wang, 1977), p. 161.

26. Roland Barthes, "The Death of the Author," *Ibid.*, p. 147.

27. *Ibid.*, p. 147.

Conrad, Ford, and the Eternity of Good Letters

George Core

Alan Judd. *Ford Madox Ford*. Cambridge: Harvard University Press, 1991. 476 pp.

The Collected Letters of Joseph Conrad: Volume 4, 1908–1911, eds. Frederick R. Karl and Laurence Davies. Cambridge: Cambridge University Press, 1990. l, 548 pp.

Jeffrey Meyers. *Joseph Conrad: A Biography.* New York: Scribners, 1991. xx, 428 pp.

We are living in the Age of the Self, with the writer often given and driven shamelessly to confessing the messiest and most unpalatable details dredged from the darkest and deepest pools of his or her psyche, and, at the same time, with biographers often equally eager to reveal the worst aspects of their subjects' behavior and to dabble in the thinnest and shabbiest speculations. Such is the shaky foundation upon which psychobiography wobbles. Some biographers, in exploring the most unpleasant aspects—actual or imagined—of their subjects' inner lives, indulge themselves in what John McCormick, who himself has forged a distinguished biography of George Santayana, has deemed the brutality of biography. We might call this proclivity—to rewrite Henry James—the brutality of low intentions. In such circumstances the biographer's excesses are comparable to the excesses of the confessional poet or memoirist.

Everyone should remember, as Mr. McCormick has said in the spring 1991 issue of the *Sewanee Review,* that the biographer "probably knows more about his subject than the subject in life knew about himself. That knowledge may tempt the biographer to the deadly sin of pride . . . and to ignore his intuition that he cannot know all about anybody. Human personality finally remains walled about with the unknowable" (pp. 180–81). And human beings often act contrary to their own best intentions and interests, which is to say illogically, irrationally, even self-defeatingly.

Joseph Conrad (1857–1924) and Ford Madox Ford (1873–1939) are two such paradoxical and mysterious figures, men alien to and alienated from their culture and society but devoted absolutely and irrevocably to the profession of letters. Although Conrad as a young man became a master mariner and earned a mate's license, after leaving the sea (which he found boring), he was beached, a sea creature almost helpless on land—and hopelessly impractical in nearly any everyday matter one could name —unable to maintain records involving his finances, insurance, and taxes; helpless with his hands; brooding and hot-tempered and almost invariably gloomy and irascible, even in the presence of friends; inarticulate as a speaker of English; and so forth. Ford was in many ways equally inept in practical matters, but he was a good gardener and cook as well as a passable farmer and carpenter; he could have been a successful dealer in art or antiques (especially as an appraiser); he performed well in wartime as an adjutant; and although he was a poor businessman who was almost as foolish as Conrad with money, he was a great editor who could handle most of the details, large and small, of running a magazine—finances aside. Unlike Conrad, Ford could also take diction and type, and in a famous instance he rescued the fumbling Conrad after he had allowed a lamp to explode and burn the manuscript of "The End of the Tether." Ford took the dictation of the hysterical Conrad, who was at the end of his tether. Although he was racked by serious depression that nearly drove him to suicide more than once, Ford had a natural optimism; and he was not locked in the chambers of the ego as was Conrad, a profoundly introverted and unhappy man who failed at suicide and then settled for depression.

One easily can argue that Conrad, who suffered greatly as a husband and father and who was worried most of his life about money, especially making enough to maintain himself and his family, had much to be depressed about, including his health and that of his wife and the older of their sons. But Conrad foolishly made his bed with Jessie George as his wife, when, as Jeffrey Meyers points out, he needed only a housekeeper and a typist—and perhaps a nurse. Meyers presents the courtship in a hilarious way, and the humor of the marriage, together with the pathos, does not abate in his account. As you read Conrad's letters, you begin to think that the Conrads must have been among the world's sickliest hypochondriacs: they seemed to revel to exotic ailments and bad health, especially while traveling (it never occurred to them to stay at home); and the worst of the lot was Conrad himself, whose terrible gout was exacerbated by his neuroses—or whose depression was deepened by his recurring trouble with arthritis.

Without Jessie to run his improvident household, Ford to help him with his writing (including the composition of one serial installment of *Nostromo* done wholly by Ford in addition to their collaborative work), and J. B. Pinker, his agent, to provide him with money for everything from cigars and milk to the rent and taxes, not to mention maintaining his records, Conrad would have been a much lesser writer; and the major works of his late middle age—*Nostromo* (1904), *The Secret Agent* (1907), and *Under Western Eyes* (1911)—would have gone unwritten or been markedly lesser accomplishments. Other people helped Conrad—notably Edward Garnett and John Galsworthy; but no one outside his family gave him the sustained support that Ford and Pinker provided. Conrad, although he felt close to Ford for many years, never repaid his friendship properly; indeed, as Meyers points out, he did not dedicate a book to Ford but dedicated several to chance acquaintances. Ford, in addition to everything else, dedicated one of his best novels to Conrad, *The Fifth Queen* (1906). Conrad also turned down the opportunity to help Ford financially when he was in great trouble but when Conrad himself was well heeled—and did not then repay Ford's financial generosity to him. (Just when you think Conrad almost monstrous in his ingratitude and niggardliness, you find he could be open-handed, as when he all but adopted a friend of Borys's, the son of an acquaintance of the Conrads.)

Conrad did not reciprocate the kindness of Ford and Pinker, who gave more unstintingly of themselves than anyone else, including Garnett and Galsworthy. No one has given either Pinker or Ford his due in his regard. Critics and biographers, especially of Conrad, have been almost as niggardly in their praise as Conrad himself. The solitary Polish genius would have found himself at sea, figuratively and literally, without these two men.

Conrad was a fair judge of literary talent, but he misunderstood Melville and dismissed the work of his greatest rival as that of a chronicler of the sea; he was wrongheaded about other writers who threatened him, especially Lawrence; and he often depreciated Ford's work, even when they worked together. In fact Ford was not only the greater man of letters (especially as critic and editor) but the greater novelist. This is heresy, needless to say; and many Conradians, especially the English who despise Ford for his irregular life and his braggadocio, will be dumbfounded and outraged. To them this heretic says: Make the most of it. *The Good Soldier* is a more fully realized novel than anything that Conrad ever wrote, and *Parade's End* is a greater novel than *Nostromo*, Conrad's most ambitious novel (and a very good one). *The Secret Agent*, which is Conrad's finest novel, in the same way that *The Good Soldier* is Ford's, would not have come into being without Ford, who suggested it to Conrad and who provided some of the details as well as the general situation. Because Conrad and Ford did not collaborate effectively, because Jessie was often galled by Ford, and because Ford's behavior, especially with Violet Hunt, often gravelled Conrad, he failed to understand Ford's genius as a novelist. He should have recognized the greatness of *The Good Soldier* even if he could not appreciate *The Fifth Queen*. Conrad misunderstood the historical novel as thoroughly as he misunderstood *Moby-Dick*, which he described as a "rather strained rhapsody" lacking "a single sincere line" (Meyers, p. 173).

Like many others Conrad overrated John Galsworthy, mistaking his money and social position for his standing as a novelist. Of the writers who congregated in and around Rye—James, Stephen Crane, H. G. Wells, Conrad, Ford, and Galsworthy—it is

Galsworthy whose work is now the slightest and most dated. In his day Galsworthy was the most popular but Wells; today he is small beer, almost undrinkable and unreadable. So Conrad's fawning deference to Jack Galsworthy, who loaned him money and did him other favors, is sometimes embarrassing to the reader of their correspondence.

Alan Judd, an English novelist, has captured Ford much more successfully than Frank MacShane and Arthur Mizener did, even though Mizener's biography is considerably longer than Judd's. Judd has given us a necessary life. On the other hand, Meyers, as was the case with his biographies of Hemingway and Lawrence, has written a biography closer to supererogatory than necessary; he has also built his work on that of others without giving them full credit and has promoted his work by claiming far more for his discoveries than is warranted.

As Judd observes in reviewing Meyers's *Conrad* for the *Spectator* (20 July 1991), Polish Joe Conrad, the deep-diving submarine, has escaped the nets of Meyers's trawler. Not so Jane Anderson, about whom Meyers obviously would like to strike a biography or a romance. In *Conrad,* Meyers argues that Anderson seduced Conrad in his old age and later replayed her promiscuity with the feckless Borys, then serving on the western front. It is a story that Ford might have used for *Parade's End,* but Meyers, who recklessly ascribes models and parallels from real life to characters and actions in Conrad's fiction, asserts that Macmaster, the treacherous Scot in *Parade's End,* is drawn from Conrad. Meyers seems more smitten with Anderson than Conrad was with any human being, including himself.

Judd has netted Conrad while presenting a sympathetic portrait of this singular man, a man mad about good writing, as he said of himself—and a man mad about women, as he did not say, being always honorable and silent about his affairs of the heart, even with the wretched Violet Hunt. Judd is good at portraiture, as is Meyers, but Meyers tends to overdraw his characters and attributes too much to physiognomy. Judd is stronger and surer than Meyers at going beyond characterizing figures major and minor to describing the relation and interrelation of those figures to the principal and to weighing the general and essential matter of literary and cultural relations. Meyers, who well understands the roles of such figures as John Quinn in the making of Joseph Conrad, does not look beyond them to what the geometry of literary relations and the pressures of the literary marketplace fully entail, even when he deals with the improbable popular success of *Chance* (1914), a third-rate novel. He tells us why *Chance* succeeded against long odds and does so persuasively, but he does not tell us anything substantive about the popular novelists of the time—and why their works sold when James's and Ford's and Conrad's did not, even in a case such as *Romance*, which Ford and Conrad wrote for the popular market.

Alan Judd, in providing a shrewd description and assessment of Hemingway's constipated response to Ford, a man who helped Hemingway enormously, observes:

Ford was not a hero in the Hemingway mould: he was vulnerable, untidy, sentimental, funny in a way that Hemingway could probably sense but not see, and genuinely heroic; he was superior in age, status, experience, knowledge of his craft, sensitivity and ability; he was unaggressive, fat and wheezing, had fought in the trenches and was unaccountably popular with women. There was much that Hemingway might have found it hard to forgive. [p. 350]

Hemingway treated Ford quite unfairly, especially in *A Moveable Feast*, in which he apparently hits the fat wheezing Ford with every punch imaginable, yet he does not score a knockout by any means. Instead Hemingway succeeds mainly in revealing himself as niggling, small-minded, unforgiving and unforgivable, a paragon of pettiness, cruelty, hypocrisy.

Ford's long friendship with Pound is charted ably by Judd. Pound wrote after Ford's death that he had been "a very gallant combatant" (Judd, p. 446) who had taken more punishment than Pound had seen anyone else absorb and who had been treated dishonestly and unfairly for being both impolitic and generous—the opposite of Hemingway and of Conrad.

Alan Judd is the better writer than Jeffrey Meyers even though Judd's punctuation is erratic, his antecedents often vague, his participles occasionally dangling, and his slang sometimes impenetrably British. Meyers's prose is the cleaner and more dependable, but he can misuse such common words as *morbid* and *bogus;* and his style is more workmanlike than felicitous.

Judd's *Ford* doesn't seem to have been edited whereas Meyers's *Conrad* has gotten careful editorial attention. But the oddest aspect of either book, more whimsical than Judd's interrupting his narrative to reprint long poems by Ford, is that Meyers provides a long bibliography about Jane Anderson but only a sketchy list of secondary material about Conrad and no primary bibliography. Meyers leaves out such essential work as B. L. Reid's *The Man from New York* and James Hepburn's *The Author's Empty Purse and the Rise of the Literary Agent,* upon which he has relied heavily for his accounts of Quinn and Pinker.

Conrad continues to get the lion's share of the attention: at least four book-length studies on his work have appeared in the past year, of which the best seems to be Richard Ambrosini's *Conrad's Fiction as Critical Discourse* (Cambridge University Press, 1991); and Cambridge continues to publish his letters. Volume 4, as its predecessors, has been edited very well by Frederick Karl and Laurence Davies. It is exceptionally interesting and valuable, especially for the letters to Pinker and Ford; and the annotation is excellent. We need a new edition of Ford's letters—although not one so comprehensive as the Cambridge Conrad. The same press is also reissuing Conrad's novels, of which the first title is a splendid edition of *The Secret Agent.*

Over the years Knopf has done more by Ford than any other American publisher—until recently, when Ecco began reissuing his work in handsome, durable paperbacks. Now Knopf has published a fine edition of *The Good Soldier* with an introduction by Alan Judd and Max Saunders, who also supply an excellent bibliography and a useful chronology of Ford's life that presents literary and historical events. This edition appears in the new Everyman's Library, which Knopf is publishing in competition with Random House's resuscitated Modern Library—a real oddity since these houses stand under the same umbrella, one provided by a publishing family as strange as any that Ford or Conrad or even Pinker ever encountered.

If Ford, as usual, has gotten the short end, at least his reputation continues to rise; and it is now as secure as it was shaky when

Knopf reissued *Parade's End* with Robie Macaulay's splendid introduction in 1950. Ford has achieved the kind of enduring recognition that can only be bestowed by important writers—in his case Allen Tate, Graham Greene, and William Trevor—and that makes it impossible to ignore his achievement. Such recognition is fortified by the extraordinarily acute criticism written not only by men of letters such as Pound and Greene and Tate but such hands as Samuel Hynes, Mark Schorer, Denis Donoghue, and William Gass, criticism on the whole that is superior to the raft of work done on Conrad, which although quantitatively is much greater is qualitatively far inferior. And think of the poets—William Carlos Williams, Robert Lowell, Richard Howard, and Howard Nemerov—who have written memorably of Ford.

An original and intelligent essay in the psychology of criticism, *Gestures of Healing: Anxiety in the Modern Novel* by John J. Clayton (University of Massachusetts Press, 1991), contains a good deal on Ford and Conrad, although more space is devoted to James, Virginia Woolf, and Lawrence than to Ford and Conrad. Within a limited compass Clayton presents remarkably comprehensive pictures of Ford and Conrad, particularly as imposters. Both men reinvented themselves constantly, changing their names; both were always alien presences in England, misfits who would have been more comfortable on the continent (Ford was in France); both indulged themselves in dreaming about, and idealizing, their defective pasts and identities as they continually remade themselves in conversation and on paper.

Conrad, the weaker and more negative personality, has emerged in the popular consciousness and in the literary mind as the stronger man. Having overcome the difficulties of writing in English and changing his profession, he has been forgiven all and so has emerged as a hero of letters. In fact Ford is the far more heroic of the two—both as a writer and as a human being. If Ford in his service to the Republic of Letters far outstrips Conrad, so too does his achievement as an officer in World War I far outdistance any public service Conrad accomplished. (The same comparison could be made about Ford and Hemingway, to the detriment of Hemingway.) Conrad, who writes very persuasively about heroes and would-be heroes, was himself as decisive and heroic as J. Alfred Prufrock—or the young Lord Jim aboard the *Patna*.

Jeffrey Meyers has not quite plumbed Conrad's essential mystery, whereas Ford emerges clearly in Judd's work and is far more human and distinct and believable than in previous biographies. Arthur Mizener lost his sympathy for the exasperating Ford and so was undone by him; in contrast Judd remains sympathetic throughout this new biography, no matter how disorderly Ford's life becomes as he changes identities and wives and magazines and moves laboriously from one phase of his endlessly complicated life to another. By his mid-fifties, Judd observes, he "was like a puppy on the loose, thoroughly enjoying himself. . . . He had reached that stage of life where his pose was no longer out of keeping with his age or appearance. He was what he seemed. He had achieved himself" (p. 374). And so, after a few more desperate years, he died in want but happy, achieving the heaven that William Carlos Williams movingly describes.

Where is the dour Pole? I am unsure but would not be surprised to learn that he is fretting in Purgatory or bridling in Hell—complaining about the accommodations, begging for money, calling for Jessie and his servants, playing for time, being as miserable in the next world as he was in this.

Hawthorne and Melville, who kicked the traces of puritanism, are together in the celestial paradise; but Conrad and Ford, nominal Catholics who finally believed in nothing but what Ford called the eternity of good letters, are probably now separated, as alien to each other as they were to England all their lives and to themselves after 1914. Is Conrad in Hell with Kurtz? It is a matter worth pondering.

Singing the Blues: The Voices of Eighteenth-Century Bluestockings and Later Literary Women

Janet Ray Edwards

Sylvia Harcstark Myers. *The Bluestocking Circle: Women, Friendship, and the Life of the Mind in Eighteenth-Century England.* Oxford: Clarendon Press, 1990. xviii, 342 pp.

Judy Simons. *Diaries and Journals of Literary Women from Fanny Burney to Virginia Woolf.* Iowa: University of Iowa Press, 1990. x, 218 pp.

The Bluestocking Circle traces the transitory life of the blues, a Pleiadic constellation of women dimly visible today. Around the edges of this scholarly book bleeds Sylvia Harcstark Myers's acknowledged yearning to claim for contemporary academic women a circle of friendships like those which supported the bluestockings in their ventures into the intellectual mainstream. She dedicates her book to the women of her generation "who struggled, often without much success, to share in the life of the mind" (p. xi). Judy Simons looks at less familiar writings by better-known writers: her *Diaries and Journals of Literary Women from Fanny Burney to Virginia Woolf* also includes Dorothy Wordsworth, Mary Shelley, Elizabeth Barrett, Louisa May Alcott, Edith Wharton, and Katherine Mansfield. Simons explores how these women constructed themselves in their private writings, examines tensions and connections between their public and private writing, and, more tentatively, seeks to elevate the diary from footnote status to that of literature.

Similar but not identical feminists—both place the experience and perceptions of the women they write about at the center—Myers and Simons differ in their disciplinary perspectives. Myers speaks social history, drawing on a wide range of primary sources and providing rich context. She takes inspiration from developmental psychologist Carol Gilligan's theory that for young women connectedness precedes autonomy. Simons speaks literary criticism. She places the texts at the center, questioning voice and audience, spaces and subtexts, what is said and left unsaid. She deciphers doubleness, resistance, and unconscious constructions of the self. Myers's feminism focuses on the bluestockings' struggle for assimilation into the dominant intellectual and culture milieu and on how their friendships served this end. Simons's feminism emphasizes women's voices as different from those of men and searches out the distinctively female in their writing. Each book is significant in its own right; taken together, they make provocative dialogue. (Regrettably, Sylvia Myers's recent death means that others must take her part in the dialogue.)

For Myers, the first bluestockings were not "earnest amateurs" (p. ix) concerned mainly to popularize the French salon, nor were they women seeking to challenge and threaten men on their own ground. She agrees with scholars who characterize them as less imitative and less competitive, "virtuous, domestic women with intellectual interests . . . striving for independence" (p. xi). Her study mutes the role of the salon or "assembly," locating it within the broader and more comprehensive concept of male and female friendships. She sees the bluestockings as innovative in using friendship to support their quest for personal and intellectual autonomy and successful in winning some general acceptance for the idea of women as intellectuals. She ties this success to their determination to write and publish in genres dominated by men. Equally important was the historical moment, in which an emerging egalitarianism allowed some reconsideration of the educational capacity of women and the formation of new ideals of rational domesticity, companionate marriage, and friendship. Myers depicts the Enlightenment as a time in which limited change was possible for "determined" women and in which at least some men were willing to assist individual women in their aspirations.

Singing the Blues

The history of the word *bluestocking*, as Myers relates it, bears on the shifting perceptions of gender central to both of these books. Sometime in 1756, one Benjamin Stillingfleet, an amiable botanist who lacked preferment, wore blue worsted rather than white silk hose to an elegant London assembly. Whether social gaffe or eccentricity, Stillingfleet's declasse attire hugely entertained his friends. "Blue stocking" became coterie speech, a tag first for Stillingfleet and then for all the men in the circle. With the "blue stocking philosophers," wrote Mrs. Montagu, she could discuss "Virgil, Milton, and Fingal" (p. 7). The term came to represent a point of view. "Philosophical blue stocking doctrine apply'd to her ear," Mrs. Montagu thought, would cure the complaints of her friend Mrs. Elizabeth Vesey (p. 8). By the 1770s, the friends used *bluestocking* for both genders. With the phenomenon of "women writing, publishing, and taking a public role in the life of the mind" (p. 244), commentators began to use the term only for the women of the circle. To this wider audience, Myers argues, it seemed evident that these women were breaching a taboo by publishing their writing on intellectual topics—an activity theretofore exclusively reserved to men. By the end of the century, a bluestocking could mean any woman with intellectual aspirations, often connoting an affected, pedantic, "female wit," slovenly in dress and puritanical in morals.

Their names will be mostly obscure to twentieth-century readers. Elizabeth Robinson Montagu, Elizabeth Carter, Catherine Talbot, and Hester Mulso Chapone were four of some dozen future friends who grew up in the 1720s and 1730s, when societal expectations were rigorous and there were still those who argued against woman's capacity for learning. However, a girl with some social status, an educated father who took an interest, and, sometimes, brothers who were being educated, might receive some intellectual encouragement. For the blues, older women friends with intellectual interests also were key. In the first and most compelling section of Myers's book, mothers get short shrift, coming across variously as preoccupied with sons, narrow in their own interests, timorous and dependent, ailing, or absent through their early deaths.

For Elizabeth Robinson, who as Mrs. Montagu would be the

catalyst for the bluestocking circle, the idea that "an interest in literature, friendships with unusual women, and even friendships with men with intellectual interests, could be developed within the context of a domestic existence" (p. 43) took its inspiration from two visits she made in her twenties to Bulstrode, the country house of her married friend, the Duchess of Portland. Here she could observe a relationship which reflected the emerging ideal of companionate marriage and enjoy elegant country living and the stimulation of being with accomplished people.

Elizabeth Carter would be their intellectual leader, a woman of wide learning, natural dignity, and independent mind. Her father, a "strong-minded and rather contentious cleric" (p. 46), gave her the same classical education as her brothers and encouraged her to make many of her own decisions. At twenty-one, astonishingly, she went alone to London, where she boarded with Edward Cave, a family friend, and wrote for his *Gentleman's Magazine*. Her Greek epigrams and verses attracted the admiration of Samuel Johnson, also seeking a literary career in London. But in little more than a year, Carter left London with its possibilities for literary recognition and friendships. The reasons are unclear: they may include Carter's discomfort at the hectoring attentions of a widowed clergyman, migraine headaches, disillusionment with city life, and her father's view that if she didn't plan to marry she should find a way to live inexpensively. From then on, Carter lived "in a kind of retirement" (p. 60) in the village of Deal, studying and writing, with family and friends, taking long walks and making occasional visits to friends in other towns.

Hester Mulso and Catherine Talbot, both several years younger, were drawn into the bluestocking circle through their devotion to Elizabeth Carter and later by Mrs. Montagu. Hester Mulso began to educate herself seriously in her twenties, and she was spurred on by her brothers, who considered her bold and clever. One brother bragged about her epistolary debate with Samuel Richardson in which she argued that parents should at some point grant their daughters as much independence as their sons. Though Chapone apologized lest she seem forward, Richardson found her overly bold, and suggested that more comments of that sort might make her unmarriageable. Catherine Talbot was witty, with poetic gifts. She and her widowed mother lived in the home of the Reverend Thomas Secker and his wife. Secker, who would eventually become Archbishop of Canterbury, treated Catherine as a kind of foster daughter and took a strong interest in her education.

To further "new-set the springs of [their] minds," as Harriet Mulso wrote to Elizabeth Carter, they looked to "chosen friends" (p. 61) from different parts of the country and of differing social status. They visited seasonally, but mostly they wrote letters, commenting on nature, history, literature, and issues of the day, including the education of women. The still-tenuous ideal of companionate marriage eluded them all. Neither Carter nor Talbot married. Carter may have feared that marriage would limit her freedom to continue her studies. Talbot refused an offer from a young man she loved deeply, convinced that the match would not meet with approval. The marriages of Elizabeth Montagu and Hester Chapone ended in partial estrangement for one and early widowhood for the other. Their letters show that all experienced loneliness and struggled with a lack of confidence and anxiety about arousing male hostility because of their intellectual interests. But their friendships, their independent interests, and their good fortune in having a degree of control over their personal lives sustained them in their vicissitudes.

To secure their intellectual and personal autonomy, the bluestockings pledged their "virtue"—prudence, modesty, and humility, chastity for single women, fidelity for married women, and usually religious piety as well. Outside of marriage, Myers finds, the blues resisted erotic relationships, whether in same-sex friendships or those with men. Their virtuous behavior ensured the respectability without which they would not have won the acceptance they did in the male intellectual world. But, as Myers shows, their inhibitions exacerbated their anxieties about publishing, possibly contributed to the paucity of their production, and ultimately failed to protect them from hostile male criticism.

When they did write and publish, they did so with trepidation, so the encouragement of friends and mentors of both genders was crucial. Elizabeth Carter translated the works of Epictetus at the request of Catherine Talbot, who like most women did not know Greek. Bishop Secker reviewed an early draft, but his criticism, though blended with encouragement, caused her to give up the translation for a time. She returned to it at Talbot's urging, however, and Talbot led the project of publishing the work by subscription. Mrs. Montagu, writing on Shakespeare, sought advice from Lord Lyttleton and Carter, and she in turn urged Hester Chapone to publish her letters to a niece on acquiring an education. Catherine Talbot was unwilling to publish but kept a "considering drawer" of manuscripts (p. 223) which her friends issued posthumously. All these works received a degree of attention from male reviewers and the public. Carter's translation brought her recognition as a woman of learning and piety and sold well enough to provide for her financial stability. Montagu's essay on Shakespeare was in certain ways the most daring of these efforts, as she attempted to be not only a female critic but to throw herself into the middle of critical controversy among male writers. Boswell's reports of sharp criticism from Johnson effectively prevented any wide influence for Mrs. Montagu's essay, though another factor, Myers judges, was the "lack of a strong, controlling, prose style" (p. 205). Chapone's *Letters on the Improvement of the Mind* was "immensely popular" for "its directness, simplicity, social conservatism, and piety" (p. 235). Talbot's essays and poems gained a small but devoted following. Myers believes that all their accomplishments as writers have been undervalued. For example, Chapone's advice to young women was neither so narrow nor so pious as that dispensed in most advice books, with which hers has been lumped. Chapone actually encourages young women to form independent judgments and suggests reading that will help them acquire an education similar to that of young men. Nevertheless, the success of these earliest blues as writers was limited. It is their use of friendship to gain a measure of intellectual and personal autonomy which is their more original achievement.

Although aware of the condition of women and valuing female friendships, the blues make uneasy company for feminists seeking political reforms. Myers links them implicitly with academic women today and, more explicitly, with the learned women humanists of the quattrocento, who were also educated largely through the interest of their fathers and attempted to participate in the intellectual life of their time. These earlier scholarly women were isolated from one another, usually had to choose between a scholarly life as a religious recluse and marriage without scholarship, and had little impact beyond their own time. In contrast, the blues had supportive friends who shared their intellectual interests, a degree of choice about how to integrate scholarly pursuits into their lives, and the satisfaction of helping younger members of the circle through their friendships and intellectual pioneering.

In *Diaries and Journals,* Simons redefines female yearning and achievement away from the "practised mimicry" (p. 195) of male genres and towards women's efforts to find literary forms and language of their own. She seeks to enrich current research on "dissident subtexts" (p. 189) in women's published writing. She also traces a change from the use of the diary for feelings women masked from public view to its development, in the hands of Virginia Woolf, into a "purely professional enterprise" (p. 170), one genre among others. Simons treats the diary as a kind of autobiography, characterized by immediacy rather than retrospection, as a literary text, and for what it may reveal about the writer's oeuvre as a whole. As Simons's chapter titles suggest, metaphorically diaries are shadows of the self, backstage views, masks behind masks, safety curtains. Earlier, journals and diaries (Simons uses the terms interchangeably) did not undertake the "intense subjective analysis" (p. 6) we now associate with them. Nevertheless, in an age when silence was a virtue, the diary was a form to which many women turned. It was more acceptable because it allowed women to write without competing with men, and because it grew out of an earlier tradition of spiritual self-scrutiny.

Simons maintains that women first emerged in a major way into the public literary world through fictions patterned after the diary, the letter, and the memoir. In these forms of writing, autobiographical rather than scholarly, familiar rather than formal, she finds a female literary tradition already in existence.

Each chapter explores the complex connection between the diaries and published writing. The diaries, by what they say or fail to say, present a sense of individual identity more complex and often more positive than their public persona. Two examples must suffice:

The young Fanny Burney, at the time that she was sharply satirizing those around her in her journal, impressed a male acquaintance as "artless, open, sincere, unexperienced" (p. 24). Later she documented in her journal the stresses of five years of inordinately confining ceremonial duties in the court of Queen Charlotte and, still later, her experiences as Madame d'Arblay, the wife of a French refugee, caught up in events surrounding the French Revolution. Simons singles out Burney's startling, ghastly account of undergoing a mastectomy without anesthetic at the hands of seven black-robed male doctors and deprived of the support of female attendants as metaphoric for her experience of female helplessness and heroism, in which the sense of identity she had developed through her journal writing helped to sustain her. Dorothy Wordsworth's devotion to her famous brother shadowed her ability to claim her own strengths. Simons moves beyond psychological inferences to discern in her journals a poetic and narrative power and a coherent personal vision. The vivid imagery and spontaneous use of metaphor in the Grasmere journal belie Dorothy's judgment that she was incapable of writing poetry. The stories embedded in the journal have the feel of an older oral tradition in which beggars and country people are not, as for Wordsworth, "timeless symbols" of eternal truths, but local individuals, exposed to poverty and harsh weather, whose suffering she presents "without sentimentality but with evident compassion" (p. 54). The juxtaposition of her household responsibilities with her descriptions of nature and country people demonstrates how limited was her time for writing. Nevertheless, the journal integrates the "rhubarb tart" and the "crooked thornbush" (p. 50) in a unified vision of the sources of life, both literal and transcendent, in the Lake District which sustained her.

Considering the diary as a literary genre enables Simons to examine the question of audience. Surprisingly often these literary women wrote with the expectation that their private writing would be seen by eyes other than their own. During her years at court, Fanny Burney sent her journal as a kind of letter to her sister; later, it became the basis for published accounts of her experiences in France during the Revolution. That Dorothy Wordsworth's journal was open to her brother, Mary Shelley's to Percy Bysshe Shelley, and Louisa May Alcott's early diaries to her parents surely plays into our sense of the writer's shaping of her material. The diary kept by Mary Shelley during the turbulent years with Shelley may reveal the repressed sensibility of its author but it equally discloses her nervousness about how it might be read by another. Its brief, enigmatic entries display an "unnatural discretion," withholding mention of Mary's anguish at the deaths of her children and making coded references to her half-sister Claire Claremont—who bore Byron's child and may, Simons speculates, have had an affair with Shelley. Curiously, it is in the anarchic passions and destructive relationships of *Frankenstein*—public, but doubly removed from the personal disclosure a diary might risk—that her emotions find explosive release.

In contrast, Elizabeth Barrett and Edith Wharton wrote with themselves as primary audience. In each case, the diaries served as catalysts for growth. In her twenty-fifth year, Elizabeth Barrett explored her own powerful feelings in connection with her search for direction as a writer. Though she ultimately found the introspection too troubling to continue, the diary provides a chart of personal and intellectual growth, notably symbolized in her account of her growing attachment to a neighbor, a middle-aged, blind scholar, married and with a family, with whom she met regularly to discuss Greek studies. The diary reveals a close bond between the two, more romantic on her part than she was prepared to admit. But as she outstripped her mentor in her facility with Greek translation, she experienced his hostile reaction and began "to perceive, however dimly, that her success could have a distorting effect on her personal relationships" (p. 104). Her breaking off of this relationship marked a decisive step towards artistic and personal independence. Edith Wharton, on the other hand, was an internationally acclaimed author known for her satirical accounts of American and European society when she began to keep a detailed narrative account of her romantic involvement with an American journalist. The conscious artistry of the diary and its expressive, romantic tone, strikingly different from her published work, lead Simons to speculate that in the diary Wharton was experimenting with a romantic persona she had not previously allowed herself to explore.

It is not until the twentieth century, with Katherine Mansfield and Virginia Woolf, that we see a more self-conscious use of the journal in the context of the writer's craft, and a lessening of dissonance between public image and private perceptions. Woolf's diary serves Simons as a touchstone for her tentative claim that the form merits literary status. Insofar as it embodied an alternative, private tradition of women's writing, the diary appealed to Woolf's sense of a developing "female literary aesthetic" (p. 171). Woolf speculated on its possibilities:

There looms ahead of me the shadow of some kind of form which a diary might attain to. I might in the course of time learn what it is that one can make of this loose, drifting material of life; finding another use for it than the use I put it to, so much more consciously & scrupulously in fiction. What sort of diary should I like mine to be? Something loose knit, & yet not slovenly, so elastic that it will embrace anything, solemn, slight or beautiful that comes into mind.[1]

Simons maintains that the journal, Woolf's longest continuous work, was central to her total artistic endeavor. Its commentary is neither introspective nor personal, but analytical, often comical in its choice of descriptive detail, mixing autobiography and fiction. Fluid, non-linear, composed of the "trivia" of daily life, her journal puts the "fabric of woman's life" (p. 178) at the center as a valid subject.

Myers's and Simons's books, read together, provide a rich sense of the private and public lives of bourgeois women intellectuals and writers over nearly two hundred years. Both writers implicitly redefine the character of virtue for women, tying it to honesty, resilience, determination, and, for Myers, the capacity for friendship; for Simons, the search for integrity. Both books raise questions not within the scope of their study to answer. By implicitly accepting the hierarchy of genres, with poetry, the essay, and translation from classical languages near the top, Myers is less able to look freshly at the letters of the bluestockings, whose flexible, lively language is more persuasive of the quality of their minds than the stiffer published works, with their painful sense of audience. Simons's claim for the diary as a "distinctively female" genre leaves unanswered questions about men as diary writers.

Myers assesses documentary evidence with a caution that evokes trust. Her idea of how the bluestockings linked friendship and the life of the mind strikes me as both original and true. If she errs, it is through a wishful generosity with regard to the accomplishment of the bluestockings and in the abundance of her praise for their male mentors. Her fairmindedness ultimately keeps all in balance. She qualifies her admiration of their publishing, for example, by a dispassionate critique of Mrs. Montagu's essay on Shakespeare, finding its ultimate value in her courage in launching into the male intellectual world. Simons's *Diaries and Journals* has a stimulating speculative quality. The interpretive risks she takes are often fruitful, as with her insight into the unique and coherent vision informing Dorothy Wordsworth's journal. In comparison with Myers, the historical context of some of the studies seems sketchy; some interpretations raise for me questions of whether the sensibility informing the interpretation is more contemporary than historical. For example, Simons considers *Little Women* as a myth of domestic harmony, celebrating "female strength that did not set out to disturb the status quo," and says that the novel "well conceals" anger and frustration disclosed in Alcott's diary (p. 128). This reading may underestimate the intensity of rebellious feeling and desire for independence Alcott embodies in Jo March along with her desire to please her family. But Simons is persuasive in showing how increasingly Alcott lived a double life, writing about happy families as a single woman and restricting her stories to the domestic sphere despite her own interests in war and politics. This and other valuable insights in Simons's book originate in her approach to the diary as if it were literature.

Note

1. Virginia Woolf, *The Diary of Virginia Woolf*, ed. Anne Olivier Bell (Harmondsworth: Penguin, 1979), I, 226, quoted in Simon, p. 176.

Not So Idle Tears: Re-Reading the Renaissance Funeral Elegy

Ronald Strickland

Dennis Kay. *Melodious Tears: The English Funeral Elegy from Spenser to Milton.* Oxford: Clarendon Press, 1990. vi, 296 pp.

I allude to Tennyson's deeply personal and rather self-indulgent poem in order to emphasize, by contrast, the self-consciously public tone of address characteristic of the funeral poems— "melodious tears"—Dennis Kay writes about. Kay himself makes a similar point at the end of the book by relating an anecdote from Wordsworth's memoirs. When Wordsworth was a student at Cambridge, the Master of St. John's College died. Wordsworth's uncle, who was visiting Cambridge at the time, expressed disappointment that his nephew hadn't taken advantage of this "fair opportunity" for distinguishing himself by writing an elegy. Wordsworth, however, had no regrets—"I felt no interest in the deceased person, with whom I had had no intercourse and whom I had never seen but during his walks in the college grounds" (pp. 231–32). As Kay points out, Wordsworth's uncle's sense of the aspiring young poet's public responsibility is opposed by Wordsworth's own sense of poetry as a personal, introspective idiom. The conflict between these two aspects of funeral elegy informs Kay's analysis of the development of the genre during the years bounded by the careers of Spenser and Milton.

Melodious Tears enters a long and distinguished line of twentieth-century scholarship on the Renaissance funeral elegy, and, for the most part, the author is content to follow closely in the footsteps of his predecessors; the study focuses on innovations by major poets such as Spenser and Donne, and on the ways in which lesser and later poets borrowed from these master elegists. Spenser's pastoral elegies develop a model of the professional "dirge expert" through which, in the funeral elegy, poets could publicly assert their personal aesthetic aspirations without seeming unduly self-serving. In Donne's hands the funeral elegy becomes less a poem of public praise about the deceased subject than an exploration of the poet's personal response to death. In this vein, bolstering his account with a series of formalist close readings, Kay traces the genre's development from a public discourse of funeral honor into a poetic vehicle through which artists could work out difficult problems of self-expression:

> Some elegists . . . confined themselves to a role that was essentially heraldic; like the heralds, they saw it as their function to ensure a respectful celebration of the status the deceased had enjoyed when alive. But more sophisticated writers recognized that the elegist faced in an especially well-defined way the problem of fitting words to the special requirements of an occasion and of arguing for uniqueness both for the subject and for the elegy. The parallel with the situation of the sonnet is evident. . . . To put it very baldly, just as the sonnet was an aggregative form, in which practitioners defined their individuality against their predecessors, so with the elegist. [p. 4]

Kay's book offers what is basically a "New Critical" theoretical framework, no less aestheticist in its assumptions than earlier books on funeral elegy from an earlier era when that paradigm was dominant.[1] Kay does depart from traditional New Critical practice in one respect, however. He includes among his readings many poems which previously have been ignored or rejected as sub-literary and not worthy of serious consideration, and he prints several previously unpublished manuscript elegies in appendices at the end of the book. Many of the extra-canonical texts are among the most specifically occasional—the most directly tied to the deaths of particular individuals—of all the elegies. Such poems blur the boundary between formal categories of aesthetic discourse and epideictic or honorific public discourse. Kay acknowledges this tension between aesthetic and epideictic categories, but, since he generally neglects to consider the ways in which the genre functions in larger networks of social discourse, he fails to account for some of the interesting, and, I think, important, discursive relationships among the aristocratic elegies of the canonical tradition and the extra-canonical popular elegies.

Perhaps due to the fact that Renaissance funeral elegies are usually tied to specific historic events, scholarship on the genre figured prominently in the historicist resistance to New Criticism during the 1940s, 50s, and 60s. Nonetheless, historically oriented scholars who wrote on funeral elegy—Ruth Wallerstein, Louis Martz, O. B. Hardison, and Barbara Lewalski—failed to mount a successful challenge to New Criticism because they accepted, by and large, orthodox New Critical definitions of aesthetic value and the New Critical emphasis upon close readings of individual texts. Though these scholars displayed a common dissatisfaction with a "purely literary" literary criticism, the New Critical privileging of literary texts as artifacts of timeless value was too deeply entrenched for them to overcome it.

In this climate, and due to its failure to make an epistemological break with New Criticism, literary historicism was relegated to the function of rehabilitating certain texts that were difficult to appropriate for formalist readings. Donne's *Anniversaries* furnishes a convenient example of such rehabilitation; here were remarkable poems by a poet of unquestioned genius, yet they seemed to have no formal or organic unity, and they seemed quite unlike other poems of the genre. Under these circumstances, they could only be judged an aesthetic failure. Then they were rescued; Louis Martz, in *The Poetry of Meditation*, discovered in Jesuit meditation exercises an external context with a pattern that could unify the poems. Soon other readers supplied alternate patterns and interpretations based on other systems of thought. Somewhat predictably, under the pressure of New Critical hegemony the conventional historicist method of seeking for reflections of external contexts in literature was reversed; now critics worked in the opposite direction, beginning with literary forms or aesthetic conventions and then searching for the suitable contextual forms and ideas to match with them.

Kay too works from the poems outward, though in his approach the historical context is limited almost exclusively to the formal evolution of the genre. Most of what I found lacking in the book stems from Kay's adoption of this relatively narrow theoretical framework. In my view, the interdisciplinary and intertextual approaches of New Historicism and discourse theory have rendered traditional aestheticist approaches to literary history and genre criticism somewhat obsolete. Perhaps it was inevitable, given this aestheticist orientation, that Kay's reading of funeral elegy would be most self-limiting precisely in his consideration of non-canonical texts. Since he tends to read the non-canonical texts through a framework of values and expectations derived from the canon, non-canonical texts can only be read as clumsy prototypes of canonical elegies or awkward attempts to imitate them. Yet Kay begins by tracing the genealogical sources of the canonical funeral elegies to the larger generic context of a popular vernacular tradition. He sketches the outlines of this tradition from the close of the Middle Ages: laments for monarchs such as Geoffrey de Vinsauf's threnody for Richard I, *de casibus* tragedies like Lydgate's *Fall of Princes*, political poems including meditations on the human condition under the headings of discussions of particular historical figures, the *memento mori* warning from the dead, and allegorical dream visions such as the *Pearl* or Chaucer's *Book of the Duchess*.

The popular tradition emerges in full bloom in the published elegies—or what Kay calls the "Tudor public" mode—of the late sixteenth century. Written by poets either outside of or relatively marginal to court circles, and sold in bookstalls alongside broadside ballads and popular tracts, the public elegy addresses a fairly broad audience of London citizens. The public elegy tends to mourn the deaths of aristocratic subjects in a highly conventional form, heavily laden with sententious aphorisms and phrases, and generally written in a relatively ponderous poulter's measure or fourteeners. Often the poets use standard ballad devices such as having the deceased subject's ghost return from the grave to tell his or her story. The poems typically begin by celebrating their subject's genealogical lineage, and then they go on to praise the subject in more or less specific personalized (though highly conventional) detail. In the elegies for men, wisdom, military skill, generosity and piety are often praised. When women are mentioned in the elegies for men, they usually appear as faithful and grieving wives and mothers, and they are frequently mentioned as a way of introducing the deceased subject's extended kinship connections—a key determinant of power in the early modern social formation. In the elegies for women, virtue, marital fidelity, generosity, and constance are celebrated. Some of the elegies for women seem to have been written as much to honor their surviving husbands as to honor the women themselves. There are no female authors listed among the one hundred or so surviving published funeral poems from Elizabeth's reign, though there are several anonymous elegies.

The most prolific writers of public elegies were Thomas Churchyard and George Whetstone. These two writers literally cultivated reputations as professional elegists, advertising previous and forthcoming works in the dedications to their elegies and collections of elegies. Though both Churchyard and Whetstone explicitly represented themselves as defenders of aristocratic standards, they wrote for popular audiences and from a social position somewhat marginal to the Court. Writing from this marginal subject position, their texts are governed by conventions and frameworks of assumptions which differ from those of the elite, belle-lettristic tradition. As Kay remarks, Churchyard viewed his function as that of "apologist for the established order," and supposed that "inadequacies of style and want of invention were to be justified by this function" (p. 17).

For the most part, Kay dismisses Churchyard's funeral poems as dull, sententious, and routine. The two Churchyard poems which Kay likes best, those on Sir Christopher Hatton and on Archbishop Whitgift, are characterized by decasyllabic lines rather than Churchyard's usual fourteeners, by "a more personal, more specifically elegiac, form," and, in Churchyard's elegy on Hatton, "an uncharacteristic metrical variety and flexibility . . . a sense of vivid movement . . . of solemn ceremony." For once, in Kay's view, Churchyard had written "a poem of moving richness, almost Spenserian in its sonorous repetition, stately in its rhyme royal" (p. 20). In fact, wherever Kay finds artistic skill in Churchyard's work, he generally attributes it to the influence of

Spenser and other courtly poets. For instance, Kay observes of Churchyard that "the achievements of Spenser and Daniel seem to have led him to cultivate a new and specifically artistic pride in his role—by the 1590's he writes as a man performing a national duty" (p. 22). Such attributions of aesthetic influence and aspiration are characteristic of Kay's analysis, but they often strike me as unconvincing projections of the author's own aestheticist framework onto the early modern texts. Certainly Churchyard saw his elegy-writing as a "national duty," but he seems to have undertaken this duty primarily as a propagandistic task, rather than as an artistic commission. What Kay often fails to notice, on the other hand, are instances in which elements of the Tudor public mode find their way into the works of more sophisticated artists. I will discuss some particular instances of this phenomenon at the end of this essay.

Turning to the elegies of Spenser and Sidney, Kay finds himself in more congenial territory. Unlike the public elegists, Spenser and Sidney see the funeral elegy as primarily an aesthetic rather than an honorific discourse. In his reading of the "November" eclogue from Spenser's *Shepheardes Calender,* Kay points to Spenser's combinations of low diction with learned allusion and of homely and primitive verse forms with more sophisticated metrical effects in a way that extends the conventional honorific style of the public elegy into a new aesthetic realm. In the scheme of Spenser's pastoral allegory the "November" eclogue is "the utterance of a professional commissioned to articulate the grief of a patron in terms which conform to the decorums of subject and season and at a level of art comparable to the poet's best in other genres" (p. 29). A key thesis of *Melodious Tears* is that Spenser paved the way for other poets to use the funeral elegy and the funeral anthology to develop public authorial personae, and to introduce themselves as "professionals"—writes who could put into words the deep, unexpressible feelings of a community of mourners. In effect, Spenser was adapting the established public persona as used by poets like Churchyard and Whetstone and turning it to a much more personal, private use. These adaptations strained under considerable tension between "terms which conform to the decorums of subject and season" and "a level of art comparable to the poet's best in other genres." But Kay neglects to consider this tension between the two discursive functions. Consequently, his formalist close readings of the poems fail to illuminate the shadowy borders of public discourse against which the belle-lettristic funeral elegy developed.

The "November" eclogue was somewhat removed from the contingencies of public funeral elegy, since it was not tied to a specific funeral. And Kay follows his analysis of this non-occasional elegy by reading another text which offers an even more self-reflexive problematization of the epideictic situation, or the relationship of a poem to a specific occasion which it commemorates—Sidney's elegies on the fictional "death" of Basilius in the *Old Arcadia*. Though he notes the potential irony in that the elegies are written for Basilius, who turns out not to be dead, he argues that the poems were "probably first read 'straight', as exemplary laments" and that they were emulated by poets such as Donne, Drummond, and Milton. These elegies were important in the history of the elegy, Kay writes,

> in that the very complexity and accomplishment of the pieces constituted a major divergence from the orthodoxy of the generation of Whetstone and Churchyard. And, even more important, the technical virtuosity was accomplished by a shift of focus, redirecting the elegy towards the speaker. Where his predecessors saw themselves as heralds, chroniclers, and moralizing historians, Sidney showed in his Arcadian elegies a speaker whose struggles with his art, and with his subject, mimed the grief he professed, both by temperament and commission. Sidney had introduced a new specificity, a particularity, into funeral lament, which made the form, like the contemporary funeral sermon, one whose decorums were (like those of the sonnet sequence) predicated on the unique qualities of the subject, speaker, and situation. [p. 47]

Here Kay overlooks an excellent opportunity to analyze the generic interplay between the Tudor public elegy and the emerging belle-lettristic elegy. Certainly his reading of Sidney's poems as a metapoetic exploration of the relationship between seemingly inexpressible grief and the power of art to mediate that grief is informative and convincing. But one wonders to what extent Sidney may be commenting on the larger functions of funeral discourse in Elizabethan society. As Peter Sacks has argued in *The English Elegy from Spenser to Yeats,* public acts of mourning are always, at some level, bids for social power.[2] This insight is particularly helpful in understanding discourses of mourning in early modern England, a highly stratified society with a rigid primogeniture inheritance system which was under considerable pressure as a result of social and economic developments such as the emergence of early capitalist modes of production and rapid urbanization of the population. Moreover, as Lawrence Stone has documented, the growth of elaborate funeral pageantry and the aristocratic funeral processions carefully staged by the College of Arms were in part a response to the aristocracy's need for ideological support.[3] The public elegies clearly played a significant role in this ideological project, and the belle-lettristic funeral poems also participated, however indirectly. Given this larger social and generic context, I suspect there is an element of parody directed at the heraldic, propagandistic, public funeral poems and other increasingly elaborate rituals of mourning in the overwrought laments of Sidney's fictional poet-character Agelastus for the still-alive Basilius.

From these poems on the deaths of fictional characters, Kay moves to Spenser's *Daphnaida,* written on the death of Lady Douglas Howard, and to the poems collected in *Astrophel,* on the death of Sidney. His main concern here is to show how Spenser struggles to accommodate aesthetic forms to poems commemorating actual deaths: how does the poet make art at such moments of crisis? In relation to the *Daphnaida,* Kay argues, Spenser turns to Chaucer's *The Book of the Duchess* as a model both for the content of his poem and for its representation of the relationship between the poet and the surviving spouse (John of Gaunt for Chaucer, Sir Arthur Gorges for Spenser) whose grief is represented. This is particularly important precisely because *Daphnaida* is a self-consciously aesthetic text mourning a fictionalized (though not a fictional) subject, rather than a heraldic commemoration in verse. There is something presumptuous about the poet's attempt to speak for other mourners and to turn grief into an aesthetic object. This presumptuousness is addressed, perhaps, in the refrain of Alcyon's (Gorges's) request for the speaker to "Weepe Shepheard weepe to make my vndersong" in which Kay sees Spenser's defense of the professional poet, whose role is the "exercise of the highest powers of his wit to console his bereaved friend" (p. 52).

In 1595, years after Sidney's death, Spenser's *Astrophel* appeared, along with several elegies by other writers, in *Colin Clouts Come Home Againe*. The *Astrophel* poems consist of Spenser's *Astrophel*, "The Doleful Lay of Clorinda" (which Kay assumes to have been written by the Countess of Pembroke), two pastoral elegies by Lodowick Bryskett, and three poems (which had been published earlier in *The Phoenix Nest*), written by Mathew Roydon, Sir Walter Ralegh, and an anonymous poet. In Kay's view, this group of poems marks a crucial turning point for the funeral elegy. In combining various forms of pastoral, public, and personal elegy, Spenser produced an exemplary anthology which departed from the stiffly formal epideictic tone of earlier published elegies and established a precedent for the experiments of later elegists such as those who contributed to collections published on the death of Prince Henry. Kay acknowledges that most of the poets who wrote on Sidney were "unreconstructed practitioners of the Tudor mode"—"drab age" writers, to use C. S. Lewis's term. But, he concludes,

Spenser's example had begun to attract followers, and they had effectively, even if on a small scale, inaugurated the fashion for elegy as a form within which praise could coexist with reflections on artistic tradition, on innovation and imitation, and through which issues could be explored that were at root cultural and political. [p. 78]

Regrettably, Kay himself never explores the cultural and political issues which circulated in and around the elegies, though such issues are never far below the surface of his analysis. He never considers, for instance, the traditionally subversive function of pastoral as political discourse in relation to the self-consciously patriotic tone of the public elegies, though he does remark, at the end of a summary of elegies on Queen Elizabeth, that the model of Spenser, with its "posture of exile, self-questioning, opposition, and obliquity" was perhaps inappropriate to use in mourning the Queen (p. 90). The pastoral elegies of the belle-lettristic tradition and the public elegies of the Tudor propagandists belong to quite different spheres of aesthetic and political discourse, but when pastoral elegies are combined with public elegies in a published anthology like Spenser's *Astrophel* poems, the two forms inevitably affect each other. Indeed, Kay notes the "processional" organization of the poems in the *Astrophel* collection, and in a footnote he remarks:

> The procession is organized on the basis of affection—"in order lov'd him best"—rather than kinship or other relationship. The pastoral fiction involves the establishment of an alternative order to the social procedures of quotidian society; it also carries with it the notion of community. [p. 61n.]

Yet he doesn't reflect upon the ways in which this processional emphasis draws upon and transforms the much more explicitly propagandistic accounts of processions found in many of the public elegies. He is simply reluctant to talk about the subliterary texts; he does not expect to find in them anything more interesting than a debased version of Spenserian poetics.

If Spenser adapts the epideictic funeral elegy as a vehicle for the expression of personal poetic ambition and as a model for serious aesthetic experimentation in a public forum, Donne all but ignores the epideictic function of the poems. This is accomplished, for example, in Donne's *Anniversaries* on the death of Elizabeth Drury, by the application of a radically "protestant" poetics:

> Donne explicitly translates the Whetstone-Churchyard notion of the elegy as "remembrance" into a new, and altogether more spiritual idiom. The focus is not the subject's fame but her soul, and the speaker is not a herald but a questioning, analyzing intelligence. [p. 101]

Donne, of course, had begun to fashion his innovative elegiac style in his earlier elegies written under the patronage of the Countess of Bedford. In these poems Donne turned away from both the Spenserian pastoral mode and the "heraldic" Tudor public mode of his contemporaries to write in a domestic, argumentative register "appropriate to conversation, satire, and the dramatic expression of inner turmoil" (p. 95). Kay acknowledges that such poems could appear "strange, inexplicable, and monstrous" when, as in the case of the *Anniversaries,* they were read outside of their immediate "domestic" setting—an elite, aristocratic audience limited to close friends of the author. But here, as throughout the book, he doesn't adequately analyze or account for the ways in which audience response and conditions of production affect the aesthetic shifts he is describing. This reticence becomes particularly noticeable in Kay's chapter on the elegies on the death of Prince Henry.

Since the number of elegies published on the death of Prince Henry, in 1612, was far greater than those upon any other death in the period, it is fitting that Kay, like Wallerstein before him, should give considerable attention to this event. Kay emphasizes the influence of Spenser and, especially, Donne, upon writers from a wide variety of political, religious, and social positions who eulogized Prince Henry. Compilers of anthologies such as Joshua Sylvester's *Lachrymae Lachrymarum,* which included elegies by Donne, Goodyer, and Sir Edward Herbert, adopt the role of spokesman for a community of mourners after the model of Spenser in the *Astrophel* poems. Spenser's influence can also be seen in the metapoetic self-reflexiveness of many elegists who questioned the ultimate value of art in the face of death, or the sincerity of highly structured poems of mourning. "Just as Sidney's Astrophil found himself torn between a compulsion to write and a conviction that writing anything other than Stella's name was futile," Kay remarks, "so elegists found themselves confronted with an obligation to write that made the act of composition seem worthless" (p. 143). Finally, the influence of Donne is widely evident. Kay presents examples of the stylistic influence of Donne in a number of poems, including those of Sir John Davies, William Drummond, Cyril Tourneur, John Webster, Thomas Heywood, and Donne's friends Sir Henry Goodyer and Sir Edward Herbert. Other elegists follow Donne's example in making their own response to Prince Henry's death the focus of their elegies at the expense of detailed praise of Henry himself.

Kay rightly sees the death of Prince Henry as the event which brings the funeral elegy to the point of aesthetic maturity as a genre, and he supplies a convincing array of examples to make this point. Yet I am disappointed, as I mentioned earlier, that he doesn't give more careful attention to the discursive interplay between the sophisticated aesthetic tradition of Spenser and Donne and the quasi-propagandistic, epideictic function which can be traced to the commemorative funeral poems of the earlier Tudor writers such as Churchyard and Whetstone. The outpouring of poetry on the death of Prince Henry is remarkable, among other things, for the number of aristocrats who risked what J. W. Saunders called "the stigma of print," venturing their literary efforts before a broad public audience, in many cases with their names affixed to the pieces.[4] The event arguably represents a turning point in aristocratic attitudes about publishing poetry. Perhaps in anticipation of publication, the poems often display elements characteristic of the Tudor public mode as opposed to either the earlier aristocratic pastoral elegies or the domestic personal elegies which were written for manuscript circulation. Furthermore, when former associates of Henry and other courtier poets allowed their verses to be published, the poems themselves were, in effect, altered simply by the exposure to the different expectations of a popular audience of readers and by the writers' conscious efforts to address the general public audience. A more properly discursive analysis of the tension between the aesthetic and epideictic demands of funeral poetry would yield a more precise historical understanding of the genre, and it might improve our understanding of elegies, such as Donne's *Anniversaries* and Milton's *Lycidas*, which have presented somewhat intractable problems for a purely aesthetic analysis.

In any case, Kay generally turns a blind eye to the conjunction of public and courtly (or popular and elite) discourse in the elegies, even as he offers an exhaustive survey which includes poems by writers from relatively low reaches of the middle class as well as the aristocracy. I would like to illustrate this point and to suggest some alternative possibilities for a discursive analysis of the genre by looking briefly at two of the most typical features of the popular (and populist) discourse of the Tudor public elegy which often show up in the elegies on Prince Henry. First, the public elegies often draw attention to other forms of funeral pomp, such as the processions, in ways which emphasize, and sometimes subtly challenge, the processions' representations of the existing social hierarchy. This may be done by providing detailed, quasi-journalistic accounts of the death and burial of the subject, or, in other cases, by producing fictionalized scenes of mourning which blur the distinction between fiction and reality. Second, the public elegies frequently include radical Protestant propaganda, sometimes mixed with populist attacks against greedy landowners and other powerful groups. In John Phillip's commemorative poem *The Life and Death of Sir Phillip Sidney*, for example, Sidney's ghost returns from the grave to relate a detailed description of Sidney's funeral, describing the appearance of the mourners ranked according to social status as they marched in the procession, and digressing along the way for a diatribe against Catholicism.[5]

Some of the elegies for Prince Henry combine representations of or adaptations of other practices of mourning with more courtly forms. Joshua Sylvester's collection, *Lachrymae Lachrymarum*, which included, in its third edition, belle-lettristic personal elegies by Donne, Goodyer, Garrard, and Herbert, also includes an allegorical poem entitled "A Pilgrim's sad Obseruation vpon *a disastrous Accident,* in his Trauaile towards the Holy-Land," written by Henry Burton, who was an officer of the Prince's household. Burton dramatizes a situation in which the narrator, a pilgrim, encounters a sort of funeral procession in which he hears Prince Henry's death lamented by the King, the Queen, Prince Charles, Princess Elizabeth, Elizabeth's betrothed, Frederick, the Elector Palatine, Prince Henry's household, the Church, the Clergy, the Gentry, and "Poets." The order of the speakers in Burton's poem, as in Phillip's poem on Sidney, corresponds and functions as a sort of adjunct to the funeral pageantry staged by the College of Arms with its hierarchical ranking of mourners by social class in the processions.[6]

Another production which crosses the line between poetry and other forms of mourning is *Great Brittans Mourning Garment,* an anonymous collection of sonnets which was addressed to (and possibly commissioned by) the Prince's household.[7] The text apparently was given to mourners at the funeral as a token reminiscent of the free black cloaks traditionally given to all participants in the procession; hence, the title represents an almost postmodern substitution of representation for substance. The published elegies, the free cloaks, and, indeed, the processions themselves, all circulated as "texts" within the highly propagandistic discourse of aristocratic funeral practices, and the belle-lettristic funeral poems of the courtier-poets also participated in this discursive interaction, particularly when the poets crossed the line from manuscript circulation to print.

Yet more clear-cut effects of intertextuality are evident in the instances of Protestant/populist propaganda which sometimes rub shoulders with more elite discursive forms of Spenserian and Donnean pastoral and personal elegy. An early example of Protestant populism is found in William Baldwin's *Funeralles of King Edward the Syxt,* where the reader eavesdrops on a conversation between God the Father and Christ in which the death of Edward is attributed to a cold he caught while playing tennis and to God's decision to punish the sinful people of England for failing to heed His warnings. Elaborating upon the theme that King Edward died for England's sins, Baldwin mounts a series of attacks against enclosures, greedy landowners, corrupt magistrates, lawyers, the misappropriation of Church property after the dissolution of the monasteries, and other offenses against the common people. Christ is identified as the champion of the poor and as their fellow-sufferer, while God rails against the leaders of Church and State:

> Behold the heades, what else do they deuise,
> Saue in our name to cloke their couetise?
> Thine herytage they have the whole bereft,
> Except thy shurt, let see, what haue they left?
> Thy golde, thy plate, thy lodgyng, yea thy landes
> That are the poores, are in the richest handes;
> They waste, they spoyle, they spill upon their pride
> That which was geven the nedy corse to hide:
> And thou lyest naked starving at their gates
> While they consume thy substaunce with theyr mates.[8]

Not So Idle Tears

When this passage is set alongside Joshua Sylvester's poem from *Lachrymae Lachrymarum*, Sylvester's clearly Donne-influenced lines also reveal similarities to Baldwin's much earlier poem:

> How-e'r it were, *Wee* were the *Moouing Cause*
> That sweet *Prince* Henry breath no longer drawes
> *Wee* All (alas!) haue had our hands herein:
> And Each of vs hath, by some *cord* of *Sinne*,
> Hal'd down from Heauen, from *Iustice* awfull Seat,
> This *heauy Judgement* (which yet more doth threat.)
> *Wee Clergy*, first who too too oft haue stood
> More for the Church-goods, then the Churches good.
> *Wee Nobles* next, whose Title, euer strong
> Can hardly offer Right, or suffer Wrong:
> *Wee Magistrates*, who (mostly) weake of sight,
> Are rather faine to feele then see the Right:
> *Wee Officers*, whose *Price* of euery *Place*
> Keeps *Vertue* out, and bringeth *Vice* in grace:
> *Wee Gentles* then, who rack, and sack, and sell,
> To swimme like *Sea-Crabs*, in a *foure-wheel'd Shell:*
> *Wee Courtiers*, next, who *French-Italianate*,
> Change (with the Moon) our *Fashion, Faith,* and *Fate*.[9]

"For," Sylvester concludes, "for the *Peoples* Sinnes, for *Subiects* crymes, / God takes away good Princes oftentimes."[10]

Since these journalistic and sub-literary features subvert the steady line of aesthetic development of the genre, Kay tends to deemphasize them, or to read them as aesthetic lapses or flaws which may pop up even in the elegies of respected poets. But a number of questions and tentative conclusions might be raised and drawn from the evident conjunction of popular and elite discourse in the poems on the death of Prince Henry. For instance, what effect did the close proximity of the propagandistic public discourse have upon the way early modern readers responded to the elite funeral elegies which began to appear from the presses, first, as a slow trickle, with the Spenserian pastorals of the 1590s, and then, in a veritable flood, with the Prince Henry elegies? It seems likely that the set of conventional expectations formed by the Tudor public elegies had something to do with the initial reaction to Donne's *Anniversaries*, both positive and negative. Further, distinctive and sometimes problematic elements such as Milton's digressive attack on the clergy in *Lycidas* or Donne's extended *contemptus mundi* theme in *The Anniversaries* may take on new and arguably richer meanings when seen in an evolving, intertextual context which looks beyond the boundaries of genre.

Melodious Tears does provide a useful and fairly exhaustive survey of Renaissance funeral elegies, and Kay does acknowledge the tension and interaction between the different registers of discourse I have been discussing. But the narrowly aestheticist theoretical framework he employs enforces a linear, progressive evolution upon the genre which tends to foreclose upon the possibility of influence from lesser poets or from discursive forces outside the confines of the genre itself. When one adds to these issues of aesthetic influence the implications of the funeral elegy's effect on non-aesthetic discourses, it is clear that much significant work remains to be done.

Notes

1. See for instance, Ruth Wallerstein, *Studies in Seventeenth-Century Poetic* (Madison: Univ. of Wisconsin Press, 1950); O. B. Hardison, *The Enduring Monument* (Chapel Hill: Univ. of North Carolina Press, 1962); Barbara Lewalski, *Donne's Anniversaries and the Poetry of Praise* (Princeton: Princeton Univ. Press, 1973); and Louis Martz, *The Poetry of Meditation* 2d ed. (New Haven: Yale Univ. Press, 1962).

2. Sacks, *The English Elegy: Studies in the Genre from Spenser to Yeats* (Baltimore: Johns Hopkins Univ. Press, 1985), pp. 36–37.

3. Stone, *The Crisis of the Aristocracy, 1558–1641* (Oxford: Clarendon Press, 1965), pp. 572–81.

4. Saunders, "The Stigma of Print," *Essays in Criticism*, 1 (1951), 139–64.

5. Phillip, *The Life and Death of Sir Phillip Sidney* (London, 1587).

6. Burton, "A Pilgrim's sad Obseruation vpon *a disastrous Accident,* in his Trauaile towards the Holy-Land," in Joshua Sylvester, *Lachrymae Lachrymarum* 3d ed. (London, 1613), pp. G1r–G3v.

7. Anon., *Great Brittans Mourning Garment* (London, 1612).

8. Baldwin, *The Funeralles of King Edward the Syxt* (London, 1560), p. A3r.

9. Sylvester, *Lachrymae Lachrymarum* 3d ed. (London: 1613), p. B2v.

10. Sylvester, p. B34.

Professionalism and Women Writers in Victorian America

Susan Albertine

Susan Coultrap-McQuin. *Doing Literary Business: American Women Writers in the Nineteenth Century.* Chapel Hill: University of North Carolina Press, 1990. xviii, 253 pp.

To what extent were the terms *professional writer* and *female* mutually inclusive in the nineteenth century? Although by no means the first study to attempt an answer, *Doing Literary Business* moves toward a more complex understanding of the social and economic context of professionalism than has been suggested until now. The book discusses the careers of five nineteenth-century American women writers: E.D.E.N. Southworth, Harriet Beecher Stowe, Mary Abigail Dodge ("Gail Hamilton"), Helen Hunt Jackson ("H.H" or "Saxe Holm"), and Elizabeth Stuart Phelps (Ward)—all of them to varying degrees influential, celebrated, and successful in their day. Since women constituted about one-third of fiction writers before 1830 and produced approximately forty percent of novels during the antebellum years, almost half of all popular works by the 1850s, and nearly three-quarters of all novels by 1872, as Coultrap-McQuin reminds us (pp. 2, 47), it seems reasonable to begin by asking, Why these five? According to Coultrap-McQuin, they are typical in social class and race, leaving it to the reader to supply the obviously intended but at first unmentioned terms *white* and *middle class* (p. xi). From the 1840s into the early 1900s they worked in different literary fields and engaged a variety of modes "from the sensational to the serious." But Coultrap-McQuin does not claim finally that they are representative. Rather, she concludes, they can teach us that nineteenth-century women "were literary professionals in the most positive sense of those terms"; their response to professionalism was, moreover, not uniform (p. xiii).

Such conclusions as these have been argued before. Earlier studies by Mary Kelley, Mary Poovey, and Sandra Gilbert and Susan Gubar, for example, have concluded that women felt ambivalence or anxiety about themselves as professional authors, having been socialized for the private, domestic realm and restricted in their use of the pen (pp. 20, 205).[1] Judith Fetterley and Nina Baym have argued otherwise, that women were comfortable and confident in their ability as writers; Lawrence Buell that women gained professional identity as authors proportionally more often than did men in the antebellum and Civil War periods; Gaye Tuchman that no author, male or female, has ever had the rights or autonomy of a professional (pp. 19, 194, 205).[2] Nor is the question of female professionalism resolved, especially if one considers race, ethnicity, class, and geographic region; or women's life cycles and age cohorts, as discussed by Claudia Goldin; or the full "communications circuit," as articulated by Robert Darnton.[3] Cultural historians have only begun to delineate the range of women's participation in the print market of the last century. In the careers of the five writers under study, however, the author has uncovered new evidence of author-publisher relations and of each writer's professional self-conception. If this seems a circumscribed contribution to women's studies, social history, and the history of the book, it is nonetheless a thoroughly useful and informed gathering of biographical evidence in service of an insightful thesis. *Doing Literary Business* encourages a most productive line of questioning.

As for what these five selected careers can teach us specifically about women's literary professionalism, Coultrap-McQuin points toward self-definition: each woman understood womanhood and professional authorship in her own way; each conducted the business of her career in a changing marketplace. It was a marketplace, she asserts, that like the society at large sent women "ambiguous cultural messages"—the topic of chapter 1—at once encouraging them to be literary professionals and at the same time limiting their range of expression. The prescriptions of True Womanhood (an ideology defining female piety, purity, domesticity, and submissiveness) and the doctrine of the separate male and female spheres, emerging together with laissez-faire capitalism, such social factors as increased literacy, and the revolutionary effects of automated book and periodical production, provided white, middle-class female authors with a complex of incentives and restrictions.[4] The Victorian belief, for example, in "moral purity, self-improvement, hard work, genteel behavior, and, in some cases, self-reliance" crossed the lines of gender and suggested to some Victorian women that they "could legitimately speak to their whole society" (pp. 12–13). The widely held opinion that writers in general were genteel amateurs not fully involved in commercial life was not incompatible with popular notions of femininity. Women who found themselves financially at risk might also choose authorship as a kind of work suited to True Womanhood. What mattered was that cultural prescriptions should be enshrined in female texts—that the writer and the writing should be womanly (p. 16). The author does not finally deny the ambivalence and anxiety that Mary Kelley documents among the literary domestics, two of whom (E.D.E.N. Southworth and Harriet Beecher Stowe) appear in *Doing Literary Business* as well as in Kelley's *Private Woman, Public Stage*. Additionally, Coultrap-McQuin finds evidence that women acquired a sense of professional status, which mitigated the anxiety and enabled feminine self-effacement to become an active, sometimes manipulative strategy (p. 97). Yet, Coultrap-McQuin argues, despite the mixed messages from the dominant culture and the mixed responses among writers, the early-century literary marketplace may indeed have been "more congenial to women than any later one"—and this was so because of the distinctive, gendered character of author-publisher relations then.

In the first half of the century, authors and publishers were understood (and I use the passive construction advisedly) to relate to each other more personally than "professionally," an understanding not inharmonious with middle-class women's socialization. Central to Coultrap-McQuin's argument here, as set forth in chapter 2, is a conception of the Gentleman Publisher, a Christian Gentleman and complement of the True Woman

(p. 38).[5] By Gentleman Publisher, Coultrap-McQuin means an advocate of "personal regard, benevolent paternalism, loyalty, noncommercialism ... and Victorian morality" who related to all writers, male and female, "in 'female' ways." This as opposed to the "more impersonal, modern and 'masculine' approach to literary business" that was to follow (p. xii). Taking as their model the Renaissance patron of the arts rather than the eighteenth-century model of the printer-as-artisan, nineteenth-century publishers strove to create a professional image that was "genial and lofty" (p. 28).[6] In the new relations fostered by the change in attitude, all writers, male and female, took the female subject position (although Coultrap-McQuin does not use this terminology), while women in that position experienced it differently from and lacked the advantages of male writers who came to occupy it (p. 39). Among other categorical splits, most obvious is the difference that remained between women as popular writers and men as literary artists (or great writers). Yet despite their doubly secondary status, women stood to benefit from such hierarchical affiliation. Based on the limited evidence available, Coultrap-McQuin suggests that women received royalties at about the same percentage as did men (p. 40). It was also crucial to the woman's professional image and self-esteem that her work outside the domestic sphere could be conducted according to the relations of power that obtained at home. If the author-publisher relationship could be construed as marital or familial, as private and intimate, with paternal authority correctly vested, then society would have less to suspect and the individual woman less to fear when engaged in the very public act of publication. Just how intimate the relationship could be is suggested in a letter from E.D.E.N. Southworth to her publisher Robert Bonner:

The first day that you entered my little cottage, was a day, blessed beyond all the other days of my life. I had some genius in popular writing; but not one bit of business tact and my pen was the prey of whoever chose to seize it. When you came to my cottage, I was dying from the combined effect of over work and under pay, of anxiety and of actual privation.... But that same winter you came to me, ... and from that time to this, nearly fifteen years, you have made my life prosperous and happy. Every improved circumstance around me, every comfort in my home, every attainment of my children, speak of your kindness and liberality to us. Among the pre-eminent blessings of my life, for which I daily and nightly return thanks to the Giver of All Good is your friendship for me. [p. 50]

Whether a writer acquiesced in such traditional, eroticized relations of power, and with what degree of awareness, or whether she found the means to resist, is by no means easy to predict or describe, as the several biographical chapters illustrate. Mary Abigail Dodge rejected a conventionally gendered female role and adopted "androgynous" behavior (pp. 128, 134). Southworth, Stowe, Hunt Jackson, and Phelps all complied, although in different ways. A firm believer in what Coultrap-McQuin calls "individuality," Helen Hunt Jackson, for example, chose True Womanhood for her female characters and often for her own conduct, and clearly preferred Gentlemen Publishers—except when she could get a better percentage. Her professional demeanor, Coultrap-McQuin observes, is marked by paradox and enigma as she worked in a market that itself "struggl[ed] to balance the older Gentleman Publisher's values with more modern commercial goals" (p. 166). As Hunt Jackson wrote to James T. Fields, "I never 'write for money,' I write for love: then after is it written, I print for money.... 'Cash *is* a vile article'—but there is one thing viler; and that is a purse without any cash in it" (p. 155). For Hunt Jackson to be womanly and artistic and financially solvent meant a reconciliation of values seemingly at odds. As woman and artist, she writes for love, demarcating her distance from commercial aims by using the appropriate clichés. Yet she forthrightly stakes out her own commercial ground by drawing a line between writing as art and printing as business. It is a fascinating maneuver.

While Coultrap-McQuin seldom offers a close analysis of primary material such as this, concluding merely—and repeatedly—that Helen Hunt Jackson is "paradoxical," caught between "individuality" and True Womanhood, the same evidence makes other conclusions possible. Hunt Jackson obviously learned how to market herself and her writing as desirable commodities, desirable to both publishers and readers. She did this by summoning True Womanhood when it was practical. Coultrap-McQuin's "individuality" seems to be typical American middle-class *individualism,* which is always predicated on a degree of conformity, no more incompatible in practice with True Womanhood than with Christian Gentlemanhood. If it seems "paradoxical," it is no more so than individualism itself. The author's unwillingness to examine her interpretive dichotomies, to pull them apart, as Myra Jehlen suggests in "Archimedes and the Paradox of Feminist Criticism," is a signal weakness of the book.[7] Here and elsewhere one wishes that Coultrap-McQuin had noted the degree to which these five middle-class women adopted individualism and modified it along the lines of gender.

The pairing of the True Woman and the Gentleman Publisher as "standards" by which to measure the relations of author and publisher is nonetheless a valuable contribution of the study. As "ideal" and "image," Coultrap-McQuin tells us (p. 32), the Gentleman Publisher has particular explanatory power. The notion that publishers should be gentlemen is, of course, not new. In *A History of Book Publishing in the United States* (1972), for example, John Tebbel noted the wide currency of this idea in the nineteenth and twentieth centuries. Both Donald Sheehan, in 1952, and John Tomsich, in 1971, observed likewise, Sheehan describing publishers as "lik[ing] to believe they were members of a profession requiring special scholarly training and a sense of dedication which rose above material gains"; Tomsich citing Sheehan: the nineteenth-century publisher, from the 1840s, "persistently distinguished himself from the rest of the business world."[8] Coultrap-McQuin's use of the idea differs significantly because it invites consideration of gender. Yet her Gentlemen Publishers, as the relentless capitalization implies, are not unproblematic. Like earlier scholars, she has had to reconcile the motives of noncommercialism or cultural philanthropy to those of a fiercely competitive market—a market that Tebbel describes (from 1800 to 1865) as "a hardnosed, competitive scramble in which it was difficult and sometimes impossible to maintain the facade of gentility that nevertheless continued to characterize publishing."⁹ While Coultrap-McQuin offers a good deal of evidence that the "ideal and image" of the Gentleman Publisher affected his conduct, she makes a much less persuasive case when she argues that publishers' sincere commitment to their values "probably perpetuated lower profits in the industry"—that they sacrificed materially for the sake of their beliefs (p. 43).

The difficulty—the very intractability of the categories—arises in her failure to see the reified concept of the Gentleman Publisher as an ideological construction. The fact that she never uses the term *ideology* to approach the concept is merely a sign of what's missing in the analysis. Hence she has trouble discussing what she continually sees as ambiguous and paradoxical in the "ideal and image": the Gentleman Publisher was motivated by the ideals of noncommercialism, benevolent paternalism, personal regard, and loyalty and at the same time compelled by competitive economic forces. Finally, though, she suggests that money mattered less to Gentlemen Publishers than did their ideals. Beyond this formulation, she apparently cannot go. It is indeed a rhetorical impasse: the Gentleman Publisher was "dedicated to the advancement of culture more than (as well as) profit" (p. 47). Had Coultrap-McQuin interpreted the Gentleman Publisher as an ideological construct, she might have been able to move farther. It would be well worth considering, for instance, that the advancement of culture and the profit motive are inseparable, together producing a "culture industry," as sociologist Gaye Tuchman puts it.[10] Certainly publishers stood at a material advantage by promoting a noncommercial image, especially when the commodity was intellectual and artistic. How much more so when the artist was complaisantly feminine—unlike Mary Abigail Dodge, whose fight with James T. Fields, documented in chapter 5, usefully complicates the gentlemanliness Coultrap-McQuin claims for Fields elsewhere in the chapters on Harriet Beecher Stowe and Elizabeth Stuart Phelps. There is more going on here than "paradox." It's worth noting, by the way, that William Charvat calls Fields's literary friendships "window dressing compared to the vital relationships which [he] built up in the world of critics, editors, and reviewers," a strategy that illustrates how an interest in promotion (a financial advantage) could mean more to a Gentleman Publisher than his constructed affiliations with authors.[11]

With some persistence, Coultrap-McQuin argues that the profit motive and the values of the Gentleman Publisher were separate entities: "The most respectable [publishers] did sacrifice personal gains by adhering to the ideal" (p. 44). More, she denies that "those lofty aims were meant to mask competitive, capitalist motives" (p. 34). Yet I must insist that in an increasingly diversified capitalist economy, the desire for profit drives ideology and it denies or obscures the very behavior on which it depends. There is, in fact, evidence of such masking in the very sources that Coultrap-McQuin uses to make her case. Tomsich handles the problem this way: "Publishing was a business, of course, but almost to a man the major publishers resisted the notion (how much they resisted the practice is another question) of setting a price upon literature."[12] Sheehan's Cold War-era justification of the ethics of Gilded Age business chronicles the "zest for cultural philanthropy" that influenced the attitude of the trade even while allowing that cultural concerns were "not the major determinant in the decision to publish."[13]

There is no doubt that most successful nineteenth-century publishers did not amass the vast fortunes of other Gilded Age magnates, but it does not follow that actual (rather than perceived) sacrifice was the cause. Market conditions in the late century were notoriously difficult, especially before international copyright laws. The development of modern techniques of promotion and advertising, succeeding the former often corrupt practices of reviewing or "puffing," had a positive effect on professionalism and author-publisher relations, as Charvat argues, but would not have required financial sacrifice.[14] Nor does Sheehan, on whom Coultrap-McQuin particularly relies, offer hard evidence of material sacrifice across the industry. Instead, he claims that "a sense of monetary sacrifice conditioned the outlook of trade leaders."[15] It must be asked if a sense of monetary sacrifice among an elite group is the thing itself, or if the perception of sacrifice conditions the very exchange on which author-publisher affiliation depends. Finally, Sheehan concludes that the biggest names in Gilded Age publishing (Frank H.

Dodd, the second Charles Scribner, George Haven Putnam, among them) acted on "self-interest that sought its salvation in self-restraint rather than in cut-throat competition and illegalisms," having inherited their values from the preceding generation (often their fathers), when noncommercial aims were considered the more genteel and scholarly.[16] If, to turn the screw just a bit, we look to Tebbel's analysis of these idealized earlier years (1800–65), we get a different view. Concerning literary piracy, in which even genteel publishers like the house of Mathew Carey took part, trade courtesy was "a pious fraud."[17]

This is not to suggest that author-publisher relations remained static through the century. An impersonal, objective "masculine" ethics of corporate capitalism clearly did succeed more personal, subjective "feminine" or familial practices, but not so neatly as Coultrap-McQuin would have it. The ideology of gentlemanly publishing, which she finds empowering for women through the mid-century, did unquestionably influence some significant author-publisher relations. At the same time, the women under study managed to work with publishers whose credentials were not genteel. Coultrap-McQuin sometimes notes this—in the background—to show that women preferred the more conventional arrangement with a gentleman. E.D.E.N. Southworth's troubles with Henry Peterson, no gentleman, allow Coultrap-McQuin to tell how Robert Bonner, Gentleman Publisher (if marginally so), offered much more satisfying relations (pp. 63–69). Yet while Southworth devoted herself to Bonner, for serial publication in the *New York Ledger,* she published her books with Theophilus B. Peterson, a rich and powerful pirate and early exploiter of the mass market whose "facade of respectability" was at best quite flimsy. Both T. B. Peterson and Southworth did well by the arrangement.[18] Noting that Southworth conducted business with T. B. Peterson throughout much of her career, Coultrap-McQuin does not remark Peterson's status in the trade. Yet an argument favoring the professional competence of such women as Southworth would be strengthened if she were seen as more flexible in her range of dealings with publishers and less dependent on Robert Bonner. One cannot help but wonder to what extent relations between women writers and genuine Gentlemen Publishers were characteristic of all relations between women writers and publishers, however gentlemanly (or gentlewomanly).

Further, one questions why Coultrap-McQuin insists that relations between Gentleman Publisher and author were based on unimpeachable sincerity and financial sacrifice. In effect this is to argue that hierarchical relations of power on such a basis were a good thing for women, or at least for women who adapted True Womanhood to suit their purposes. Despite other differences in their conduct, all but Mary Abigail Dodge were more True Women than New Women on the continuum between the two types that Coultrap-McQuin delineates in chapter 1; and Dodge, who opposed woman suffrage, does not herself qualify as a New Woman. I would like to suggest that an extension of the traditional gender hierarchy opens up but limited opportunities for a limited class of women—above all in the interests of the class itself. A few more rungs added to the ladder means for most women a longer climb to the top. Coultrap-McQuin implies an apology for the inequities of the relationship: women writers accepted inequality; publishers accepted less money. Most telling is the fact that not a shred of evidence of financial sacrifice on the part of the Gentleman Publisher appears in the biographical chapters.

If Coultrap-McQuin had seen how the ideology of True Womanhood, itself a construction, works to foster middle-class hegemony, she would make better sense of "the ambiguous cultural context" for women, notably that the ambiguity is sometimes more apparent than real. As Linda Kerber concludes in her historiographic essay "Separate Spheres," based on work by Gerda Lerner and many other women's historians of the last twenty years, the rhetoric of True Womanhood and the spheres is itself a sign of "a particular and historically located gender system" that could be at once "prescriptive" and "useful and emotionally sustaining" for middle-class women.[19] Although Coultrap-McQuin acknowledges that the women under study were members of the middle class, she discusses neither ideology nor rhetoric and seems puzzled about the intersection of class and gender—the extent to which women constitute a class in themselves and to which their behavior is determined by social class apart from gender. "Like all subordinate classes," she observes, "women had knowledge of the dominant class' views, including its Victorian ideals and its concept of authorship, which were not wholly distinct from the ideals and concepts of woman's sphere." This, she suggests, is "the overlapping nature of the ideals and concepts" (p. 25). While hegemony is indeed implicit here, a more useful reading would consider the complex interaction among factors of gender, sexuality, ethnicity, and race that fosters class dominance. Both True Womanhood and New Womanhood exist within parameters of the middle class; both perpetuate that class, the one conservatively, the other liberally. Although some conservative Victorians, male and female, wished to keep middle-class women out of the paid workforce altogether, others could see that True Womanhood had marketable value, that True Women had to be active participants in the economic life of the class, that True Womanhood had to be compatible with individualism. What else to do with widows and abandoned wives, often mothers of middle-class children, like E.D.E.N. Southworth? It would have been more surprising if female professionalism had failed to emerge under such conditions. Four of the five writers had to support themselves and sometimes their husbands. Only Mary Abigail Dodge was an unswerving careerist, and she chose a career because, Coultrap-McQuin suggests, she thought herself ugly and unmarriageable.

To ask for this sort of analysis is not to deny Coultrap-McQuin's achievement. She has provided the means for further discussion of women's professionalism. Her extensive archival work, particularly with correspondence between writers and publishers, uncovers telling differences in professional conduct among the women. One appreciates how each writer acquired the skills to negotiate her business while preserving for herself a female identity not incompatible with True Womanhood and also not rigidly bounded by that ideology. Both E.D.E.N. Southworth and Harriet Beecher Stowe were True Women, but Stowe, a domestic feminist, was far more assertive in her dealings with publishers (p. 80). Mary Abigail Dodge's fascinating ambivalence—her anti-suffragism, her choice of masculine (or androgynous) identity, her female pseudonym ("Gail Hamilton")—suggests just how warping the most commercially successful values could be. Elizabeth Stuart Phelps's increasing conservatism, her movement toward True Womanhood even as she supported woman suffrage and prided herself on always having been a working woman (pp. 178–84), is likewise an object lesson in the complex and sometimes wrenching effects of female professionalism. At the same time Helen Hunt Jackson's mostly traditional feminine behavior seems not in the least incompatible with her successful accommodation to the market. While agreeing with Mary Kelley to a point, that women use disguises and self-effacement because they feel anxious about public exposure, Coultrap-McQuin also makes the important observation that professionalism is dynamic, something gained over the course of a career. It might be mediated by anxiety, but it can be shown to evolve. Female professionalism requires a seriousness about and commitment to writing as a career, and a consequent growth of self-esteem. Often, professional behavior includes a willingness to receive advice from mentors and to give it, especially to other women. Not only does the writer develop literary expertise, but she also learns how to conduct business directly in the marketplace, which demands flexibility, judgment, and bargaining skills. Coultrap-McQuin's particular group of women justify themselves as professionals by citing the moral or cultural uses of their writing. Finally, professional conduct for these five women often depends on an intertwining of private and professional concerns, which, Coultrap-McQuin argues, could best occur in their relations with Gentleman Publishers (pp. 195–97). If these characteristic behaviors do not meet Tuchman's strict definition of professionalism, they are nonetheless definitive signs of conduct within a realm of gendered, class-based economic relations.

Was the market finally more congenial to women at mid-century than thereafter? Did the "personal relationships, non-commercial aims, and moral guardianship" that characterized author-publisher relations then not only give way to more masculine ethics ("competition, profits, and timeliness" [p. 192]) but also "edge women out" as professionals by the end of the century? Citing Tuchman and Christopher P. Wilson, Coultrap-

McQuin closes by asking that such a hypothesis be tested further.[20] It's worth speculating about what could be done, for instance, with a study combining literary biography or career criticism and the new sociological approach to the production of culture. Tuchman's quantitative analysis of the Macmillan (London) archives, the *Dictionary of National Biography,* and the *British Museum Catalogue* leads her to dispute the received literary historical view that in the nineteenth century women writers "came into their own." She finds instead that English women writers born after 1814 "had to work harder than men to achieve less acclaim," that the very success of women novelists at mid-century encouraged men to invade the genre and "gentrify" it, so that by the turn of the century, the high-culture novel had been defined as a nearly exclusive male preserve.[21] If this narrative is also accurate for the American high-culture novel—as remains to be seen—it fails to address the participation of women in print culture, whether "high" or "low," at every point in the communications circuit: writers, editors, publishers, reviewers, promoters, booksellers, and readers.

Notes

1. See Mary Kelley, *Private Woman, Public Stage: Literary Domesticity in Nineteenth-Century America* (New York: Oxford Univ. Press, 1984); Sandra M. Gilbert and Susan Gubar, *The Madwoman in the Attic: The Woman Writer and the Nineteenth-Century Literary Imagination* (New Haven: Yale Univ. Press, 1979); and Mary Poovey, *The Proper Lady and the Woman Writer* (Chicago: Univ. of Chicago Press, 1984).

2. See Nina Baym, *Woman's Fiction: A Guide to Novels by and about Women in America, 1820–1870* (Ithaca: Cornell Univ. Press, 1978); Lawrence Buell, *New England Literary Culture: From Revolution through Renaissance* (Cambridge: Cambridge Univ. Press, 1986), p. 378; Judith Fetterley, *Provisions: A Reader from 19th-Century American Women* (Bloomington: Indiana Univ. Press, 1985); and Gaye Tuchman, with Nina E. Fortin, *Edging Women Out: Victorian Novelists, Publishers, and Social Change* (New Haven: Yale Univ. Press, 1989), pp. 19, 35.

3. For a discussion of technology and its effects on the reading public which might be applied to a class and regional analysis of women's participation in the print market, see Ronald J. Zboray, "Antebellum Reading and the Ironies of Technological Innovation," in *Reading in America: Literature and Social History,*

ed. Cathy N. Davidson (Baltimore: Johns Hopkins Univ. Press, 1989), pp. 180–200. See also Robert Darnton, "What Is the History of Books?" in Davidson, ed., *Reading in America*, pp. 27–52 (reprinted from *Daedalus*, 3 [Summer 1982]); and Claudia Goldin, "The Changing Economic Role of Women: A Quantitative Approach," *Journal of Interdisciplinary History*, 13 (1983), 707–33.

4. On True Womanhood, see Barbara Welter, "The Cult of True Womanhood, 1820–1860," *American Quarterly*, 18 (1966), 151–74. On male and female spheres, see Linda K. Kerber, "Separate Spheres, Female Worlds, Woman's Place: The Rhetoric of Women's History," *Journal of American History*, 75 (1988), 9–39. On labor history, see Alice Kessler-Harris, *Out to Work: A History of Wage-Earning Women in the United States* (New York: Oxford Univ. Press, 1982).

5. On the Christian Gentleman, see Charles E. Rosenberg, "Sexuality, Class, and Role in Nineteenth-Century America," *American Quarterly*, 25 (1973), 131–53.

6. Zboray argues otherwise, that an artisan ideology remained definitive for nineteenth-century publishers; it justified the industrialization of printing while at the same time obscuring it. See Zboray, pp. 181–82.

7. See Myra Jehlen, "Archimedes and the Paradox of Feminist Criticism," in *The Signs Reader: Women, Gender and Scholarship*, ed. Elizabeth Abel and Emily K. Abel (Chicago: Univ. of Chicago Press, 1983), p. 83.

8. John Tebbel, *A History of Book Publishing in the United States*, 4 vols. (New York: R. R. Bowker, 1972), I: 207. John Tomsich, *A Genteel Endeavor: American Culture and Politics in the Gilded Age* (Stanford: Stanford Univ. Press, 1971), p. 19. Donald Sheehan, *This Was Publishing: A Chronicle of the Book Trade in the Gilded Age* (Bloomington: Indiana Univ. Press, 1952), p. 5.

9. Tebbel, I:207.

10. Tuchman, pp. 22–26.

11. William Charvat, *The Profession of Authorship in America, 1800–1870: The Papers of William Charvat*, ed. Matthew J. Bruccoli (Columbus: Ohio State Univ. Press, 1968), p. 180.

12. Tomsich, p. 19.

13. Sheehan, pp. 5–6.

14. Charvat, pp. 298–316.

15. Sheehan, p. 4.

16. Sheehan, pp. 8–9, 12–14.

17. Tebbel, I:208.

18. Tebbel, I: 247–48.

19. Kerber, pp. 39, 26.

20. See Christopher P. Wilson, *The Labor of Words: Literary Professionalism in the Progressive Era* (Athens: Univ. of Georgia Press, 1985).

21. Tuchman, pp. 207–08, 211, 215.

Of Making Many Books on Chaucer

D. S. Brewer

Peter Brown and Andrew Butcher. *The Age of Saturn: Literature and History in* The Canterbury Tales. Oxford: Basil Blackwell, 1991. xii, 296 pp.

Katherine Heinrichs. *The Myths of Love: Classical Lovers in Medieval Literature.* University Park and London: Pennsylvania State University Press, 1990. 270 pp.

Erik Hertog. *Chaucer's Fabliaux as Analogues.* Medievalia Lovaniensa. Series I/Studia XIX. Leuven: University Press, 1991. x, 290 pp.

Charles A. Owen, Jr. *The Manuscripts of* The Canterbury Tales. Cambridge: D. S. Brewer, 1991. x, 132 pp.

Lee Patterson. *Chaucer and the Subject of History.* Madison: University of Wisconsin Press, 1991. xix, 489 pp.

Sabine Volk-Birke. *Chaucer and Medieval Preaching Rhetoric for Listeners in Sermons and Poetry.* Scriptoralia 34. Tübingen: Gunter Narr Verlag, 1991. 315 pp.

Katharine M. Wilson and Elizabeth M. Makowski. *Wykked Wyues and the Woes of Marriage: Misogamous Literature from Juvenal to Chaucer.* Albany: State University of New York Press, 1990. x, 206 pp.

The extraordinary richness of Chaucer's writings with their many ramifications into all aspects of fourteenth-century culture has throughout the twentieth century been better recognized in the United States than in Britain. It may be because the culture of the United States has always retained a thread of interest in rhetoric and in the social implications of literature, whereas in England the development of Romanticism led to a concentration in poetry on the lyric, on personal expressiveness and introspection. Although nineteenth-century English literature is marked by many fine narrative poems, the essence of poetry was felt to be lyrical. The climax of such tendencies came paradoxically in *The Waste Land,* demonstrating T. S. Eliot's view that even an epic poem should be very short. Chaucer's genius, on the other hand, though it encompasses the lyric note especially (and paradoxically in *Troilus*) is narrative and needs space to develop. In the nineteenth century in England the neoclassical novel with its realism reached its height. Chaucer could be seen to relate in some ways to the realist strain in the narrative literature of prose, and to that extent his genius was recognized, but Chaucer's realism is intermittent and conceived on a non-materialist base. It was not well understood. Meanwhile in the twentieth century in England narrative itself came to be regarded as a lower form of literature. John Stuart Mill in his too little known essay *On Poetry* in 1833 dismissed almost all of Homer as mere narrative, not poetry. E. M. Forster in *Aspects of the Novel* took a similarly patronizing attitude to narrative in 1933.

Scholars in the United States, often under the guidance of the French, may well since the Second World War say *"Nous avons changé tout cela."* Narratology, still supported by rhetoric, seems almost to dominate the field of literary theory, although it is a narratology that in almost every case disregards the most fundamental form of narrative, which is "traditional story"—a quite different kind of narrative from the usually rather few nineteenth- and twentieth-century novels which are taken as the basis of modern literary theory. But even that is changing. Furthermore, the intellectual vein in literary scholarship of the United States has also fastened on Chaucer with benefit.

Meanwhile there has also been since the war an increased interest in Chaucer on the part of scholars in continental Europe. Up to the middle of the twentieth century Chaucer was worthily studied in Germany but, with some notable exceptions, mainly from a philological point of view. We do indeed owe to German scholarship of the late nineteenth and twentieth centuries the recovery and presentation of many medieval English texts including some of Chaucer's. From the point of view of literature, however, Chaucer seems not to travel south as well as the claret

Of Making Many Books on Chaucer 89

which the English developed in the Bordeaux region in the fourteenth century travelled north. Such prestige as Chaucer had tended to be attributed not without truth to his French models. Nowadays, a number of scholars from European nations north and south have made quite remarkable contributions to the study both of Chaucer and of Medieval English literature in general. In this respect we have all benefited from wider European horizons.

The present clutch of books under review illustrates many of the trends of modern Chaucer criticism, yet still with some flavor of national style. It should be said immediately that all these books are good. It is most heartening to see such a flow of learned, intelligent books on Chaucer with fresh and developing insights. The continental (if I may use that now rather old-fashioned-sounding adjective) scholars are characterized by a high level of technical interest and a scientific but always humane approach to their subject-matter. They are systematic and informed by contemporary scholarship. They have in the most general sense of the term a "rhetorical" approach.

The American books are varied. They are all intellectual to a high degree and are well grounded where relevant in the literary history of the period, sometimes going back to antiquity. I also have a sense that they are at the same time strongly engaged with current political issues. The most obvious of these is Lee Patterson's *Chaucer and the Subject of History* which is a product of the "New Historicism." Nevertheless, it seems driven by political interests. Patterson's is the most powerful of the books under review, written in a highly modern language owing much to French influence, notably Derrida. I sometimes think that the "New Historicism" is an interesting variant of the "Old Marxism," which has obviously undergone a bit of a blow recently, but Patterson has a subtle and deeply engaged mind.

Katherine Heinrichs's *The Myths of Love: Classical Lovers in Medieval Literature* is much concerned with the development of classical mythology in European vernacular poetry, and mythology is very much a contemporary concern. The situation of women is an important topic in it as it is in Katherine Wilson and Elizabeth Makowski's excellent historical survey of *Wykked Wyues*. This book better responds to the current surge of interest in women's writing but is splendidly balanced and judicious, considering the inevitably distasteful hostility to women shown by so much traditional medieval literature.

Charles Owen's consideration of the manuscripts of *The Canterbury Tales* is highly technical in a way that has been characteristic of a vein of United States scholarship since Manly and Rickert. Its technicality is formidable but leads to important literary considerations. One curious fact to me is that I found the English in both Hertog's *Chaucer's Fabliaux* and Volk-Birke's *Chaucer and Medieval Preaching Rhetoric* a good deal easier to understand than Patterson's. I find I have continually to explicate Patterson's language to myself before proceeding to the next stage of finding out if I agree. Peter Brown and Andrew Butcher's *The Age of Saturn* remains within the personal pragmatic English tradition, although heavily influenced by criticism from the United States. It is more informal and less formidable than Patterson's. Amongst all these books there is a great deal to learn and, as far as I am concerned, quite a bit to disagree with.

One general problem for me, which arises particularly with the books by Patterson and by Brown and Butcher, is the lack of historical sympathy which they sometimes show. It is surely right in modern times to condemn the attitudes that virtually every traditional society has maintained towards women. In a traditional society which by definition has primitive technology and virtually no medicine it is inevitable that women should suffer greatly. Such societies are also deprived of long historical views and of much self-criticism. They achieve within their own terms a *modus vivendi* which is not suitable in modern high technology societies. High technology has mercifully liberated women.

Yet it is absurd to take a high moral line against such societies. The very pluralism of which we are now so proud ought to allow us to sympathize rather than to condemn. It is true that traditional societies are not pluralist. They have a strong sense of absolutes which we think we have abandoned. Yet the high moral tone of condemnation which is taken by Patterson, for example, against the father Virginius in *The Physician's Tale* is in itself an absolute based upon modern standards. There are a number of critics of this kind both in the United States and in Europe (including Britain) who sacrifice their historical sympathies to their virtuous championing of modern causes of equality between the sexes and so forth. Such writing, especially when developed with such zeal, intelligence and learning as Patterson deploys, makes for exciting reading once one has decoded it. It will surely be greatly influential. In some ways this is the best kind of criticism, honest, energetic, partisan, deeply engaged, which makes one realize how important and how human are the issues which Chaucer is dealing with. It avoids that kind of false historicism which places painful questions safely in the past. It also makes Chaucer's own concerns modern. That is its strength. That is equally its weakness. Chaucer was writing in the fourteenth century and there seems no doubt that he was fully meshed into the culture of his time, as indeed Patterson argues. Yet the core of Patterson's book is to develop, as he expresses it in his introduction, Chaucer's "specific cultural problem—the need to liberate writing and the writer from the constricting social environment of the court" (p. 22).

There is no doubt a truth in this, as I have myself argued recently and no doubt less powerfully in the Göller Festschrift (*The Living Middle Ages*, ed. Böker, Markus and Schöwerling, Stuttgart, 1989). Yet it seems to me to fit more easily into a modern North American democratic, egalitarian frame than into Chaucer's hierarchical society. After all it is clear that *The Canterbury Tales* is designed for courtly and gentry society, not least the so-called *fabliaux*. This could still leave Chaucer in his latter days as an "anti-Ricardian poet." But internal criticism has always distinguished European medieval society. Criticism of Richard, or even of the court, is not disengagement from the court. Again, there was undoubtedly hostility on the part of peasants against the gentry—a hostility, incidentally, occasionally supported by members of the gentry, as in the Peasants' Revolt. What society does not have its internal dissensions? But that was rather different from a hostility which could be called "class-warfare." In the Revolt the peasants were notably loyal to the young king, except for John Ball, who wanted to be king himself.

The obsession with class and particularly with the bourgeoisie seems to me to be an inheritance from Marxism that has become quite noticeable in post-war criticism. "Bourgeois" is a highly pejorative term. But the medieval bourgeois was a town-dweller, and there is ample evidence of the interpenetration of the upper levels of town-dwellers, such as Chaucer's family, with the court in the fourteenth century. It is equally clear that, although there was plenty of concern in the fourteenth century with the levels of society revealed in various ways, not least in poll tax lists, there was on all sides an emphasis on maintaining hierarchy. The divisions so maintained were accepted by everybody. There was not an "ideology" (favorite modern word) of class in anything like the same form as that which has persisted in the second half of the twentieth century, partly sociological and partly mythological. It is clear that Chaucer was a "new man" in some ways. The case has been known and accepted for many years. To this may well be attributed his detachment and also the range of his knowledge of society insofar as that was not the product of unique genius. But when we return to Chaucer's "Complaint to his Purse," we do not see him detached from the court. Indeed, he is here making a witty petition to the fountainhead, not only of honor but of reward. He is making a petition as a courtier, not as a poet. (Incidentally, it would be interesting to know if anybody has attributed this poem to a stupid and uncomprehending narrator. It is just as stagey in its way as the narration of *Troilus and Criseyde*.) The truth of the matter is that, as Patterson and many critics recognize, Chaucer writes as it were in a multiplicity of voices. He switches from one to another and there are not always very clear signals to tell us how he is speaking. This is no doubt the source of much of the ambiguity and neutrality of his tone. It is also the source of much fruitful discussion of Chaucer's meaning. I will freely agree that in the past I may often have read Chaucer too simply and without recognition of ironies or alternative possible readings. But such ironies and alternatives are often modern anachronisms. True interpretation requires that one think oneself into a different historical situation, take account of what was and was not thinkable, and use the past, in the old cliché, as a window rather than as a mirror. Naturally, complete identification with another culture will never be possible.

Of Making Many Books on Chaucer

The multiplicity of voices that Chaucer legitimately deploys (as do other poets) allows him particularly to indulge his dramatic genius. It is this which gives so much variety to *The Canterbury Tales* and allows for so much freedom of interpretation. Despite longstanding attacks on the "dramatic fallacy," i.e. the notion of the tales as being so to speak dramatic soliloquies expressive of a character, there are still critics who take the tales as psychologically fully expressive. Some parts of the tales seem indeed to have this quality; other parts do not. Much of this variability can be interpreted in terms of "traditional story-telling" which escapes from the nineteenth-century concepts of dramatic characterization. What is remarkable about Chaucer is that he maintains so much drama which can be psychologically interpreted.

Patterson is of course deeply interesting in this respect. He is fully involved in the modern American concern with "the self" and "subjectivity," and is particularly interesting on *The Wife of Bath's Prologue*. He takes its basis to be a preaching model, thus linking up, though in a very different style, with Volk-Birke's more specialized work. (One of the many virtues of Patterson's book is the way it links into a variety of such topics as are treated in the other books under notice here.) At the same time he is much influenced by deconstructionist notions. A good deal of his account of the Wife's *Prologue* and indeed her tale is a witty deconstruction in pregnant metaphors. In summary, "At the heart of the Wife's dilated discourse, then, rests the subjectivity that it both masks and discloses" (p. 310). This is part of a subtle argument that I am not always sure I understand. On the other hand, much of the energetic and learned argument does lead to a gratifyingly "natural" reading. It is impossible to summarize this rich and impressive book in a review; there is no doubt of its importance as a contribution to Chaucer studies, in placing many topics in interesting contexts, both modern and ancient.

By contrast *The Age of Saturn* offers a more personalized, less modernistic approach. It is also more deliberately limited in scope and discusses only five tales. The book begins with a disarming confession by the authors of how they came to write the sort of book they have done and has an excellent summary of both traditional and new approaches to the literature. They invoke such new approaches for themselves, but a good deal of what they write about the poetry is fairly obvious commentary without much historical depth, or with totally unconvincing historical connections. For example, *The Merchant's Tale* is seen (as usual) as a black and bitter comedy and is said to be written with reference to the historical situation in 1377. "History" is often a summary of political events and it is the events of 1377 which are said most improbably to be paralleled also by the opening of *The Knight's Tale*. The thesis about Saturn, the planet which brings disaster, though it can also in certain circumstances be benevolent, does not seem to me to be very penetrating. The view taken of *The Knight's Tale*, for example, is fairly well established and, although I am in a minority here, quite wrong. It is indeed true that Chaucer presents in this tale an unsentimental, harsh view of reality and of the chivalric life but it is far from being a view of total despair. Life is what it is, with much sorrow; but joy follows sorrow just as sorrow follows joy. To concentrate only upon the sorrow, that is, upon the end which is death, is sentimental. It is also from the point of view of Chaucer's culture inaccurate. Whatever people felt "naturally," they were well enough indoctrinated, as all the evidence goes to show, in the fourteenth century, to believe that death was not the end.

There is also real virtue in necessity, and much of the sententious wisdom expressed in *The Knight's Tale* by both Theseus and his father is perfectly good sense. Modern critics may call it banal and platitudinous but so is much of Shakespeare's, like Chaucer's, greatest poetry. The criteria of the New Criticism are anachronistic and untrue, in this respect, of natural human response. Existential despair that rejects such wisdom is merely kicking against the pricks, which Chaucer deplores in biblical reminiscence, in his short lyric "Truth." Modern critics may not believe that God will deliver them and perhaps he won't, but Chaucer surely had such a belief. This is not merely personal impressionism, it is a judgment which can be backed by reference to cultural commonplaces of many kinds. As far as *The Knight's Tale* is concerned, the poem can be called optimistic in that the general lesson of the story is that you have a 50/50 chance of survival and success, even if you suffer on the way. Brown and Butcher, against all likelihood, since the poem almost certainly existed before the Knight was thought of, regard the Knight as "an unreliable narrator." The dramatic fallacy comes in again even though it makes the preceding arguments in favor of existential despair less logical. For if the Knight is unreliable, so may be a message of despair attributed to him. The modernistic attack on the "ideology" of Theseus is by the same token weakened. To summarize, both these books are politically correct. At times, however, they are historically and anthropologically misguided, but most modern critics will agree with them.

Charles Owen's book on the manuscripts of *The Canterbury Tales* is far too technical for me to attempt even a summary of his views here. I would just pick up the interesting implication that among other matters the Retraccioun is not genuine. The arguments are complicated and I am not convinced by them, though my resistance is mainly on literary grounds and by the pricking of my thumbs, rather than by analysis of the textual argument for which there is no room here. The interest of this textual work is intrinsically very great, but here the important thing is the literary implication. Norman Blake's view that *The Canon's Yeoman's Tale* is not by Chaucer because it is omitted from the Hengwrt manuscript is rejected and surely must be so. The Retraccioun is a more tricky matter since our view of its authenticity can fundamentally alter our view of Chaucer's total outlook. The genuineness of the Retraccioun can be supported by cultural references of various kinds. What we can see of Chaucer's multiple poetic personality would easily allow us to accept a change as death approached. Nor need one be too certain that this was the very last thing that Chaucer wrote. It would be quite possible in relatively old age after a bad dose of flu to feel conscious of a misspent life, but to revive and write a little more of the former kind of poetry without destroying the literary last will and testament. Leaving that aside, however, we note how certainty or uncertainty about the canon of Chaucer's work (a canon of a different sort from him who had a yeoman) can greatly affect our view of Chaucer's work.

The classic example of how basic scholarly detailed work can affect our whole estimate and understanding of a writer is the establishment of a reasonably certain chronology for Shakespeare's plays in the nineteenth century. (Such detailed work is rooted in larger changes of cultural outlook, but that is a further question not to be pursued here.) In Chaucer's case we would benefit from a clearer understanding of the chronology of *The Canterbury Tales;* meanwhile, the relatively marginal uncertainty about the canon is a useful check on our understanding. It is also a useful reminder of how important the notion of the canon is, though nowadays sometimes under attack. Patterson, as so often, manages to take into account some of these matters as well.

The other books deal with matters of literary history of perhaps a more traditional kind, but they are fully armed with the apparatus of modern scholarship. Hertog's book on Chaucer's *fabliaux* is excellent. Again it is very complicated and defies summary. In essence he takes the well-known cases of the *fabliaux* existing in several analogues and organizes them in terms of the narrative rather than in what may be called the "verbal realization." The analysis is painstaking but highly readable. There are four "case-studies" which establish these traditional stories as having certain cores which Chaucer varies in different ways. There is a fruitful analysis of each story which both indicates its general sources of effectiveness and brings out vividly the quality of Chaucer's own individual handling of "commonplace" material. Hertog remarks that the originality of the framework of *The Canterbury Tales* provokes the reader into setting up links and making connections among the tellers and their tales. These connections are very extensive indeed. They involve traditional topics as well as stereotyped characters and individualizing traits. Hertog finds a transition from a traditional symbolical model to a more "modern" one reflecting contingency and the reality of material experience. In the course of this demonstration we learn a great deal about the treatment of traditional stories and about the way in which Chaucer really does manage to disengage himself, as Patterson reasons, from certain traditional attitudes. The book is densely argued but highly readable and follows a method, partly borrowed from the folklorists, which could be pursued with profit in relation to other stories and poems of Chaucer's.

Volk-Birke also takes a kind of analogy, this time between the medieval sermon and some of the rhetorical uses of the poetry. Her work comes within the general tradition of studies initiated in recent years at the University of Freiburg-im-Breisgau on the relation between orality and literacy. There is a good deal of technical rhetorical analysis and *The Pardoner's Tale* naturally comes into its own for such analysis. The interaction between the Pardoner and his pilgrim-audience, the formulas he employs, his structural organization, his narrative and his patterns of development are analyzed in terms of the practices of sermons. These are not matters simply of surface structures but of deeper meanings and Volk-Birke moves easily between the larger structures of rhetoric and detailed analysis of individual phrases. Her final chapter deals with *The Nun's Priest's Tale,* which is seen as a transformation of preaching. We are, of course, defended from taking the moral seriously. *The Pardoner's Tale* is taken, as Patterson showed it to be, on a different level altogether. And *The Parson's Tale* is dreary. One might put a *caveat* in here. *The Parson's Tale* is called by Chaucer a "meditation" and it is very unlike a normal medieval sermon. That is no doubt intentional. Modern critics find it drab and dreary and I would not wish to recommend it as the most delightful reading. It is a clear case where the historical-anthropological approach of sympathetic insight into an alien culture is required. One could make a strong argument for the compulsions of chastity, sexual restraint and so forth, even for hierarchy and control, in the technologically primitive, traditional medieval society. It is even possible that modern society could find some advantages in such constraints.

Wilson and Makowski's excellent *Wicked Wyues and the Woes of Marriage* takes up another aspect where a great deal of sympathy has to be found. The authors show remarkable restraint in dealing not only with the mysogyny but, in a way, the more interesting misogamy, which characterized a good deal of medieval clerical satirical writing. The book is anchored in the classical antecedents and in particular the inheritance of misogyny and misogamy from Latin. We are then conducted through ascetic, philosophic and general misogamy with full references and much quotation. It is a thoroughly useful handbook on this dismal subject. It is historically well-informed and gives an excellent basis for understanding some of the cultural factors which lie in particular behind *The Wife of Bath's Prologue*. On reading the account of all these misogamous tracts, which often merge into straightforward and to us outrageous anti-feminism, one can only be grateful (contrary to the university teacher's usual habit), for the extraordinary unteachability and natural vitality of ordinary people. Surely most men and women disregarded a whole millenium of biased and miserable condemnation. One must inevitably feel dismay at the sufferings of women in such a period, though one might also add that these are sufferings imposed mainly by nature. What Christianity did in part was to attack and condemn "nature." The anti-naturalistic stance of so much Christian thought in the Middle Ages was misguided in some ways, but one can see how it arose in so absolutist an otherworld religion. The paradox has been its ultimate development into our modern conquest of nature, with its attendant pluralism and materialism. When considering misogamy, it is worth recalling (as Patterson shows some authors did) the real sorrows of marriage. It is always worth remembering Emily in *The Knight's Tale,* who prayed so heartily not to be "made a wife and bear a child." It is worth remembering that before the end of the eighteenth century or even later, even in Europe, four children out of five who were born died before the age of five. As Chaucer shows, this did not destroy mother-love nor even paternal care. It may even have intensified them, and their agony. The stresses and strains of such life, such death, the effect upon personal emotional structures, is extraordinarily hard for us to imagine and to recreate. It is equally hard for us to recreate what was for millennia the "normal" attitude to sex in fairly advanced societies. We know, of course, from the "sexologists," that virtually every imaginable and indeed unimaginable variation of sexual activity has been practiced somewhere at some time and regarded, if not as inoffensive, at any rate as acceptable. But the long Western tradition of hostility, or at least disapproval, of sexuality, with its roots in Greek, Latin and Jewish thought, and which is now so unimaginable at least to the young, had great power. It demands an effort to recreate it imaginatively and to understand how perfectly decent ordinary men and women (so far as ordinary or indeed extraordinary people are decent and normal) could come to accept it. We have lost the concepts of awe and fear and "women's mysteries" which underlay not only so much mysogyny and misogamy but also that strange and beautiful flower, equally dead, "romantic love."

We turn finally to another treatment of that romantic love, of which, strangely enough, one of the many roots was the corpus of stories of obsessive and disastrous love which were so frequent in classical mythology. Western civilization is based upon a profound and doubtless fruitful self-contradiction. After the collapse of the Roman Empire, Christianity salvaged classical learning in the West. The Church needed such learning since Christianity is essentially a religion of the Book and books. The problem obviously is that the learning was pagan and that the main Christian tradition, as it arose out of its other, Judaic strand, was deeply hostile to the pagan character of the learning it could not do without. In consequence classical mythology, which had underlain the structure of so much classical thought, was taken over, but had to be sanitized in various ways. Heinrichs takes the history through the various themes of classical lovers and Christian morality, through their treatment in pilgrimage, and, as she calls it, the foolish lover, concluding after a long treatment of French poets with classical lovers as portrayed in Chaucer. She notes the combination of the moral, the religious and the courtly in Chaucer and finds that their internal contradictions give humor. Humor is a problem for me in this book. She finds, for example, that Machaut's *Fonteinne* is an elaborate Boethian comic parody at the expense of Venus. This seems to me to be a very long-winded joke but I suppose it is possible. *The Book of the Duchess* is seen as part of the inherited comic tradition and the narrator is inevitably silly. Heinrichs finds the story of Ceyx and Alcyone given "an even sillier application" by the narrator in *The Book of the Duchess* than is found in Machaut. All this hilarity is rather in the Robertsonian tradition and most of the medieval mythologizing is seen as comic or simply absurd.

There is a good deal of moralization. Dido is seen as an example of lust and irrationality. Much of the interpretation of these poems, including *The Parliament of Fowls,* seems to me to be crude and over-simplified. Laughable absurdity is found everywhere, but no delicacy nor any sense of love. Heinrichs shows that medieval poets did indeed see more and different things in classical mythology than did the original classical authors and she recognizes the plurality of voices. On her showing, however, the medieval vernacular poets are mostly dull univocal jesters. She disregards her own argument for multiplicity. Despite my disagreements, however, I found this book a full and useful survey of some classical mythology in medieval vernacular poets. Heinrichs's scheme allows her to make, for example, sensible observations on the mixture of autobiography and fiction in such poets' writing about what is apparently themselves. The book is in effect a series of studies, with Ovid's *Amores* as the given original theme, on which later authors play their own variations. Historical comparisons of this kind are always valuable and variety of interpretation inevitable.

Among such recognized differences, not to speak of *différances*, and while recalling Cardinal Gasquet's cheerful remark to the Pope that "no one is infallible," it seems worthwhile to assert again that even in these delicate and complex investigations, intersubjective as they are, it must be possible to be right—or, of course, wrong. Otherwise discussion and even thought are useless.

Vital Signs: Humanist Scholarship, Literary Theory, and the Body of Knowledge

L. M. Findlay

Alvin Kernan. *The Death of Literature*. New Haven and London: Yale University Press, 1990. ix, 230 pp.

When the Avalon Professor Emeritus of Humanities at Princeton writes a book entitled *The Death of Literature,* one might be tempted to wonder whether this will be a sustained Jeremiad from someone increasingly aware of his own mortality, or shrill alarmism from a senior scholar badly out of step with recent developments in his discipline and in the culture at large. However, anyone who has read Kernan on Shakespeare, satire, Samuel Johnson, or *Literature and Society* ought to know better. His work has seldom (if ever) been unduly sour or glib, and he has not allowed success as a scholar and teacher to excuse him from reading widely and thinking critically about his chosen profession and its relations to literature and to the contemporary university. Himself a strong exemplar of the humanist tradition, he knows that this tradition cannot long survive if it simply averts its gaze from the modern world or sees but a whirl of epigones where (some humanists may fondly surmise) beauty, truth, and goodness once held undisputed sway. Kernan is not averse to a dash of sensationalism to grab our attention, but once he has secured that attention he does not waste the opportunity; instead, he contrives literature's death scene with a strong sense of how satire and drama can be effectively enlisted in the double cause of complication and vividness. In an introduction, eight chapters, and an epilogue, Kernan contributes intelligence and balance as well as candor to a debate that has too often degenerated into sectarian conflict. I will deal in what follows with the major challenges issued in his introduction, connecting them to particular chapters to bring out the local and cumulative force of his arguments.

Kernan begins by justifying his sensational title as not so much his own invention as the echo of a slogan widely employed in the 1960s and confirmed regularly thereafter in books such as Leslie Fiedler's *What Was Literature?* (1982). Meeting audacity with audacity, Kernan claims that there has been a complete reversal of "traditional romantic and modernist literary values" (p. 2), and that this has been attended by a thorough demystification of the author, art, the canon, and a cultural continuum originating in ancient Greece. Here we see the scholar of satire at work, perhaps too sanguinely accepting the strategy of reversal as a means of challenging, clarifying, exposing, and then rehabilitating persons or practices. Kernan insists that his emphasis will be factual rather than judgmental, a claim that seems to sit well with his desire to locate the literary, as imaginative product or commentary on that product, in a wider context of cultural change. However, the promised contextualizing is far from sober, not least because Kernan is unable or unwilling to curb his talent for trenchant, witty, manifestly interested as well as interesting characterization. In conceiving recent developments in literary studies as "complex transformations of a social institution in a time of radical political, technological, and social change" (p. 10), Kernan seems to disperse individual culpability in larger patterns of social determination, but he retains the satirist's affection for the representative instance, the far from innocent example which hovers between ad hominem animus and curative pursuit of a widely distributed vanity, hypocrisy, or evil. The result is eminently readable, the demonstration of a particular position on the question of the intelligibility of academic discourse, and on the capacity of the concrete instance to resist or refine the schematizing tendencies of the cultural historian. Modesty and mordancy, erudition and engagement, abound in this book; however, that abundance is an imperfect consolation for what is ignored, misconstrued, or too readily dismissed. In *The Death of Literature,* Kernan reveals himself to be, in the words of his dedication to A. Bartlett Giamatti, a "Staunch Defender of Good Sense," but that notion proves on this as on other occasions to be more exclusionary and problematic than its advocates are usually willing to admit.

In characterizing the changes of the past thirty years, Kernan makes one of his most damaging preliminary charges with deconstruction clearly in mind: "What were once the masterpieces of literature, the plays of Shakespeare or the novels of Flaubert, are now void of meaning, or, what comes to the same thing, filled with an infinity of meanings, their language indeterminate, contradictory, without foundation; their organizational structures, grammar, logic, and rhetoric, verbal sleights of hand" (p. 2). Maybe deconstruction is another word for death, for the death of literature as determinate meaning (and the accountability that derives from such determination). Kernan's tactical overstatement takes the impasse of *aporia* from its rhetorical moorings in Derrida and de Man and pushes it to the extreme of the simultaneously full and empty text, asserting the identity of opposites in a single net effect, "the same thing." But is Kernan really intent on attributing to deconstruction the chaotic collapsing of distinctions hitherto essential to the judgments of "good sense"? There is certainly an attempt to reify the effects of deconstruction and render them deficient through an appeal to experience or a pragmatic standard. Equally clearly, there is little sympathy for the possibility that deconstruction may escape from the bind of the binary by reconstituting logical difference as the play of *différance,* or by understanding identity not as a property of things that are the same (*idem*) but as the process of generating representations *identidem* (that is, recurrently, but in an infinitely differential series which never "comes to the same thing"). The nature of Kernan's quarrel with deconstruction becomes clearer later.

In chapter 3, "Authors as Rentiers, Readers as Proletariat, Critics as Revolutionaries," Kernan elaborates on his earlier claim:

The razor-close readings of deconstruction always eventuate in discovering that all texts, because of the indeterminate nature of language, contradict themselves in ways that cancel out even the possibility of any meaning, however ironic or ambiguous, and this is about as far away as it is possible to get from the position of the new criticism that works of literature are sacred texts so intensely meaningful that any paraphrase is heresy. Jacques Derrida and J. Hillis Miller, along with Jonathan Culler and other notorious deconstructors, regularly deny the nihilistic tendencies of deconstruction, insisting that they do not so much deny the possibility of meaning as they free the readers from the burdens of imposed and illusory single meanings to make possible a variety of meanings suiting human needs. In this, as in much else, they follow Nietzsche, who spoke of a "gay science," a "happy and dexterous negotiation of a surplus, or excess of meaning." [p. 81]

The earlier claim about the annihilation of meaning is reiterated here in spite of the explicit demurs of some very distinguished (or "notorious") scholars. Kernan shows a rather uncritical allegiance to traditional logical categories in his move from contradiction to cancellation of even the possibility of meaning, a move that seems to fly in the face of, for example, such difficult but intelligible notions as Derridean *erasure* (a derivative not of Nietzschean nihilism but of Hegelian *Aufhebung*), or the Derridean *pharmakos* as both disease and cure (a radically revisionary reading of Plato's *Phaedrus*, to be sure, but a reconstitution of meaning rather than its utter abandonment). Is the Law of Non-Contradiction any more sacrosanct, one might ask, than any other law, including the Law of the Father? Logicists like John Ellis clearly think so, and hence the aggrieved sectarianism of their assaults on deconstruction. Kernan emphasizes the social more than the logical dimensions of "good sense," insisting on the practical outcome of particular reading practices: the "always eventua[lly]" rather than deconstruction's "always already."

Even though his interests and emphases are socially pragmatic rather than severely philosophical, Kernan shows little inclination to repeat the criticisms from the left about deconstruction being in cahoots with new criticism and other formalist evasions of the stench and viciousness of the real world. Indeed, Kernan attributes to deconstruction social consequences of a quite different kind, linking it to a Nietzschean conscription of that "unmasking" (p. 81) traditionally associated with the reconstructive acerbities of satire. Kernan counters deconstruction's colonizing of satire with an appropriation of his own, aimed at reconfining displacement within narrative, in this instance within the plot of academic politics. He admits to the dislodging of single, privileged interpretations by deconstruction but insists that the demystification of the canon and its most authoritative commentary has been at the same time a remystification of critical discourse and the "creation of sophisticated mandarins teaching in the more prestigious universities" (p. 83), mandarins whose devotees are the legions of the disenfranchised on the edge of the profession and exemplars of alienated labor in emphatically lesser institutions. Kernan recognizes the intellectual elitism of a methodology which works with a recondite minicanon and an unremittingly difficult rhetoric of its own, and he lives up to his opening promise to connect such critical practice to larger social patterns and concerns. However, it is worth noting that the idea of hierarchy seems to pose a problem for him only when the 'wrong' people are in power at the 'right' places, when distinction becomes notoriety and its appeal inflammatory rather than reassuring. It is not intellectual mastery *per se* which must be deplored, but rather the subversive masters of the new arcana.

For Kernan, the power of print has given way to the crisis of literacy. Drawing on his work on Dr. Johnson's *Dictionary,* Kernan affirms that "literature has historically been the literary system of print culture" (p. 133), and that a move away from print implicates even (or especially) print's most privileged messages, namely literature and literary criticism, in the fate of their medium. In the eighteenth century, Samuel Johnson could virtually create the English language while in no way denying the continuing power and unruly nature of spoken English. By the late twentieth century, so the argument goes, the links between ordinary language and literary discourse have become so attenuated, the attempt to subsume speech in writing so concerted and zealous, that writing now concerns itself principally if not exclusively with questions which, when placed (as they must be) within the electronic matrices of the information age, are swept to the margin or appear to vanish altogether. Kernan can perceive differences between American and British lexicographical practice in our own time, but neither the *OED* nor the most recent *Webster's* would deny or permanently delay the arrival of the referent in the way that deconstruction seems to do. The process of putting difficulties in the way of reading and interpretation is a double movement, creating an ever wider chasm between academic discourse and the dialect of the tribe, but at the same time joining both varieties of language in a common fate at the hands (or on the screens) of technology. There is an evident disjunction between deploring limited reading at the level of functional literacy while celebrating its incompleteness at the level of deconstruction (p. 145). But this disjunction can also be viewed as a conjunction of sorts at a historical moment when economics, chemistry, and above all technology are poised to claim cultural primacy from print and for television.

Kernan is sensitive to the vanities of dogmatizing, and endeavors to keep an open mind on issues such as this: "Whether deconstruction has saved literature remains in doubt, but it seems unlikely" (p. 146). He bases his skepticism about the preservative or redemptive capacities of deconstruction on two contrasting but equally unacceptable notions: safety-through-secession (literature is as forbiddingly indeterminate and estranged from the ordinary as deconstruction alleges it to be, and therefore not bound for hell in a handbasket like the rest of the culture); and privilege-as-quintessence (literature encapsulates more thoroughly and intensely than any other form of representation the dominant and irreversible tendencies of the culture, and hence will remain the supreme means by which we understand ourselves). But even if one accepts that these are the only options available to deconstructionists and that they are vulnerably elitist, there are still problems with this account. Most obviously, deconstruction seems not to have been much concerned with the preservation of literature at all. Indeed, deconstructionists have proved as willing as structuralists to read any text no matter how 'lowly' or avowedly unimaginative or anti-imaginative—beer mats and post cards as well as medical, legal, and philosophical works—and hence they can hardly be accused of harboring an ambition to save literature as traditionally understood. If de Man, for example, aimed to affirm the linguisticality of the literary as ideological critique, using literature's connections to grammar and writing to expose symbolic wholeness and aesthetic disinterestedness as, respectively, allegorical contrivance and rhetorical suasion, then he can hardly be taken to task as a fairweather friend or ineffectual defender of literary tradition. Of course, there may be some legitimacy and point in attributing intention to deconstructors who vanish from accountability into the conundrums of decentred selfhood, the death of the author, and the tyranny of indeterminacy. (As we shall see, this point is made more forcibly later in an extended discussion of de Man.) But we can discern nevertheless that Kernan is trying to have it both ways, blaming deconstruction as socially transformative discourse (serving the interests of the political left) *and* as socially impotent or escapist obscurantism. In so doing, he is not necessarily wrong, but he is at the very least paying inadvertent, quasi-deconstructionist tribute to logic's elasticity or to its limited capacity for making sense of a very complex set of circumstances. The most serious devotees of a hermeneutic of suspicion might immediately declare, "I told you so! The learned professor is of the devil's party without knowing it!" However, it is neither fair nor accurate to brand Kernan a crypto-deconstructionist.

Kernan situates various contradictions, including his own and those of the academy more generally in the United States, in the context of massive social change. He is not interested in suppressing difference; neither is he interested in reducing difference to *différance* as the inescapable property of language and of all the layerings, inscriptions, and erasures of the venerable palimpsest that makes up human society. When Kernan sticks his neck out, it is not to make extravagant claims for what he knows and still loves to study. Not literature but society is the residually mysterious, protean plenum which elicits from him one of his most daring and self-revealing claims:

The computer might almost be treated as an advanced form of writing and printing, but television is an openly revolutionary force, pictorial rather than verbal, vigorously at work everywhere in the world, changing all it touches, politics, news, religion, sports, "life-styles," and consumption. Such common culture as we still have comes largely from television. [p. 147]

Kernan's version of cultural critique makes generous allowance for the importance of the means of production to our understanding of what counts as knowledge or as credible grounds for community. He can even extend the notion of textual production to include computer technology, but he is no naively or ruthlessly literary pantextualist. For him the word is succumbing to the electronic image which (in a revealing instance of synesthesia) "touches" all aspects of life and all corners of the world. However, for Kernan's reader there remains a problem with the characterization of television as "an openly revolutionary force." First of all, how open a medium is it? Is it not as susceptible as any other medium of communication to manipulation and ideological reduction or closure? And is it inescapably revolutionary as a simple consequence of its ubiquity, its penetration, its share of the semiotic pie? One might say that it is potentially revolutionary, certainly, but one cannot generalize about its impact in different parts of the world unless one defines "revolution" in apolitical ways. In North America indeed it might be argued that television has been the enemy of revolution and the defender of the status quo, a marketing tool which protects the interests of business while making of the public interest little more than homage to catatonia: soaps and game shows, much muzak for the Pepsi Generation, the clamorous banalities of the commodity wars interspersed occasionally with bytes of simplistic, slanted, and apologetic seriousness.

Now television might be read as the product of electronic interleaving and editing which extends the hegemony of print culture rather than marking its imminent demise. Kernan's example of the television interview in 1988 between Bill Moyers and Joseph Campbell, an interview which gave a dramatic boost to sales of *The Hero with a Thousand Faces,* leads him to the conclusion that "if you want people to read, or at least buy, a book, nowadays, advertise it on television" (p. 147). He appropriately broaches the question of what buying a book signifies, a question that has been with us since the beginnings of print culture, and this difficulty is suggestively linked to clear evidence of the power of television as a marketing tool. But the evidence adduced by Kernan might easily be interpreted as confirming the power of print and the prestige of authors rather than as reducing both to curios in a fiercely competitive marketplace where the only form of memory is nostalgia, and the only evidences of continuity are the consumer habits and sales figures for the last quarter. It might even be argued that the act of buying the book-behind-the-interview is a response to the tenacity of the written as still the most authoritative cultural form if no longer (if it ever was) the most 'real'.

Such a sanguine, if not complacent, view of the continuing health of literature and prestige of the literary needs more serious consideration than Kernan gives it. Moreover, his own cultural fatalism would have been more persuasive for many a reader if it had engaged with the kind of media critique one associates with Horkheimer and Adorno's salutary challenges to the culture industry or with Benedict Anderson's more recent work, *Imagined Communities* (1983). Kernan needed to make clearer the implications of his assessment of technology. In fact, his list of cultural forms revolutionized by television concludes with a missed opportunity for just such clarification, an apparently inadvertent but nonetheless revealing pun on "consumption," a term which, with modern medicine's virtual elimination of tuberculosis, no longer signifies the artist's disease par excellence but rather the defining activity of consumer society. However, this semantic shift does not necessarily work against the interests of literature via the de-aestheticizing of language; indeed, it can be seen as a welcome change of status for literature from dubious distinctiveness on the margins of an otherwise healthy body politic to a more integral role within a larger cultural economy, the role of cautionary, stubborn subtext within the rapidly destabilizing contexts of late capitalism and postmarxism. Many diseases can be cured, but what about those that afflict the body of society? Is this latter notion naive vitalism relying on metaphors which have no bearing on the way people have collectively lived and will continue to live their lives? If this is indeed the case, then the notion of society's health or sickness, like the idea of the death of literature, is an illusion, a presumptuous or pathetic fallacy, an irrelevance, a category mistake.

But is it *merely* a metaphor? It may well be that literature aligns itself with this very question and has always done so, within a historically changing cultural field where dependence on figurality is inevitable but not uniformly respectable. It may well be that literary scholars, as custodians of semantic history (however problematic) and all that it entails, including the power of rhetoric and the necessity of reference, are in the best position to determine when metaphors are live and when they are dead, and what flows from either designation. This is a claim that plainly runs counter to Kernan's sense of things, but then he is too little concerned with the kind of reading and cultural interpretation that television can promote, both in itself and beyond itself, even in America where the medium promotes more passivity than in some other countries. Or perhaps Kernan too readily assumes that what America does today the rest of the world *will* do tomorrow. His resistance to the readability and complexity of electronic images certainly gets him into a number of difficulties, including the transposition of associations of life and death in the following: "The truth of television images is not *engraved in stone* but is provisional, contemporary, transitory" (p. 150; emphasis added). If the genuinely vital truth is lapidary and monumental, then that would seem to suggest that death has triumphed as a kind of writing, that literature *of* death and *as* death endures while all else is increasingly ephemeral. Kernan resorts to a colloquial version of the formal and durable (that which is written in stone), but the opposition this makes possible can be deconstructed by doing what he thinks deconstruction too seldom does—namely, letting history back into the scene of interpretation.

Like the rest of us, Alvin Kernan can be read otherwise than he intended, and this raises issues about the responsibilities of writers and readers which he himself examines in his seventh chapter, "The Battle for the Word." Here he devotes eight of his most moving and powerful pages to the problem of Paul de Man. This example of professorial practice hits close to home in a number of ways, not least because it complicates the history of European exiles in the American academy. Kernan offers a remarkably controlled account of the principal features of de Man's career in four of America's finest universities, but the Belgian antecedents to this immigrant's success require nothing less than saeve indignatio of a Swiftian kind. The return of the repressed in this case is the return of the personal, as culpability and the unapologetically ad hominem, in a compelling exposure of what de Man did and what underlies some of the special pleading on his behalf by Derrida and others. Kernan establishes the need for workable (if imperfect) notions of identity, agency, accountability; but then he extends his argument as follows:

The de Man case removes deconstruction from the realm of pure intellect and puts the theory, protesting and wriggling, in a full living human context. It confronts deconstruction with the monstrous and passionately felt *fact* of the Holocaust and asks, is this too only a *text*. Can its meaning be endlessly deferred? Can it too be interpreted in any way deemed suitable? To all these questions, of course, despite the staggering revelations of the de Man case, the logician can and does answer "yes." . . . The language of the world where things are done and made and sold looks at language from a practical rather than a strictly logical viewpoint. The result is an awe-inspiring, often daunting, linguistic overconfidence, sometimes cynical and exploitative, regularly immoral, irreverent, and greedy, but quick, clever, thoroughly alert to the possibilities of what can be done with words. Words are not pale isolated things but magical in their ability to evoke, shape, control things. To the eye of the philosopher it is all a vast swindle, but what privileges the casuistries of the philosopher over the evidence of all our lives to decide what is real and true? Words work in the world, they make people rich and poor, happy and sad, wise and foolish, and what better proof can there be of their meaningfulness and power? . . . Of course we no longer live in the dawn of pure linguistic enthusiasm, we have heard too many words, and learned to distrust them. But though it would not appear so from our poetry and novels, the world is still filled with confidence in words. Which side is likely to prevail, which view comes closest to the situation in which we actually live and with which literature should be identified, became overwhelmingly clear in the tragedy of Paul de Man's writings. [pp. 187–88]

This blend of passion and pragmatism encapsulates the virtues and deficiencies of Kernan's book. On the positive side, he sustains effective links between literature and society, rightly insisting that meaning is constantly determined and therefore in significant measure intelligible and reconstructable. The linguistic and the historical referents are complexly determined rather than incurably fugitive, and they cannot be easily or entirely elided, especially within an academy where *ars memoria* is not always distinguishable from the nursing of grudges. Kernan uses the fact that Paul de Man made his way so easily in the American academy to remind us of its best traditions but also of its susceptibility to certain myths about European scholarship and the separability of knowledge from social contexts and political interests. Kernan is above all impressive for the way in which he conveys the importance of language as an overwhelmingly social medium, and for the way in which his moral outrage can lead to generosity and concern, as when this leading student of Shakespeare and Jonson chooses to speak finally of "the *tragedy* of Paul de Man's writings" (emphasis added).

Kernan has a strong case here, but I think he overstates it in several regrettable respects. First, he continues to appeal to a naive organicism as the moral alternative to "pure intellect." Such an appeal willfully ignores the fact that the most effective recent challenges to the Cartesian *cogito* have come from Foucault, Derrida, and feminist scholars. Again, in associating deconstruction with the "logician" he ignores the challenges to logic so prominent in Derrida's early work on Husserl or in de Man's mature work on Hegel; and, in extending that association to philosophers more generally, he preserves his own preference for clear disciplinary boundaries only by resorting to Laputan caricature. The opposition between the "strictly logical" and the practical requires the remystification of everyday life as "awe-inspiring" and of words as "magical." In his impassioned defence of a moral and practical "good sense," Kernan accepts the inevitability of an imperfect social order while suppressing the connections between "linguistic overconfidence" (hubris) and tragedy of a kind perhaps analogous to de Man's. He conspicuously avoids any mention of discourse (and hence any suspicion of sympathy for the critical practices in which this term so prominently features); but in preferring to discourse "words [which] work in the world" he sounds ironically close to Heidegger's version of linguistic autonomy (*die Sprache spricht*), if not to de Man's reflexive modification thereof (*die Sprache verspricht sich*). The difficulty is one of deliberate misprision by a scholar who chooses, like many others and not without reason, to identify the trace and erasure with disappearance rather than problematic persistence, and to insist that meaning is determinable rather than interminably deferred. But which determinate meaning, when, and for what reasons? The Holocaust was not and is not a text, strictly speaking, but it was and is inevitably, crucially connected to texts of all kinds from the full to the fragmentary, from the almost unbearably graphic to the despicably fraudulent. It is in this sense that Derrida can claim that "il n'y a pas de horstexte." Everything exists not *as* language but *in relation to* language; and this does not mean the denial of history in some heinous appropriation of de Manian forgetting or Derridean deferral, or the travesty of truth and history in some hermeneutic free-for-all. It means, rather, at least for this reviewer, that the generation of linguistic accounts and interpretations will not and should not cease, lest we forget, lest we forget to dissent, lest we attempt to avoid the responsibilities that come to us with language. I hence conclude, with all due respect to Alvin Kernan, that writers and literary scholars have as rosy/grim a future as they have ever had, and that rumors of the death of literature, like claims about its life, are greatly exaggerated.

Coleridge and the Retreat from Democracy

Norman Fruman

John Morrow. *Coleridge's Political Thought: Property, Morality, and the Limits of Traditional Discourse.* New York: St. Martin's Press, 1990. xi, 215 pp.

One of the stranger controversies in Coleridge studies over the past twenty years has been whether or not he was a political radical in his youth. Despite the overwhelming evidence of contemporary letters, journals, publications, and the testimony of those close to him at the time, all clearly demonstrating that Coleridge was a fiery Jacobin in his twenties, some eminent scholars continue to take him at his retrospective word to the contrary, unwilling to accept the idea that Coleridge could deliberately and consistently have misrepresented his past.[1] The point is worth emphasizing because any persuasive discussion of Coleridge's views on politics or society must deal not only with *what* Coleridge wrote, which, like many complex texts is open to conflicting interpretations, but *why* he wrote what he did.

In this short and concentrated study, John Morrow, a senior lecturer in Politics at the Victoria University of Wellington in New Zealand, provides an admirably clear survey of the dominant themes in Coleridge's extensive political writings. Morrow has an intimate knowledge of the political contexts in which these works appeared, and an impressive familiarity with political texts from preceding centuries now known only to specialists. The result is a book useful not only to students of political science, but also to literary scholars, who come to Coleridge primarily as a poet and critic.

Morrow's study is divided into five chapters, framed by an

introduction and conclusion. The first chapter deals with Coleridge's early activist writings, specifically the Bristol Lectures (1795) and the short-lived *Watchman* (1796). Chapter 2 deals with the crucial 1799–1802 period, immediately following Coleridge's spectacular *annus mirabilis* as a poet, which saw the abandonment of radical politics and the beginning of his *volte face* with regard to almost everything he had believed before. Chapter 3, entitled "Principled Morality and Prudential Politics," focusses on *The Friend* (1809–10), the intellectually demanding periodical the ailing Coleridge conducted as a one-man operation. The period 1810–1819 (Chapter 4) deals with "Politics, Property and Political Economy," as seen primarily in *The Statesman's Manual* of 1816, and the *Lay Sermon* of the following year. The last chapter continues the earlier themes in the context of later political issues, as seen in *On the Constitution of the Church and the State* (1829), in which Coleridge put forward what were to prove his highly influential ideas on a national church and "clerisy."[2]

Unfortunately, Morrow shows almost no interest in or knowledge of Coleridge as a man or artist. The reader will learn almost nothing about the personal circumstances which might have played a role in the many twists and turns in Coleridge's thinking. Coleridge's closest friend during the most creative period of his life was William Wordsworth, another youthful radical with strong political convictions. Wordsworth is mentioned just twice in this book, and only in passing. William Hazlitt, who remained loyal to Napoleon and the French Revolution to the end, and who wrote voluminously on politics, was for a time a close friend and became one of Coleridge's most bitter critics. Nevertheless, he is unmentioned both in the text and the ten-page bibliography. Neither Coleridge's wife nor children appear, nor does Charles Lamb. Thomas Poole, a friend and benefactor of great importance in Coleridge's life, is mentioned once. James Prior Estlin, the Unitarian leader of a group of Coleridge's Bristol benefactors, is not mentioned at all. In that, as is now widely acknowledged, the ever-ingratiating Coleridge tended to write his friends, and especially his benefactors, what it would please them to hear, the absence of personal context in a study of Coleridge's political writings tends to place them in a psychological void.

Early in 1795, when Coleridge was just twenty-two years old,

Coleridge and the Retreat from Democracy

he embarked upon a series of political and religious lectures, mainly delivered in Bristol, the home town of his closest friend, fellow poet and political radical, and soon-to-be brother-in-law, Robert Southey. Although Coleridge's personal involvement with practical politics up to this time was nil, he was not averse then, or ever afterwards, to instructing humanity on how to conduct its affairs. At twenty-two, he already regarded himself as a fit teacher of mankind. Between the ages of nine and seventeen he had scarcely stirred from the grim cloisters of Christ's Hospital, a famous London school for orphaned or indigent boys, mainly the sons of clergy. After fifteen months at Cambridge he impulsively enlisted in the army, where he languished for four months before being rescued by his older brothers. After eight months more at Cambridge he left again, this time for good.

Raised as an orthodox Anglican, the young Coleridge was radicalized as an undergraduate and became a convert to Unitarianism, then a passionately Christian denomination that denied the divinity of Jesus, rejected such doctrines as original sin, believed ardently in the essential goodness and benevolence of humanity, and made major contributions to progressive political thought and action throughout the eighteenth and nineteenth centuries.[3] Since religion was always to play a central role in Coleridge's thinking about politics and society, it would be of great interest to know what prompted his conversion from the religion of his youth. The same is true of his later conversion to a strictly orthodox version of Trinitarian Christianity. On neither of these important topics does Morrow add anything to the little that is currently known.

It is hardly surprising that the young, ambitious, and indigent Coleridge, a man with no important social connections in a rigidly class-conscious society, was a bitter critic of things as they were. He was just seventeen when the French Revolution changed Europe and politics forever. If it was bliss to be alive in that dawn of hope, and to be young was very heaven, it was also a dangerously turbulent time, especially for opponents of the government. England was at war with France through all of Coleridge's young manhood, and this circumstance profoundly shaped his view of politics and the world.

Coleridge and nine other Bristol youths, including Southey,

formed a utopian plan. Together with ten young women, all properly married, they proposed to found an ideal community on the banks of the Susquehanna River in Pennsylvania. It was supposed that a morning of farming would be sufficient to feed and clothe the group, and the rest of the time would be spent in reading, writing, and other forms of intellectual and social improvement.

All property was to be held in common, for which the term "aspheterism" was coined, and the project itself given the name of "Pantisocracy." "The real source of inconstancy, depravity, & prostitution," Coleridge wrote to the radical John Thelwall in 1796, "is *Property*, which mixes with and poisons every thing good—& is beyond doubt the Origin of all Evil."[4] Two years earlier Southey wrote to his brother Tom that he and Coleridge had "preached Pantisocracy and Aspheterism everywhere. These, Tom, are two new words, the first signifying the equal government of all, and the other the generalization of individual property."[5] The whole pantisocratic program was based, Coleridge said, "On the scheme of the abandonment of individual property."[6]

The intensity with which Coleridge held this and yet more radical opinions (as compared with his later life), appears in a note to his long, youthful poem "Religious Musings" (prudently dropped after 1803): "I am convinced that the Babylon of the Apocalypse does not apply to Rome exclusively; but to the union of Religion with Power and Wealth, wherever it is found" (*PW*, I, 121, n. 1). As Morrow points out, Coleridge's six "Lectures on Revealed Religion, Its Corruptions and Political Views," contain "an attack on the doctrines and practices of the Established Church, and portray it as the purveyor of a corrupt and oppressive form of Christianity."[7] He even dared to equate the Church of England with the Church of Rome.

Coleridge's millenial hopes and absolute conviction that mankind was basically benevolent are everywhere apparent in these early lectures: "Vice and Inequality mutually produce each other," he declared; "vice is the effect of error and the offspring of surrounding circumstances," and "the evil must cease when the cause is removed."[8] Coleridge in this early period, Morrow justly writes, "thought that inequality lay at the root" of most social evils (p. 23); "as long as anyone possesses more than another," STC wrote, "Luxury, Envy, Rapine, Government & Priesthood will be necessary consequences, and prevent the Kingdom of God—that is the progressiveness of the moral world" (*Lectures: 1795*, p. 227).

Morrow notes that the "treatment of revealed religion in the lectures on the subject was heavily dependent upon standard sources of both orthodox and Unitarian origins" (p. 21). Further: "The distinctly theological parts . . . depended upon arguments and illustrations which were the stock-in-trade of Unitarians such as Priestley" (p. 28). Moreover: "Coleridge frequently drew upon Moses Lowman's *Dissertation on the Civil Government of the Hebrews*" (p. 29), and so forth. Here as elsewhere, Morrow is content with general statements of this type, leaving one to wonder just what "heavily dependent" and "drew upon" might actually mean. Let us examine a single instance as an example of what may lie hidden behind such vague terms.

Coleridge's "Lecture on the Two Bills," we learn, "leaned heavily upon Burgh's *Disquisitions*." Morrow adds, "Burgh's work was, as Lewis Patton says, 'a popular Whig sourcebook'" (p. 33). This sort of comment, like "stock-in-trade" where borrowed ideas are involved, has been characteristic of Coleridge's commentators down the generations, for it has the effect of drastically reducing the force of any imputation of improper use of sources. After all, one could hardly present as one's original thoughts and research the contents of "a popular Whig sourcebook" and expect to get away with it. Neither Morrow nor Lewis Patton, however, indicates just what sort of work Burgh's *Disquisitions* was, or provides evidence that it was in fact widely used.[9]

James Burgh's *Political Disquisitions,* now very scarce, originally appeared in 1794 and 1795, in three thick volumes, each over 450 pages, hardly one's idea of a handbook. By the time Coleridge was lecturing in 1795, Burgh's work was already twenty years old. Lest the unwary reader suppose that authors in the late eighteenth century had casual notions of authorial property and were indifferent as to acknowledging sources (as is often asserted), be it noted that in the "General Preface" of his first volume, Burgh lists the many works he used as background (I, vii), and provides a four-page list of "Books quoted, or referred to in this First Volume." In Volume II, p. vii, Burgh again provides a four-page list of books quoted or referred to.

Conversely, the young Coleridge rapaciously plunders Burgh and mentions his name just once, toward the end of a long footnote in *The Plot Discovered* (which may not have formed part of the spoken lecture), and in a way that could not possibly lead one to suppose that he was massively indebted to Burgh for the vast reading and political judgments so lavishly on display.[10]

In a note Morrow cites a two-page article by Lucyle Werkmeister: "Coleridge's *The Plot Discovered:* Some Facts and a Speculation."[11] The rare reader who follows up on this note will find that Werkmeister prints in parallel columns some dozen direct borrowings from Burgh, and acknowledges that the young Coleridge may well have lifted more. But she insists, almost grotesquely, that all this shows neither dependence nor desire to suppress a source![12]

Morrow asserts that Coleridge's "early political thought contained a far-reaching critique of contemporary political and social institutions, and demands for their reformation" (p. 39), a judgment that seems to me characteristic of the exaggerated claims made for the importance of Coleridge as a political thinker. Coleridge's "critique" consisted of the commonplaces of radical thought then and now: private property must be abolished and government regulation (like later utopian belief in "the withering away of the state") must give way to benevolent relations among individuals. These were also the views of John Thelwall, widely regarded as the most notorious Jacobin of the time, who, Morrow supposes, shared with Coleridge "a concern to avoid rabble-rousing and bloodletting" and emphasizes that despite the "radical character of his analysis and goals," Coleridge was really all for "moderate procedures" (p. 39). This may be true, but Morrow ignores or is unaware of the later testimony of Thelwall himself, written into his copy of *Biographia Literaria,* wherein Coleridge claimed that friends of his youth would "bear witness for me, how opposite even then my principles were to those of jacobinism or even of democracy, and can attest the strict accurancy of the statement which I have left on record in the

10th and 11th numbers of THE FRIEND."[13] This is false, as the contemporary record abundantly shows. In the margins of this very passage, Thelwall, who at the time was one of Coleridge's closest political allies, wrote: "that Mr. C. was indeed far from Democracy, because he was far beyond it, I well remember—for he was a down right zealous leveller & indeed in one of the worst senses of the word he was a Jacobin, a man of blood."[14]

Coleridge's early political writing, like much of his prose, is rich in metaphor and vivid images, sparkling with apt quotation and apposite poetic extracts drawn from a remarkably wide range of reading. The general dazzle of language, together with the arresting power of mind that glows in many passages, make it difficult not to resist assigning these texts an exaggerated importance. They are texts which, after all, can only have an antiquarian interest, irrelevant as they are to any contemporary political or social concern. When STC cobbled together these early lectures (often under great pressure of time), he had never owned a square foot of land, or held public office, or been anywhere in the world outside of Great Britain. His moral principles had been shaped first by the orthodox precepts of the Anglican church, the narrow stringencies and hypocrisies of English society, and the millenial dreams of the early Unitarians. Characteristically, he delivered his beliefs, hopes, judgments, and prejudices as "bottomed" on "first principles," on the immutable laws of universal logic, or on the authority of sacred texts whose truths were either self-evident or beyond criticism because divinely sanctioned. Later, having changed his beliefs as to almost everything but the supreme importance of religion, and having fallen under the spell of Kant and transcendental idealism, he was to locate the authority of both Anglican Trinitarianism and his personal political doctrines in the supposed nature of the human mind itself.

Coleridge's supreme achievement as a poet took place over a remarkable fourteen-month period bridging 1797–1798, during which he wrote "The Ancient Mariner," "Kubla Khan," "Christabel," "Frost at Midnight," and almost every other poem for which he is today remembered outside of professional circles. During this time, in almost daily association with William and

Dorothy Wordsworth, his political journalism, understandably, was markedly reduced. Moreover, a lifetime annuity of £150 was conferred upon him by the two wealthy sons of the famous potter Josiah Wedgwood, in part to free him from the necessity of preaching or writing political journalism for a living. Nevertheless, in early 1798 Coleridge, always short of money, began writing for Daniel Stuart's *Morning Post,* a liberal, sometimes radical newspaper, opposed to the government and to the war with France. "Over the next year, however," Morrow writes, "both Coleridge and the *Morning Post* became increasingly hostile towards France and towards the forces of reform at home" (p. 43). By the following year "the radical perspectives that had informed both the Bristol lectures and *The Watchman*" (p. 53) had been abandoned. By the end of 1799, in a complete about-face with respect to everything he had previously maintained, both publicly and privately, Coleridge declared:

For the present race of men Governments must be founded on property; that *Government is good in which property is secure and circulates;* that *Government the best, which, in the exactest ratio, makes each man's power proportionate to his property.*[15]

By early 1800 he could write:

Has not the hereditary possession of landed estate proved, by experience, to generate dispositions equally favourable to loyalty and established freedom? Has not the same experience proved that the moneyed men [i.e., those whose wealth derived from commerce] are far more malleable materials? that Ministers find more and more easy ways of obliging them, and that they are more willing to go with a Minister through evil and good?[16]

These astonishing changes should not be "seen merely as a retreat into conservatism," Morrow believes, but rather as a "theoretical reorientation" (p. 45).

That prudential or self-serving motives might have played some role in Coleridge's political shifts is simply not considered. For example, on 1 October 1803, the thirty-one-year-old Coleridge sent Sir George Beaumont, an influential new friend, a painter and patron of the arts, a man of strong conservative leanings, and a wealthy potential benefactor, a long and anxious account of his former political views and activities (unmentioned by Morrow). At the age of twenty-four (the period of *The Watchman* and the Bristol lectures), Coleridge wrote, "I was retiring from Politics, disgusted beyond measure by the manners & morals of the Democrats." He alleged further that he had always been "utterly unconnected with any party or club or society.... All such Societies, under whatever name, I abhorred as wicked Conspiracies—and to this principle I adhered immoveably, simply because it was a principle." He described himself in earlier years as "insulated" from political affairs, "at Stowey, sick of Politics, & sick of Democrats & Democracy."[17]

Coleridge clung tenaciously to this position for the rest of his life, much to the dismay of Southey and some of his early Bristol friends, who knew better. Sadly, among the many scholars who have taken Coleridge at his word are the editors of the Bristol lectures and *The Watchman*, who declare in their influential Introduction to the former: "By reason of his Christian, moral, and philosophical principles, which he attempted to clarify and justify in his lectures, Coleridge found himself in a state of "insulation" (to use one of his own expressive words) from the democratic movement and its ideas."[18]

Coleridge's rejection of democracy surely had much to do with his rooted distrust of the wisdom and judgment of the common man, to whom he never appealed directly, as did, for example, Thomas Paine. Coleridge was now to accept, however reluctantly, the necessity of the war against revolutionary France. By the end of 1806, Morrow notes, "Coleridge's break with Unitarianism was complete . . . and his acceptance of the full doctrine of the Trinity allowed for a complete reconciliation with the orthodoxy of the Established Church" (p. 73).

Some commentators have argued that because Coleridge thought a government good "*in which property is secure and circulates,*" he therefore envisioned and desired a society with substantial social mobility and economic opportunity. But if property was to be "secure," in Coleridge's sense, it had to be protected not just from the depredations of mobs, but also from the encroachments of government. During Coleridge's lifetime, the overwhelming source of wealth was land, a commodity that does not circulate easily. If property was to be secure, and passed on by the law of primogeniture exclusively to the eldest son (as was true in England), and if moreover political power was to be "*in the exactest ratio*" to how much property one possessed, then such an arrangement guaranteed the continued control of public affairs by a landed aristocracy and gentry, and of course exclusively by males.

It may seem curious that Coleridge should ever have believed such an arrangement socially desirable in any sense. But the modern reader rarely considers how great a gulf exists between ourselves and even the most enlightened thinkers of the past on certain social issues. For Coleridge and his contemporaries, it required an act of imagination to believe that an uneducated laborer with calloused hands or an impoverished mother grieving over a sick child could have feelings as complex and intense as those of the privileged classes. Wordsworth's series of poems in *Lyrical Ballads* about the joys and sorrows of ordinary men, women, and children alarmed many critics precisely because they posed a political threat. If these uneducated laborers could think the thoughts and feel the feelings Wordsworth attributed to them, then what was the justification for the rigid and exploitive class system under which Great Britain groaned? On 14 January 1801, Wordsworth sent a copy of the second edition of *Lyrical Ballads* to the influential statesman Charles James Fox. In a remarkable accompanying letter, he called attention particularly to the poems "Michael" and "The Brothers," which "were written with a view to shew that men who do not wear fine cloaths can feel deeply."

Coleridge never really shared this attitude. The tradesman was always for Coleridge a vulgar or faintly comic figure (a prejudice shared by most of his contemporaries). In *Biographia Literaria,* "a ludicrous instance" of bad imagery comes from "the poem of a young tradesman" (I, 24). In an attack on literature as a trade, Coleridge mocks those in the business who "had failed in the lowest mechanic crafts" (I, 41). Among the many anecdotes in the autobiographical Chapter 10, those about tradesmen are

Coleridge and the Retreat from Democracy

characteristically scornful, as in references to "the mere man of the world" (I, 170), to the "rigid Calvinist, a tallow-chandler by trade" (I, 180), and to the fatuous "and opulent wholesale dealer in cottons" (I, 182). In an astonishing passage on language, he asserted, "The best part of human language, properly so called, is derived from reflection on the acts of the mind itself"! Cerebrations of this kind, obviously, have little "place in the consciousness of uneducated man; though in civilized society, by imitation and passive remembrance of what they hear from their religious instructors and other superiors, the most uneducated share in the harvest which they neither sowed or [sic] reaped" (II, 54).

These were the common beliefs of Coleridge's time and for generations thereafter. They still prevail more widely than we like to believe. Even to so fierce a democrat as William Hazlitt, an opinion was "vulgar that is stewed in the rank breath of the rabble." There is a vicious attack on "persons of low estate" in his essay "On the Disadvantages of Intellectual Superiority," and a worse one in "On the Knowledge of Character," in which he writes, "I would lay it down in the first place as a general rule on this subject, that all uneducated people are hypocrites. Their sole business is to deceive. . . . They have no fellow-feeling, they keep no faith with the more privileged classes."[19] Attitudes like these must be kept in mind when reading political treatises of the past. Without some such compass to keep one's bearing, one will consistently misread the true meanings of passages which admit, so far as the words themselves are concerned, of various interpretations.

The major political document of Coleridge's middle period is the immensely demanding periodical called *The Friend* (1809–1810), a potpourri of theology, metaphysics, scientific speculation, literary criticism, politics, and anything else that interested the polymathic STC. In *The Friend*, Morrow justly observes, property became "the central element in his political theory" (p. 100). Among its more surprising pages are those describing the "positive" and "negative" ends of government. "The negative ends of Government," Coleridge declared, "are the protection of Life, of personal Freedom, of Property, of Reputation, and of

Religion, from foreign and from domestic attacks."[20] Strangely, he had almost nothing further to say about these "negative ends," which most theorists would surely regard as fundamental to any just society. As to "positive" ends, there were four, the first three dealing with the government's responsibility to "make the means of subsistence more easy to each individual"; the fourth "was to encourage moral, intellectual, and religious education." Admirable as these objectives always appear in the abstract, few people would place them before "personal Freedom," without which all other qualities of life are constantly threatened. How to account for Coleridge's views here? Surely not by abstract reasoning from "first principles," but by realizing that throughout his anxiety-ridden life, Coleridge always had to struggle to provide "Bread and Cheese" for himself, and was often humiliatingly dependent on handouts from friends and benefactors. In the grip of such struggles, the primary responsibility of government will always seem to be to make life easier for its citizens, if necessary at the expense of their personal freedom.

In 1817, at the age of forty-five, and now living as a permanent semi-invalid in the home of Dr. James Gillman of Highgate, Coleridge published two "Lay Sermons."[21] The first, entitled *The Statesman's Manual*, "was intended to encourage the upper classes to inform their actions by a 'philosophy of history' derived from reading the Bible in 'the spirit of prophecy'" (p. 101). It was subtitled "The Bible the Best Guide to Political Skill and Foresight," and was "Addressed to the Higher Classes of Society." Sarah Wedgwood, the younger sister of Coleridge's longtime benefactor Josiah Wedgwood, responded thus is a personal letter (26 February 1817):

I have been reading a pamphlet by Mr. Coleridge, which, he calls "The Statesman's Manual, a Lay Sermon." It would quite have killed us if it had come out some years ago, when we were fighting in his cause against his despisers and haters. I do think I never did read such stuff, such an affectation of the most sublime and important meaning and so much no-meaning in reality. I can't see how any human being could possibly learn anything either about their duties, or anything else, by the whole sermon. . . . He is as insolent as his brother-lakers [Wordsworth and Southey], takes the same high ground, no mortal can tell why, except that it pleases them to think that their proper place is on a throne, and he writes more unintelligibly, more bombastically, than any of them."[22]

Coming from an intelligent contemporary, long one of Coleridge's friends and champions, this is a revealing outburst. That Coleridge could seriously argue that the Bible in any practical sense could be "the best guide to political skill and foresight" twenty centuries after it was written, if only one read it in a "spirit of prophecy," strongly suggests that he was no longer in touch with sublunary politics but had given himself over wholly to the role of seer.

"He argued that the discipline of political economy was intellectually flawed and morally pernicious," Morrow writes, and pointed to the "fuller, more relationally informed ideas found in the Bible. In the Scriptures, political economy was generated by 'living *educts* of the Imagination; of that reconciling and mediatary power, which incorporating the Reason in Images of the Sense, and organizing (as it were) the flux of the Senses by the permanence and self-circling energies of the Reason, gives birth to a system of symbols, harmonious in themselves, and consubstantial with the truths, of which they are the *conductors.*' Modern political economy was, by contrast, merely the '*product* of an unenlivened generalizing Understanding'" (p. 103).

It is unlikely that more than one reader in a hundred can have more than the vaguest conception of what all this can mean, and what relation the passage quoted from *The Statesman's Manual* might have to the real world of politics or commerce. Without a searching examination of what the Kantian Reason and Understanding meant to Coleridge (which he stated over and over again in many contexts, from politics to aesthetics, from science to philosophy) the key terms carry little if any of their crucial metaphysical freight. Morrow makes little attempt to clarify these difficult matters, apparently assuming that, because he is addressing a professional audience, his readers do not need such help.

Despite its Stygian obscurity, the passage quoted above on the symbol was, for almost fifty years, a *locus classicus* in literary criticism, quoted repeatedly when the symbol—one of the key concepts of the New Criticism—was discussed. And for almost fifty years it was useless to complain that the passage was "fertile in unmeaning," as Lamb said about some of the miracles in "The Ancient Mariner." Today, as the New Critical edifice crumbles, contemporary "theorists" regard with lofty scorn the whole nexus of romantic doctrines, including the symbol, imagination, and organicism.

The point is worth emphasizing not because today's consensus is any more valid than that which reigned supreme during the heyday of the New Criticism, but because it has been the aura of transcendent genius Coleridge has carried for the past half century that has resulted in the massive cascade of books on every aspect of his intellectual life: poetry, criticism, aesthetics, politics, theology, science, metaphysics, and sociology. In each area there have been those to hail his work as of exalted importance, even when the sources from which he drew many of his leading ideas have long since sunk into obscurity. Morrow writes that Coleridge regarded "the discipline of political economy [as] intellectually flawed and morally pernicious" (p. 112). He then quotes a passage from *The Friend* to the effect that a genuine science derives its principles from "a truth originating in the mind, and not abstracted or generalized from observation of the parts." Only in such instances, Coleridge insisted, can we "affirm the presence of a *law*" (I, 459). Here as elsewhere, following Schelling and other post-Kantian idealists, Coleridge scorned empirical evidence, sandy generalizations deriving from mere facts. "It is among the miseries of the present age," he wrote, "that it recognizes no medium between *Literal* and *Metaphysical*. Faith is either to be a dead letter, or its name and honors usurped by a counterfeit product of the mechanical understanding" (*Lay Sermons*, p. 30). Now the "mechanical understanding" was, for Coleridge, precisely that which derived from concrete experience, from the "notices of the senses." The major misery of the age was thus its acceptance of Newton, Locke, and other "mechanist" scientists and philosophers, instead of the German *Naturphilosophen*, whose fantastic views of how nature worked are of interest today only to a few historians of science.

In these "Lay Sermons," Coleridge's jeremiads extended even to the landed classes, in which he found many flaws of character, especially—as he explained in a letter to Daniel Stuart—"the self regarding application to themselves of the Jew Principle— Mayn't I do what I like with my own?" (*CL*, IV, 711).[23] He passionately exhorted the privileged to recognize the social obligations imposed by their good fortune. "This required that the upper classes adopt an intellectualised, Platonic form of Christianity in place of Lockean materialism," Morrow writes, "but it also meant, as the conclusion of *A Lay Sermon* made clear, that they should purify their own characters" (p. 125). There is much richly figured writing in these tracts, which on the whole fit far better one's sense of a Jonathan Edwards in an eloquent rage, than a political philosophy with any practical application to the conflicting goals and desires of a diverse citizenry in a modern society.

On the Constitution of the Church and the State (1829), the last of Coleridge's prose works, was occasioned primarily by the national crisis created by the parliamentary move towards Catholic emancipation. The complex details of the bitter controversy need not concern us here; suffice it to say that English Catholics could not serve in either house of parliament or attend British universities (among other disabilities) without abandoning their religious beliefs. Grotesque as the necessity for such a battle now seems to us, it is instructive to observe just how "universals" and "first principles" worked out in practice. For Coleridge, Catholic emancipation did not rest on a basic right of all citizens to worship freely and not be excluded, on the basis of religion, from any of the rights of other citizens. Rather, Catholic emancipation, and related issues involving the British Constitution, rested on a "regulative Idea," of the "*Ultimate* Aims implied in the Constitution."[24] "The real question," as Morrow puts it, "was whether, and under what conditions, the emancipation of Catholics was compatible with the fulfilment of the ultimate end that the Constitution existed to serve" (p. 132). Translating this into contemporary terms, an Afrikaner might argue that the emancipation of blacks was not a question of inherent justice but could only be determined on the basis of what purposes the South

African constitution, as it had developed since the nineteenth century, was intended to serve. Again, it would be a moral anachronism to judge Coleridge's views on the public issue of "Catholic Emancipation" from the perspective of the late twentieth century. At the same time, however, it would be a mistake not to recognize that Coleridge's views of an ideal state were incompatible with democracy, a criticism which would not have disturbed him in the least.

Coleridge's conception of the "clerisy," developed in this final statement of his political philosophy, has often been cited as an attractive ideal. This clerisy was to be a kind of national lay church, consisting of a small learned class akin to our own academic faculties, and a

> far more numerous body . . . to be distributed throughout the country, so as not to leave even the smallest integral part or division without a resident guide, guardian, and instructor; the objects and final intention of the whole order being these—to preserve the stores, to guard the treasures, of past civilization. and thus to bind the present with the past; to perfect and add to the same, and thus to connect the present with the future; but especially to diffuse through the whole community, and to every native entitled to its laws and rights, that quantity and quality of knowledge which was indispensable both for the understanding of those rights, and for the performance of the duties correspondent.[25]

Writers as diverse as the Anglo-Catholic, royalist T. S. Eliot and the marxist Raymond Williams have found much to praise in this general scheme. Is not its attraction precisely its blueprint for a society wholly organized to achieve specific moral and political goals, the character of which have been predetermined? Despite the relentless evidence of history, neither Coleridge nor innumerable others have understood that any kind of "clerisy"—a concept that can be generalized to include any group thought to be a repository of benevolence or wisdom—would no more insure the harmonious functioning of society than the Universal Church was able to do during the ages it ruled supreme in Europe, or the party commissars who monitored every aspect of politics and much of social life during the seventy-five years of communist control of the Soviet Union. Coleridge's call for an extremely powerful national church completely independent of elected government, not liable to regulation or taxation—"Coleridge wished to insulate the Church from the interference of a legislative body which might contain an increasing number of enemies of the Church of England" (p. 147)—would give such a church and its clergy vastly more power than is compatible with democratic societies. Among those powers was to be, ideally, control over education, for "Coleridge was dismissive of all non-Anglican educational initiatives because they were tainted by the 'mechanic philosophy' that it was the Church's role to counteract" (p. 148).

The England and Europe Coleridge knew have vanished forever, as have many of its moral and social assumptions and practices. Here in the final decade of the twentieth century, which has witnessed previously unimaginable changes in the scope and violence of war and social conflict of all kinds, the transformation of daily life by technology, the threat of exploding population levels, and unprecedented ecological degradation, one might well ask why anyone should have more than antiquarian interest in Coleridge's political thought. The answer, of course, is that Coleridge is one of the major figures in English literature, one who, for a variety of complex reasons having to do primarily with the sociology of academe, came to be seen as an intellect of the order of Da Vinci and Goethe, as one of his most influential editors asserted. Morrow's excellent bibliography includes some 125 books, book chapters, and journal articles, devoted in whole or in part to Coleridge as a political thinker. The present volume, and Morrow's judicious, recently published selection from all the major texts in *Coleridge's Writings on Politics and Society* (Princeton Univ. Press, 1991), perform a valuable service in providing an informed guide and the basic documents. It is difficult to imagine that anything more will be needed for a long time to come.

Notes

1. For example, See Thomas McFarland's "Coleridge and the Charge of Political Apostasy" in *Coleridge's Biographia Literaria: Text and Meaning*, ed. Fred Burwick (Columbus: Ohio State Univ. Press, 1989), pp. 191–232.

2. Key selections from these five periods, together with relevent passages from Coleridge's "Table Talk," can be found in the recently published *Coleridge's Writings on Politics and Society*, ed. John Morrow (Princeton: Princeton Univ. Press, 1991).

3. See R. V. Holt, *The Unitarian Contribution to Social Progress in England* (London, 1928, 1952).

4. *Collected Letters of Samuel Taylor Coleridge*, ed. Earl Leslie Griggs, 6 vols. (Oxford: Oxford Univ. Press, 1956–71), I, 214. Further references will be in the text to *CL*.

5. Quoted from J. D. Campbell, *Samuel Taylor Coleridge, a Narrative of the Events of his Life* (London: Macmillan, 1894), p. 35.

6. *The Complete Poetical Works of Samuel Taylor Coleridge*, ed. E. H. Coleridge, 2 vols. (Oxford: Oxford Univ. Press, 1912), II, 1137. Further references in the text will be to *PW*.

7. Morrow, p. 23. Subsequent references in the text will be to page number alone.

8. *Lectures: 1795: On Politics and Religion*, ed. Lewis Patton and Peter Mann, Volume 1 of *Collected Works of Samuel Taylor Coleridge* (Princeton: Princeton Univ. Press, 1971), pp. 217, 40, 19. Further references for the early period will be to *Lectures: 1795*, *CC* for the *Collected Works*, and *The Watchman* ed. Lewis Patton, *CC*, II (Princeton: Princeton Univ. Press, 1970).

9. *Lectures: 1795*, p. xlvii. The editors state that Bristol Library records for 1773–1784 show that Burgh's *Political Disquisitions* was borrowed thirty-eight times, thus slightly more than three times a year. Coleridge was twelve years old in 1784.

10. *Ibid.*, p. 302.

11. *Modern Philology*, 56 (1959), 254–63.

12. John Colmer, in *Coleridge: Critic of Society* (1959) put the matter this way: "The wealth of illustrative material and facts concerning British Constitutional history with which *The Plot Discovered* is adorned, came from a single source. Reference to Burgh's *Political Disquisitions*, which Coleridge had borrowed from the Bristol Library in November [1795] enabled him to amass a great deal of information at small intellectual cost" (p. 29). Colmer did not, however, particularize—a tendency endemic in Coleridge studies, a fact that bears repeating. With the publication of *Lectures: 1795* in the *Collected Coleridge*, however, readers can determine for themselves the extent of Coleridge's debt to Burgh (and others, of course), keeping in mind always what is very difficult to keep in mind, namely that the discovery of new sources in Coleridge appears to be a never-ending process (including overlooked debts, some of them important, in sources long known), and also that scholars, particularly in the *Collected Coleridge* edition, consistently present the evidence in a way that minimizes lack of originality, as when outright unacknowledged borrowings are referred to as mere "background reading," or as when they assert that because certain general ideas are, so to speak, in the public domain, the specific formulation of them can be considered public property also.

13. *Biographia Literaria,* ed. James Engell and W. Jackson Bate, 2 vols., *CC,* VII (Princeton: Princeton Univ. Press, 1983), I, 184.

14. Burton R. Pollin, "John Thelwall's Marginalia in a Copy of Coleridge's *Biographia Literaria,*" *Bulletin of the New York Public Library,* 74, (1970), 81.

15. *Essays on his Times in 'The Morning Post' and 'The Courier,'* ed. David V. Erdman, 3 vols., *CC,* III (Princeton: Princeton Univ. Press, 1978), I, 32. Morrow, p. 46.

16. *Ibid.,* I, 143–44. Morrow, p. 57.

17. *CL,* II, 999, 1001.

18. *Lectures: 1795,* p. lxxix. As Nicholas Roe forthrightly puts it, "This would have delighted the author of *The Friend* [where Coleridge asserted this position repeatedly], but it seriously misrepresents Coleridge as an active political figure in Cambridge, London, Bristol, and the Midlands between 1792 and 1796." (*Wordsworth and Coleridge: The Radical Years* [Oxford: Oxford Univ. Press, 1988]), p. 12.

19. *Selected Writings,* ed. Ronald Blythe (New York: Penguin, 1970), pp. 468, 104–05.

20. Ed. Barbara E. Rooke, 2 vols., *CC,* IV (Princeton: Princeton Univ. Press, 1969), II, 201.

21. *Lay Sermons,* ed. R. J. White, *CC,* VI (Princeton: Princeton Univ. Press, 1972). Further references in text to *Lay Sermons.*

22. *Emma Darwin, A Century of Family Letters, 1792–1896,* ed. Henrietta Litchfield, 2 vols. (New York: Appleton, 1915), I, 109–10.

23. Quoted from Morrow, p. 112. Anti-Semitic remarks of this kind, lamentably characteristic of his age, are strewn throughout Coleridge's writings, particularly his letters and journals, together with attacks on the national character of the French and Scots, among others. He was also to have eloquent second thoughts about his anti-Semitic prejudices after meeting Hyman Hurwitz, the learned rabbi of the Jewish congregation in Highgate.

24. *On the Constitution of the Church and the State,* ed. John Colmer, *CC,* X (Princeton: Princeton Univ. Press, 1976), p. 31, n. 2. Morrow, p. 132.

25. *Ibid.,* pp. 43–44.

The Refeminization of Dickinson

Bruce Michelson

Judy Jo Small. *Positive as Sound: Emily Dickinson's Rhyme.* Athens: University of Georgia Press, 1990. xiii, 261 pp.

Joanne Feit Diehl. *Women Poets and the American Sublime.* Bloomington and Indianapolis: Indiana University Press, 1990. xvi, 203 pp.

Mary Loeffelholz. *Dickinson and the Boundaries of Feminist Theory.* Urbana and Chicago: University of Illinois Press, 1991. viii, 179 pp.

Obtusely eating marinelife, cooked convention-style, with a Grey Eminence of American academic feminism, I mentioned to her that I was planning to review these three books, and a cold front instantly swept in across my crab cakes. "Really!" I heard. "And what do you assume to be your qualifications?" Oh dear. As pals we go back to simpler days, before she found professional identity as a feminist, and before my growing unease with elegant formulations drifted me into those dubious currents which are dubiously called the mainstream. Times have certainly changed for us all, and my friend's wariness had grounds. "If the 'women's tradition' means anything," observes Mary Loeffelholz, "it means a common set of problems—of definition and ambivalence. It is a relational, not an absolute, identity" (p. 110). Though that well-said premise seems inherent in all three of the books under review—and in much of the better feminist discourse of the past decade—some of our "mainstream" floaters still choose to ignore the complex, self-scrutinizing discussion which the "women's tradition" in letters has become. When they publish inane dismissals, they earn bad, depressing replies, calls for them to be silenced, disenfranchised, even fired. The hyperbole on both sides needs to stop because it obstructs the reception of careful, sharp-minded scholarly work, theoretically supple, historically aware, and essential for readers of any political or aesthetic stripe who claim an interest in literary-historial subjects, like Emily Dickinson and nineteenth-century American letters.

With the most straightforward ambitions of these three books, Judy Jo Small's *Positive as Sound* calls for reinvigorated thought, feminist and otherwise, about Emily Dickinson's prosody. Lamenting that "feminist critics have occasionally fallen into facile generalizations that identify formal features of her poetry as gender-based linguistic maneuvers intended to subvert male authority" (p. 3), and that nonfeminist scholars have had imperfect luck with similar problems, Small calls for recognition that Dickinson's "daringly innovative handling of traditional poetic forms" establishes a presence that "is not just 'woman' but a voice uniquely her own" (p. 4), and that her heretical practices in rhyme are crucial to understanding that presence. Small's strategy is to study a broad array of Dickinson's "strangely deviant rhymes" (p. 5) to observe "correlations between meaning and sound" (p. 8) throughout the poetry.

What Small discovers is equally straightforward, and useful: Dickinson's consonantal rhymes signify uprisings of doubt in her personae, and her rhymes which break from expectation or convention suggest breakouts from rationality, from Emersonian cults of the intellect, from received and stifling cultural assumptions which permeated Dickinson's world. The general findings have this cast: the "proportion of partial rhymes intermixed with full rhymes is fitting, broadly, to a poetic based on the precarious admixture of joy and pain in all the highest experience, on the impossibility of grasping all we must long for. Thus, her rhymes contribute aurally to the search for [the] 'hauntedness' of her art" (p. 58).

At times Small seems uneasy that such arrangements might not hold neatly through hundreds of poems and many years of Dickinson's life, and she can seem to plead for durable rules, rather than to find them: "Until we grasp some sort of general principles governing the relation of partial rhyme to aesthetic possibilities," she warns, "how can we begin to understand whether Dickinson, or any other poet using partial rhymes, demonstrates technical brilliance or technical ineptitude?" (pp. 12–13). Since we've been averaging three to five laudatory books on Dickinson per year for the past decade or so, many good critics have apparently found their way around such worries; but for Small much hangs on answering the question, and so a certain anxious rigidity haunts the study. The homework has unquestionably been done: the biography, the extant letters, and the historical context have all been considered, and Small's prose is direct and clear. Approaching Dickinson's rhyme as a species of music, Small hears "epistemological uncertainty" and the "bitter sweets of skepticism"—findings which, though not thunderously new, she details with gusto. Here and there that verve leads to pronouncements which seem either gratuitous or odd. Paragraph blocs sometimes warm up slowly: "Rhyme," we are told, "is not only a phonetic repetition, a pleasant musical chime. It is also an indicator of poetic structure, a marker of units and patterns of verse. Rhyme shapes a poem in a reader's ear" (p. 71). Elsewhere we are informed that "To the extent that one strives to be a precise user of the language, one avoids wordplay, instead structuring statements according to the principle that for everything there is one exact word that denotes it clearly" (p. 144). Were such a statement plugged into poets as precise as Frost, Robert Lowell, Bishop, Plath, or Wilbur, the test-lights might not come on. Good referees are supposed to catch and delete indiscretions like that in draft manuscripts of younger scholars; but such compassionate hunters seem to grow scarcer every year.

Small's general thesis doesn't admit of much development, and later in the book Dickinson's "calculated disruptions of structure" (p. 104) tend to be noted and tallied without strong indications of a poetic strategy ripening or varying over time. Uncomfortable with Dickinson's puns and paradoxical word-choices, Small spends a chapter lamenting such moments; and some readers might take issue with interpretations in which reader-response is prescribed a bit absolutely. Even so, Small is ever willing to compare her own findings with those of other critics, and her book includes ongoing conversations with a wide range of scholarship on Dickinson. Well-grounded, precise, and self-aware, Small's long look into Dickinson's rhyme will lead discussions of her prosody to new levels of sophistication.

Small and Loeffelholz both look to Joanne Feit Diehl's 1981 book *Dickinson and the Romantic Imagination* as a text to be reckoned with; Feit Diehl is a scholar of such demonstrated depth and individuality that her subsequent moves will be watched closely. Her newest work, *Women Poets and the American Sublime,* may trouble some people much as the earlier one did, for Feit Diehl again ventures too far for some tastes, not far enough to suit others. Her thinking about nineteenth-century poetics flourishes in a neighborhood which Elaine Showalter redlines as "gynocriticism," meaning feminist discourse which relies on methodologies essentially borrowed from other (male) systems, whether traditional or contemporary. Accepting certain influence-anxiety premises from Harold Bloom, Feit Diehl has also been questioned for endorsing heterosexist models of the father-daughter relationship as relevant to her descriptions of the predicament of nineteenth-century American women writers, who have the likes of Emerson and Whitman set before them to worship, resent, and displace. Yet with the battle over methodologies so far from resolution, Feit Diehl seems to have grounded her own reading in a strategy more central, durable, and appropriate to the age in question. If she seems Bloomian and post-Freudian at times, she also seems at least as consistently Fullerite. She reads Dickinson, Bishop, Plath, and Adrienne Rich as acts in an unfinished drama which the first great voice of American feminism began: a drama of recognizing, resisting, and proclaiming the exclusionary complacency—meaning the paradoxical limits—in American Transcendental "gender-inflected poetics," and of extending, correcting, and humanizing that model of the sublime. "For the woman reader," Feit Diehl observes, "Whitman's poetics presents an especially frustrating double bind: at once offering the woman of imagination a potential equality while committing her, within his own work, to an archetypal, hence restrictive role as a procreative force" (p. 9). Dickinson's reply, therefore, is couched in her "fusion of bodily sensation and the workings of the mind, her elision of poetic influence with the process of the experiential Sublime, and her reshaping of the transformative experience through the redemptive possibilities of a woman-to-woman encounter" (p. 28). The quest is to escape from fables of subjugation into fables of union—to make Transcendentalist ideology more transcendental than, at least in Emerson's parlance, it ever could become. In Dickinson, she says, "The crux of the matter is power, how to wrest independence from a patriarchal universe" (p. 39).

At times there does appear to be a measure of affection, on Feit Diehl's part, or at least compassion, for the old, stultifying fathers and values of the American sublime. The expansion and refreshment of American poetics, and of literary history, are what Feit Diehl has in mind, not their overthrow, and her command of that history, and of its gender-inflected configurations, is entirely convincing. In fact, because she is so astute in her reading of Dickinson and her cultural context, readers might lament that the chapters on that poet are too short to satisfy, and that the three chapters following, on Marianne Moore, seem written with diminished zest and conviction. The trouble lies perhaps with Moore herself: Feit Diehl finds there an "aesthetics of renunciation," which at times slips into outright evasion of trouble or even into something like a Modernist brand of hypocrisy; Moore's "naturalness" is half-excused as "a defense against the combativeness of a world in which publication can be interpreted as a usurpation of the will" (p. 51). It won't boost Moore's reputation much to be lauded as "a heteroglossia of textual voices that itself functions to displace authorial point of view" (p. 49), though that is about the highest praise these chapters muster. The energy and conviction seem to return with the Bishop and Plath chapters, the Plath readings being the more radical; the graphic descriptions of "surgical procedures, shock treatments, and bodily injury" (p. 130) which have long made students cringe are read as dramatizing conflicts over the "bodily ego" (p. 136), the empowering, threatening mind-body mergence which Whitman prescribes (with a threatening male cast to it) and which Emerson expels from his own model of sublimity, in favor of bodiless intellect. If Feit Diehl's readings of Plath seem at times almost reckless, they are also something of a gift, as they release our reading from dreary concern with what might otherwise seem the self-indulgent morbidity of Plath's metaphors. If Plath is going to stay with us, it's gratifying to have a richer Plath to read.

Compared to Feit Diehl's broad, confident motions through the fabric of the American renaissance, Mary Loeffelholz's *Dickinson and the Boundaries of Feminist Theory* might seem cautious or narrow in its designs. This is a book of tight-focus comparison of texts with texts, Dickinson moments set against passages from Wordsworth, Higginson, Elizabeth Barrett Browning, Emily Brönte, and, of course, Emerson, who plays familiar obstructionist roles—and some intriguing new ones. For Loeffelholz and Loeffelholz's Dickinson seem soulmates in the delights of subversion and paradox, and the Emerson-bugbear who vexes Dickinson here is the oppressive, denying Father, the aesthetic-materialist-political Lawgiver, and the lover as well, who must be challenged and desired in a volatile, dangerous emotional intrigue enacted in the poems. Emerson won't stay put in Dickinson's poetry; neither does anything else, and if Loeffelholz limits the texts under scrutiny, she does so to show us a grander Dickinson, a poet whose sensibility is broad and changeful and psychologically full enough to outrun or overthrow a host of assumptions popular in critical discourse, feminist and otherwise. It is no easy task to present, or rather to pursue, a poetry which "speaks back to all theories, deconstructive, feminist, materialist, psychoanalytic—that would address it" (p. 6), and in showing us such scope and depth, Loeffelholz demonstrates compassionate mastery of the jumbled theory-landscape we must wander in. Though she isn't averse to borrowing typology from many formulations, she does so without loose-minded pluralism, for each term and method adopted is eventually scrutinized in the bright light of Dickinson's reply. For all its attention to Freud, Lacan, and the ferment of psychoanalytic theory, the method which emerges seems essentially New Historicist, in that Emerson, Dickinson, and their forebears and contemporaries are viewed as firmly in and of a specific time and marketplace; and the ideologies of entrepreneurial capitalism, raw and reified by the Transcendentalists, seem to bay at midnight from the commons near the Amherst front door. Yet the Dickinson whom Loeffelholz presents is neither overwhelmed nor psychologically disfigured by such forces, as weaker social-constructionist readings tidily assert must be the case with American writers. This Emily Dickinson rises higher, and eats critical systems like air, especially new ones. Loeffelholz asserts that "a classically Oedipal psychoanalytic theory, even Lacanian terminology of the Imaginary and the Symbolic orders, resonates more fully with Dickinson's body of apocalyptic love poetry than does most current revisionary, mother-centered, object-relations psychoanalysis, even as informed by feminist thinking" (p. 67). That is a bold affirmation, in touchy times, and it is a tribute to Loeffelholz's understanding of the current ferment, of Dickinson, and of artifacts in her imaginative experience, that any method-happy reader can find something to be troubled by in this uncompromisingly clear-headed discussion.

There is urgency of all the right kinds in this book, and from some perspectives a radical agenda: Loeffelholz sees academic feminism as having obstacles to burst if it is to continue to live and grow, and she prescribes redoubled effort and a better sense of direction, insisting that a new "tradition" of feminist reading must be one which "encompasses differences among and within women, different readings of separateness and connection, different attitudes to and figurations of power," (p. 170) and outgrows a predicament in which, as she observes elsewhere, strong readings languish alone, "each to each a sealed church, not yet communing" (p. 118). But, happily or otherwise, each of these works has its conservative side. Each affirms, after all, that there *is* a somebody or a something that can be called Emily Dickinson; that there are intentions to impute, powerful relationships to be recognized, rather than concocted, between a text and an author's personal and cultural history, and meanings to be achieved, meanings which require little apology. The fact that none of these studies shudders at the inherent uncertainty of the reading process may bother some ideologues. But these books should please widely, as together they suggest a place of rendezvous, if not reconciliation, between academic feminist reifications of the American nineteenth century and a mainstream discourse—which eventually must recognize how the gender-inflection of our most cherished texts, and the rejoinders they have lately provoked, make the whole heritage richer, more complete, more genuinely human, and open venues in which conversation between the sexes can thrive.

The Body and the Body Politic in Lawrence

Virginia Hyde

James C. Cowan. *D. H. Lawrence and the Trembling Balance.* University Park: Pennsylvania State University Press, 1990. xiii, 306 pp.

Tony Pinkney. *D. H. Lawrence and Modernism.* Iowa City: University of Iowa Press, 1990. x, 180 pp.

Tony Pinkney says issues of *content* "can no longer be confronted head-on" in a post-modernist critical climate (p. 2). Fortunately, however, both of these authors care about content, engaging it deeply notwithstanding the times. Cowan employs an informed and somewhat daring psychoanalytic and epistemological context to explore how a reader's mind may interact with a literary work and gain "empathic understanding" (p. 9). This approach, handled with Cowan's broad insight and detailed knowledge, seems to me a sophisticated response to the post-structuralist challenge. Pinkney himself arrives at content "obliquely, secondarily" through a "literary-formal" means of examining modernist trends and "structures" that Lawrence illustrates and subverts. Both critics know the psychoanalytic theories of Melanie Klein[1]—as Cowan shows in the present volume and Pinkney in his earlier book, *Women in the Poetry of T. S. Eliot* (1984), though Klein is nowhere in sight in his new book. Ultimately, Cowan is more interested in Lawrence—and his holistic vision of the human individual—while Pinkney, who acknowledges the inspiration of Terry Eagleton and Raymond Williams, is more concerned with the cultural forces discernible in and around Lawrence.

Both critics have taken the writer at his word in important

respects. Cowan's title *The Trembling Balance* comes from a Lawrence essay entitled "Morality and the Novel" (1925): "Life is so made, that opposites sway about a trembling centre of balance," and the novel is an art form demanding "the trembling and oscillating of the balance" most of all.[2] Beyond illustrating these points with a large range of the novelist's writings, Cowan works in the vein of Lawrence's claim, in another essay of the same year, that "the novel, and the novel supremely can help you" not to be a "dead man in life."[3] Art in a therapeutic or "Aesculapian" tradition is Cowan's broadest subject. Pinkney writes from the most "deconstructive" Lawrentian advice to the reader (in the introduction to essays on American literature [1923]), "Never trust the artist. Trust the tale."[4] Pinkney not only quotes this maxim approvingly (and repeatedly) but he also forges some of his arguments "against the grain" of Lawrence's apparent intentions—and he is even more iconoclastic in his application of broad abstractions like "Englishness," "Northernness," and "classicism."

Cowan ranges into several scholarly fields. Besides utilizing Freud and Jung in the course of the book, he refers to philosophers and critics as well as to literally a score of medical or other scientific authorities bearing upon his attempt to establish how reading may accomplish communication and effect change. But this interdisciplinary breadth is only one welcome aspect of Cowan's work. The founder of the *D. H. Lawrence Review* and the compiler of the two-volume *D. H. Lawrence: An Annotated Bibliography of Writings about Him* (1982, 1985) as well as the author of *D. H. Lawrence's American Journey: A Study in Literature and Myth* (1970), he is massively well-informed on Lawrence; and his years of scholarship bear important insights in *The Trembling Balance*. Eight of the twelve chapters contain material that has appeared before, yet the volume is far more than a mere collection, being unified by extensive revision and by the broadened perspective that contains and enhances the individual units—that is, the idea that Lawrence's sensitivity to the dynamic flux and flow of life directs his aesthetics and provides paradigms of the "quick" and the dead by which readers can apprehend the difference.

Cowan fully acknowledges how Lawrence as psychologist—in *Psychoanalysis and the Unconscious* (1921) and *Fantasia of the Uncon-*

scious (1922)—disapproved of the Freudian attempt to make conscious the deep impulses of the unconscious. Although the young Lawrence himself initially gave some support to the Oedipal reading of *Sons and Lovers* (1913), he later declared his hatred of a clinical view of that novel written by Alfred Booth Kuttner in the 1915 *Psychoanalytic Review*.[5] Thus Lawrence might be surprised at the number of psychoanalytic studies that have followed him over the years, but Cowan's work is of a different order, being most aimed at epistemological insight. "Textual reading of any kind places the reader in an object relation to the author," he states (p. 1). Showing by Klein's theory how readers must therefore bring "projective responses" to their reading, casting upon the text their own subjective imagos, Cowan suggests that this deep reader engagement, despite its apparent remove from the text, may contribute to an interchange: "the reality of the text is answered by the reality of the reader's response" (p. 5). Theories on empathy by such authorities as Alfred Margulies and Ralph R. Greenson help to explain how projection can become not an isolating bar to the "real" but an empathic bond with the other. "The kind of critical reading I propose," says Cowan, "is not reducible to extraspection of the text considered solely as objective artifact," for "the act of reading itself internalizes the text" and can be performed "empathically rather than only projectively" (p. 12).

Cowan finds that Lawrence's metaphor for the "trembling balance" of life is the human body—indeed the male body so prominent not only in some of his writing but also in paintings like *Contadini* (1928), showing the head and torso of one naked man with the back of another in the background (reproduced on the book's dust jacket). It is the body that forms the Libra-like "balance" uniting life's polarities and allowing the individual's experience not only of selfhood but of the very elements. "Balance" may also arise between two or more individuals (as the jacket's *Contadini* is meant to illustrate). Lawrence's eye for the human body is that of an artist as well as a "philosopher," and Cowan's chapter on his artist characters and their humane (or mechanistic) vision (chapter 3) points toward Lawrentian organicism and a "myth of the body" (chapter 6). This "myth"—placing the soul not in some intangible realm but in the blood and locating specific body centers that Lawrence believed to regulate human "sympathetic" and "voluntary" faculties and even to link the human being to the non-human cosmos—combines scientific and fictive materials, along with yoga, theosophy, and pre-Socratic cosmology. This view of the body leads naturally into a discussion of touch as the most important of the senses to Lawrence (chapter 7). The need for human wholeness is highlighted further in chapters 8 and 11—the former an account of phobia in "The Thorn in the Flesh" (1914) and the latter a perceptive look at "epiphanies" in *Lady Chatterley's Lover* (1928). Again, in chapter 12, the "resurrection" of the body, bringing life's "trembling balance" to "the man who died," is the central point of *The Escaped Cock* (1929).

Perhaps the best opportunity to further the metaphor of the body comes in chapter 10, a luminous demonstration of alchemy in *The Plumed Serpent* (1926) in which Don Ramón/Quetzalcoatl turns out to be the restored Anthropos or universal man (known in alchemy as the perfected phoenix, cast in cabbalism as the perfect Androgyne before the "fall," and somewhat resembling the figure of the zodiacal man connecting the human form to astrological influences). More might have been done to connect the metaphor of the naked Lawrentian men (and perhaps women) to this view of the Anthropos.[6] Since Lawrence often depicts women's bodies, too—like those of Lady Chatterley and the Priestess of Isis—in stages of healing or achieved "homeostasis," one may wonder if his body metaphor is indeed limited to the masculine form or if, like the Anthropos, it includes both aspects of the Androgyne.

Writing on Lawrence's fondness for the phoenix (chapter 9), Cowan shows how this emblem, in psychology, traditionally "integrates both masculine and feminine components of the psyche" (p. 172). Yet Lawrence, he finds, may sometimes use it to denote manhood, as when Lilly urges Aaron Sisson in *Aaron's Rod* (1922) to be true to his own "phoenix," a "'self-form,' resembling Jung's archetype of the self" (p. 170). In its most complex Lawrentian form, though, the phoenix—an image of Christ to Christians and of resurrection and immortality to Lawrence, too—has a "numinous" dimension associated with "a syncretic deity lying beyond and encompassing" it (p. 175). If both man and woman are required to form one angel, as Tom Brangwen says in *The Rainbow*, it should be no surprise if Lawrence's phoenix ultimately embraces both sexes, too. No critic is better than Cowan on Lawrence's "de-Christianization" of hackneyed aspects of Christianity in order to resacralize them, transforming static emblems into true archetypes that can be dynamically experienced. Cowan's other chapters—on dualism in *The Ladybird* (1923), Melville as a myth-making influence on Lawrence, movies in *The Lost Girl* (1920) and elsewhere in Lawrence—all fill their places well in the book and provide valid insights.

While Cowan's main point is the relevance of Lawrence's work to life, Pinkney claims that "the post-structuralist critics" have been "scandalised by the naïvete of Lawrentian appeals to 'life,' the 'blood,' 'intuition'" (pp. 1–2). His own interests, however, are in some ways no less ideological than the novelist's. If Cowan sees the human body as a metaphor for Lawrence's ideal of balanced unities,[7] Pinkney, on the contrary, finds fragments of the body politic scattered throughout his works. Unlike Cowan's relatively optimistic Lawrence, Pinkney's Lawrence grows so darkly disillusioned by the First World War and the rise of a brittle "mass-culture" that he can scarcely keep faith with his own creed: "Whereas Lawrence had once believed—in later tales residually still does believe—that he could invoke the 'lived,' the 'blood,' as a human alternative to the vapid abstractions of mass-modernity, he now discovers under the duress of war that the 'lived' is in fact the very terrain of modernity, in its mass-cultural rather than liberal-rationalist forms" (p. 116).

The hyphenated words typify the book's proclivity for constantly mutating and unstable definitions. Pinkney has occasionally written almost in code necessitating a knowledge of his particular sources—or, better yet, of his own work as editor of *The Politics of Modernism* (1984) or of *News from Nowhere*, a periodical. *D. H. Lawrence and Modernism* is not a careful book, though at times an inspired one, with an "off-the-cuff" manner that both excites and exasperates. Greater care in offering definitions, wider reading in Lawrence critics (including Americans), less selective use of materials—all would have improved his presentation and widened his audience. No less than a theory of history lies behind his readings, but not invariably *in* them directly.

Pinkney holds that certain native features of English literature have waged a long, uneven struggle—seldom in "balance"—with "classicism," which proves to have amazing resilience and adaptability. Modernism itself, while attempting new directions, gave the classical mode a refuge when transmitting Matthew Arnold's Hellenism to T. S. Eliot's orthodoxy and to stranger tributaries like Frazer's mythology (and, ultimately, even Lawrence's phallocentric primitivism). Lawrence, while often seemingly "a modernist," is also a "counter-modernist and meta-modernist" (p. 3). Picking and choosing among multiple "modernisms," he employs major modernist "structures," including the Image (as in Imagism), seen in the visually realized *Sons and Lovers* (1913); the encyclopaedia of diverse cultures (an attempt to compensate for the absence of broad social cohesion), found in *Women in Love* (1920); the "male pseudo-couple" (providing a cranky verbal dialectic instead of plot and theme), incipient in *Women in Love* but fully present in *Aaron's Rod;* and the "mythic method," exemplified and parodied in *The Plumed Serpent*, a massive allusive structure recalling *Heart of Darkness* (1902), *The Waste Land* (1922), and *Ulysses* (1922)! Maybe so. Some of Pinkney's examples fully persuade; others leave one perplexed.

Among the most interesting discussions is the one about Lawrence's experiments with the "pseudo-couple" (of which Samuel Beckett would provide the later type)—not primarily as a homoerotic indulgence but as a means of maintaining narrative by substituting "dreary metaphysical tirades" or "non-conversation" (p. 107) for all that is lost to the novel in a world without significant feelings, actions, or meaning. Pinkney credits Lawrence with exploring the limits of this bleak doubling device and exposing "a version of human relationship so impoverished that one cannot live—cannot *read*—within it" (p. 123). In works like *Aaron's Rod*, *Kangaroo* (1923), and *The Plumed Serpent*, the novelist seeks the impossible—a "politics" for a couple created by the very loss of political hope (chapter 3).

Pinkney pursues historical trends to explain why Lawrence the

The Body and the Body Politic in Lawrence 149

coal miner's son seems to veer away from the Ruskinian or Morrisian social vision that might be seen as his English birthright (chapter 1); *Sons and Lovers,* after all, "looked as if it might inaugurate a new genre of 'proletarian realism'" (p. 164). Pinkney posits a social and artistic dichotomy between classical and Gothic forms, no doubt the same that arose in the Renaissance and manifested itself in the eighteenth-century conflicts over Palladian and Gothic architecture and in the eclectic Victorian "Medieval Revival." He even invokes (without fully explaining) the "Saxon myth" that had political and literary currency for some centuries—the idea that the indigenous, quintessential English virtues were Anglo-Saxon rather than "classical," more obvious among the hardy yeoman class than among its Roman or Norman (or other elitist) rulers. It is a surprise to find vestiges of this myth in Lawrence's first novel, *The White Peacock* (1911), in the contrast between the Saxtons (Saxons) and the more genteel Temples, who prevail (chapter 1). Pinkney has just been discussing George Eliot.[8] Perhaps he means that she could be a source for Lawrence's treatment of the down-to-earth "Saxons"—and so she could.[9]

But mere myth and literary influence do not satisfy Pinkney. He shows how Lawrence's "Englishness," partly sharing Eliot's realistic fidelity to local detail, modulates into experimental forms at its apex in his greatest work, *The Rainbow* (1915), a monument to "Northernness" (finely balanced, for once, with elements of "classicism"), in which the importance of the Gothic cathedral bespeaks the tradition of Ruskin and Morris—and also the German Expressionism of Walter Gropius, who in creating the Weimar Bauhaus after the war championed craft guilds and "a return to medieval roots" (p. 76). This chapter (2) is well represented by the book's cover design, reproducing Lyonel Feininger's woodcut, *The Cathedral of Socialism* (1919), an illustration of the Bauhaus Manifesto. But *Women in Love,* never achieving the same large cultural balance, returns to an Imagist style; far worse, Lawrence has become convinced that real "Englishness"—that of ancient, primordial, "blood-conscious" rusticity—is gone, having yielded utterly, during the war, to a rigidly "classical" official England (as suggested in "England, My England"

[1915] and in the "Nightmare" chapter in *Kangaroo*). Despite the fierce struggle Lawrence's texts often wage with "classicist abstraction," Pinkney states, they must at last be seen not as balancing their disparate inclinations but as falling "captive" to the very tradition the writer had sought to eschew in his preference for the Sax[t]ons and the Gothic cathedral (pp. 165–66).

This is no doubt a crude sketch of what Pinkney wants to demonstrate, but his book resists straightforward explication. Complications abound, and definitions run rampant. Medievalists will cringe, for example, at this indiscriminate account of "Gothic": "The Gothic is a rich notion, encompassing medieval cathedrals (Lincoln, Ely) at one end, and a specifically female subversive literary form at the other (the Brontes)" (p. 36). When Pinkney explains "classicism" early in the book, it is "a culture that defines 'reason,' 'truth' or the 'essentially human' as situated in a transcendental realm beyond history, beyond what it regards as the superficial distractions of local custom, class, gender, race, sexuality" (p. 3). But this somewhat temperate tone hardens until "classicism" is charged with "repudiation of neighbourhood, custom, community, Nature, sexuality" (p. 165); and instances in Lawrence of "buggery," suppression of female orgasm, and even ritual murder are laid at its door as "thematic consequences" of Lawrence's resurgent classicist urges (p. 167). Unlike the feminist Margaret Storch, who has separated her own position from the shrill assault on Lawrence in Kate Millett's *Sexual Politics* (1970), Pinkney comes to endorse it.[10] He concludes, with a hurried sense of paradox and contradiction, by discovering that Lawrence's central preoccupations (like the phallus) always inevitably allied him with the Greeks.

Unlike Cowan's ample bibliography, providing international scope, Pinkney's sources and suggestions for further reading are narrowly selective, almost entirely devoid of American scholarship. This may be why he believes that "Lawrence's reputation has suffered a deep slump" (p. 129) even though one recent five-year bibliography on him lists more than 200 items. One example of Pinkney's omissions may suffice. Despite his book's central preoccupation with the meaning of Gothic form in Lawrence (and he is atypical of Lawrence critics since Horace Gregory in making no distinction between the Romanesque Norman forms and the Gothic, no distinction between the arch of a rainbow and that of a cathedral), he never broaches the thirty-five-year debate about "The Shape of an Arch" (as Mark Spilka phrased it in 1955 in *The Love Ethic of D. H. Lawrence*). In the chapter that should be Pinkney's strongest—the one on *The Rainbow* as Lawrence's highest achievement—well-rehearsed arguments are either repeated or entirely ignored. A few of the books that offer useful comments on Lawrence's arches and cathedrals should be consulted along with Pinkney's: for example, Julian Moynahan's *The Deed of Life* (1963), Marguerite Beede Howe's *The Art of the Self in D. H. Lawrence* (1977), Robert W. Millett's *The Vultures and the Phoenix* (1983), Keith Sagar's *D. H. Lawrence: Life into Art* (1985), and Cornelia Nixon's *Lawrence's Leadership Politics and the Turn Against Women* (1986). Judith Ruderman has even emphasized, in *D. H. Lawrence and the Devouring Mother* (1984), that the writer's "leadership" period marks a change in his preference—from the rounded Norman arch (womb-like) to the pointed Gothic arch (phallic), apparently illustrating visually not only the power of the lingham but also a pyramid-like social hierarchy such as the novelist advocates at this time. Such details might have been useful to Pinkney, for he approaches the gender issue several times, referring to the Gothic cathedral as "a female body" (p. 67) and to the language of *The Rainbow* as an utterance seeming to issue from a "fertilized female body" (p. 94). But he never proceeds to the architectural images, or their implications, in later Lawrence.

Cowan and Pinkney are generally unlike. Interestingly enough, they even make different assessments of the ongoing *Cambridge Edition of the Letters and Works of D. H. Lawrence* (1979–present, ed. James T. Boulton and Warren Roberts), around which controversy has circled for some years now. While the American scholar scrupulously cites it, Pinkney terms it "scholarship run riot" (p. x) and opts for the cheaper (and sometimes textually different) Penguin edition. As unlike as Cowan and Pinkney are as critics, both seem to agree in valuing "balance" in Lawrence—Pinkney in the rare instance of *The Rainbow* and Cowan in the canon at large. To Cowan, this balance is most intense at the individual level, being represented visually by the human form and experienced empathically by the reader. But his book is not limited to the individual level, for he easily commands the Lawrence *ouevre* in depth and also provides a wealth of specific cultural details from several disciplines. To Pinkney, vast cultural tendencies weight the scales of history, as they do Lawrence's pages, yet some of both the history and the literature goes unexplained in this broadly conceived but short volume. One may wish, nonetheless, to read a provocative book—and this one, already existing in paperback, can reward the careful reader. Above all, one must not miss Cowan's scholarly achievement, a book to read with confidence and the informed "empathy" it encourages.

Notes

1. Margaret Storch's *Sons and Adversaries: Women in William Blake and D. H. Lawrence* (Knoxville: Univ. of Tennessee Press, 1990) also makes use of Melanie Klein's theories. Cowan, whose interest is in Klein's view of the process of projection, presents a far broader psychoanalytic and cultural context. Storch's feminist approach deals with the ambivalent hostility of the infant in mother-child relationships that influence later patterns of thought. Both Blake and Lawrence are said to reveal aspects of "splitting" (projecting both "good" and "bad" mother-images), envy of the female body, Oedipal disturbances, and "reparation" of the destroyed female love/hate object. See my forthcoming review in the *D. H. Lawrence Review*.

2. Lawrence, *Study of Thomas Hardy and Other Essays*, ed. Bruce Steele (Cambridge: Cambridge Univ. Press, 1985), p. 173.

3. Ibid., p. 197.

4. Lawrence, *Studies in Classic American Literature* (New York: Viking, 1966), p. 2.

5. *The Letters of D. H. Lawrence*, ed. George J. Zytaruk and James T. Boulton, (Cambridge: Cambridge Univ. Press, 1981), II, 659. Storch, who does not complicate her argument with these claims by Lawrence, provides the latest psychoanalytic approach through the "object relations" school of the basically Freudian Klein. Of course, Lawrence has often received good psychoanalytic criticism despite his own distaste for the method, but it is not Cowan's method.

6. See also Leonora Woodman, "D. H. Lawrence and the Hermetic Tradition," *Cauda Pavonis*, n.s. 8.2 (1989), 1–6, and my forthcoming book, *The Risen Adam: D. H. Lawrence's Revisionist Typology* (1992).

The Body and the Body Politic in Lawrence 153

7. See also Storch's Blakean view of Lawrence's attempts at unification, discussed in *Sons and Adversaries*, p. 115: "As Blakean man suffers separation of the vital functions that can be healed only with the redemption of Albion, so too are Gerald and Birkin [in *Women in Love*] two halves of a broken person who can come together only in a close male relationship that is envisaged but never realized."

8. When discussing *The Mill on the Floss*, Pinkney seems to accept the mistaken claim of Jessie Chambers (and, by her account, of Lawrence himself) that Maggie Tulliver marries Philip Wakem (p. 11).

9. See, for example, my article on a "Saxon myth" in the portrayal of the Garths in *Middlemarch*: "George Eliot's Arthuriad: Heroes and Ideology in *Middlemarch*," *Papers on Language and Literature*, 24 (1988), 404–11. But Sir Walter Scott is a likely source for both Eliot and Lawrence.

10. Storch, *Sons and Adversaries*, p. 192.

E Pluribus Unum

Ilan Stavans

Earl E. Fitz. *Rediscovering the New World: Inter-American Literature in a Comparative Context.* Iowa City: University of Iowa Press, 1991. xiv, 275 pp.

A frontier is inherently an artificial division, a sign set out by humans to divide. It separates the unseparable: two segments of land that are a unity, part of a whole. Take for instance the Río Grande, a natural line marking the limits between the United States and the rest of the Americas. North of it is Texas, California, Arizona, New Mexico; Anglo-Saxon culture with Great Britain as the mother country; Protestantism; English; the 1776 Revolution. South of it is a reality conquered by the Spaniards in 1524 and onwards; Catholicism and the Church; Spanish and Portuguese; Simón Bolívar and his nineteenth-century dream of unification; today's political instability, human poverty, and economic disaster. It's only a river that separates the two universes, a geographical line. And yet, and yet. . . . "Distant neighbors" is the term coined by Alan Riding: one territory and two civilizations.

A way to perceive the cultural difference between the two sides is through their literatures. Besides the fact that their novels and poems are written in different idioms, their themes, motifs, and symbols are self-contained—an expression of the two idiosyncracies, each of them unique. Or at least that has been the accepted view. Washington Irving, in 1726, looked to Spain for inspiration. He couldn't begin to imagine that a far richer, perhaps more complex reality, one more akin to his own, existed south of the border. And think for a moment of how Christopher Columbus is seen as a hero in the United States while Latin America makes of him one of the most villainous, dishonest personalities in the continent's difficult history—a scoundrel. In 1887 Walt Whitman, who was according to Ralph Waldo Emerson the greatest poet of the United States, wrote "Prayer for Columbus," later included in *Leaves of Grass*. In the poem he assumes the voice of the old Genoese admiral the moment he is about to die and is insecure about his own life achievements. This is a poem about personal goals, about fame and success, about recognition—a chant to individuality. Only a few years later, in 1892, the year of Whitman's death, the Nicaraguan stylist Rubén Darío, the greatest poet of Hispanic America according to the Uruguayan *modernista* critic José Enrique Rodó, was in Spain. And it was there when he wrote "To Columbus," later included in *El canto errante* (*The Wandering Song*). He used the same topic that inspired Whitman—the mariner who in 1492 thought he had found a new European route to the West Indies. Yet even a superficial reading of both texts shows how fundamentally different they are: while the U.S. poet celebrated the courageous spirit and character of the Spanish voyager, the Nicaraguan attacked him for having opened the door to an ecological and religious holocaust in the "newly discovered colonies." Darío vilifies Columbus, ridicules his endeavors, and condemns him for having set the stage for a tremendous tragedy. Whitman, on the other hand, sings to his glory. Thus, in a Rashomon-like sum of perspectives, the same historical figure is seen from two opposing viewpoints that ultimately create a double-faceted mariner, simultaneously a villian and a semi-god.

Every so often, North American writers have looked for themselves in Mexico and South America. Katherine Anne Porter collected some of her more tantalizing stories about poor Hispanic peasants and talented filmmakers in *Flowering Judas;* Ernest Hemingway found an oasis in Cuba; John Reed, Michael Gold, and John Kenneth Turner were fascinated with the 1910 Socialist Revolution of Pancho Villa and Emiliano Zapata; Harriet Doerr set her novel *Stones for Ibarra* in a tranquil Mexican town near an abandoned copper mine; the Beat generation and, earlier, Ambrose Bierce went to Mexico to meet their fate or to run away from justice; and Peter Matthiessen located his 1965 novel *At Play in the Fields of the Lord* in the rain forests near Bolivia and Brazil. But the rustic and urban exoticism of these geographies has been more than a mere narrative stage for outlaws, missionaries, and soul-searchers. Many United States novelists of the twentieth century, especially after World War II, have revisited their literary notions, and even discovered one or two of their own literary forefathers, thanks to the help of authors from Argentina, Brazil, Mexico, or Peru. That's because some U.S. authors keep a high profile south of the Río Grande. In an interview with John Updike (*Diario 16*, Madrid, 27/IV/1991), the author of *Hugging the Shore* persuasively explained how his knowledge of Nathaniel Hawthorne, so influential in the writing of his trilogy *A Month of Sundays, Roger's Version*, and *S.*, came to him, not thanks to Henry James' 1879 booklet for the series English Men of Letters, but through a Jorge Luis Borges lecture given in Buenos Aires in 1946 and later included in *Other Inquisitions*. No doubt this is a reversal of considerable importance. The fact that a North American appreciates one of his precursors with the help of an Argentine fabulist indeed does tell something about the immense bookishness of Borges. But it also goes to show how we are living in a global mass culture in which the so-called Third World may have an awkward political and financial reality but literature there is "simultaneous" with that of Europe or the United States. Fast, readily made translations facilitate the expansion and osmosis of ideas from one hemisphere to another, from one linguistic area to the next. High-brow readerships are no longer the properties only of major capitals such as Paris, Rome, and New York, as was the case before 1950. With the emergence of independent states in Africa, Asia, Oceania, and South America after World War II, but especially because of the collective awareness of the division between rich and poor nations, of the haves and have-nots, writers such as V. S. Naipaul, Wole Soyinka, Mario Vargas Llosa, and Nadime Gordimer have acquired international reputations, and they can illuminate, even influence, a writer in Connecticut or South Carolina. The superiority of the industrialized nations isn't a ticket to the production of better, more technically complex novels. In Octavio Paz's words, "Latin America is finally a contemporary of the rest of the world." Argentina, Brazil, or Mexico, nations in which the writer has long had an antagonistic position *vis-à-vis* the State, is now the object of world curiosity and scrutiny. Although their fiction has become a door to the understanding of this struggling, unstable social dynamics, always on the brink of civil war, authors there are not altogether obsessed with internal affairs. They also read Hawthorne, Giambattista Vico, Marcel Proust, and Robert Musil; they are enlightened and sophisticated readers, not the owners of underdeveloped minds.

Of course, the artistic influence that the United States has had over culture in Río de Janeiro, Lima, or Buenos Aires is unquestionable and reaches back to the late eighteenth century and the beginning of the nineteenth. In his *Facundo: Civilization and Barbarism,* a half-fictional, half-authentic study of his nation's identity, Domingo Faustino Sarmiento, a Argentine writer and diplomat, is said to have imitated the craft of James Fenimore Cooper, the so-called "North American Sir Walter Scott." In his detective short stories, Borges openly emulated Poe's "Murder in the Rue Morgue," in which August Dupin displays his ratiocinative logic. And it's a well-known fact that Yoknapatawpha, William Faulkner's fictitious region in the Deep South, so afflicted by the Civil War and the Depression, had a strong impact on the creation of Macondo, Gabriel García Márquez's town on the Caribbean coast that is at centerstage in *One Hundred Years of Solitude,* as well as on Santa María, Juan Carlos Onetti's dump of prostitutes and down-and-outs near the River Plate. The Colombian and Uruguayan saw in the Mississippi writer a dimension of defeat, of decades of repression and pain, and identified with his views. They adapted them, remodeled his roots, and made them their own.

Other than Faulkner, Ernest Hemingway and John Dos Passos were almost the only two United States authors who were read south of the Río Bravo. Yet that was a far better situation than the other way around. During the nineteenth century and the first half of the twentieth, no one from Argentina or Nicaragua was even known in the literary circles of New York, Chicago, Boston, or Philadelphia. Not even Rubén Darío, the *Modernista* poet *par excellence,* author of *Azul . . . (Blue)* and *Prosas profanas* ("*Unsacred Texts*"), highly revered in Spain by Juan Valera and Juan Ramón Jiménez, was known. In other words, the south knew about the narrative and artistic endeavors of the north, but not vice versa. Power, it may be concluded, promotes a certain narrow-mindedness and parochialism. Fortunately the panorama is now different. In "The Literature of Exhaustion" (*Atlantic*, August 1967), John Barth prized Borges as one of his personal tutors, and in "The Literature of Replenishment" (*Atlantic*, January 1980) he celebrated Gabriel García Márquez as an unforgettable master in the tradition of the anonymous author(s) of the *Arabian Nights,* and believed, together with Susan Sontag (*New Yorker,* 7 May 1990), that Machado de Assis, Brazil's early Modernist, is an unsurpassed genius in the landscape of world letters. In "The Writer as Librarian" (*New Yorker,* 30 October 1965), John Updike introduced Borges to English-speaking audiences and established his influences as comparable to those of Franz Kafka and Lewis Carroll. What all of this attention to Latin American letters means is that finally there is some reciprocity.

Already for quite a while and with intense passion during the last decade, scholars have been prompt in examining the points of coincidence between the aesthetics and literary motifs of both continents: Alfred J. MacAdam, for instance, in *Textual Confrontations* (University of Chicago Press, 1987), made comparative studies of the works of W. H. Auden and Pablo Neruda; Edna Aizenberg edited *Borges and His Successors* (University of Missouri Press, 1990), a book that contained an examination by Geoffrey Green on the similarities between Borges and Barth, Robert Coover, Updike, Thomas Pynchon, John Hawkes, and Don DeLillo; Lois Parkinson Zamora, in *Writing the Apocalypse* (Cambridge University Press, 1989), looked at contemporary U.S. writers like Pynchon and Walker Percy, and equated their understanding of disaster themes and techniques with those of Carlos Fuentes, Julio Cortázar, and García Márquez; Bell Gale Chevigny and Gari Laguardia edited *Reinventing the Americas* (also issued by Cambridge, 1986), a mesmerizing volume that included essays on the correlations and bridges between Alejo Carpentier and Herman Melville, Cooper and Rosario Castellanos, Alice Walker and Elena Poniatowska, Wallace Stevens and Octavio Paz; finally, *Do the Americas Have a Common Literature?*

(Duke University Press, 1990), edited by Gustavo Pérez Firmat, a Cuban poet and scholar, is a recent collection of essays dealings with Walt Whitman, José Lezama Lima, Cirilo Villaverde, and other writers of the Americas. Interestingly enough, all of these texts are the product of U.S. researchers and scholars with a Brazilian and Hispanic background or area of specialization. That is, with few exceptions, the desire to compare the literatures north and south of the Río Grande with one another is being carried on by culturally diversified North Americans. Yet their adventure is only an echo of the interest that began with Updike and Borges and the other authors who, through their own fiction, ignited the whole process.

Undoubtedly the most important comparative text to date is that of Earl E. Fitz, *Rediscovering the New World: Inter-American Literature in a Comparative Context.* A professor at Pennsylvania State University and a veteran in the art of collating literatures, Fitz has written one book-long monograph on Machado de Assis in which he discusses his place in the playful tradition of Lawrence Sterne, and another on Clarise Lispector, a Ukranian-born Brazilian-Jewish author of intimate, sensitive novels and short stories who died in 1977. While the above-listed studies by Alfred MacAdam, Gustavo Pérez-Firmat, Lois Parkinson Zamora, and the rest are fragmentary, often examining only a handful of authors or symbols or a single aesthetic movement, the volume by Fitz is the most ambitious attempt ever by a single critic to unify both literary cultures. The author not only includes the narrative legacies of the U.S., the Hispanic, and the Brazilian nations south of the Río Grande, but also that of Canada as well, another crucial player in the creation of a true "Inter-American library" written in at least four languages: English, French, Portuguese, and Spanish. Too, while the essays in the previously listed academic collections were based on the assumption that the Americas have "different" histories, *Rediscovering the New World* supports the thesis that the two continents constitute "a community of literary cultures related to each other by virtue of their origin, their sundry interrelationships, and their sociopolitical, artistic, and intellectual evolutions" (p. xi). Fitz claims that "their very real differences notwithstanding, the nations of the

New World share enough of a common history that they can legitimately be studied as a unit, as different manifestations of the Americanism or New Worldism that each represents" (p. xi). Hence his methology is thematic and historiographical. He identifies a handful of crucial issues that interrelate these literatures—the narratives of discovery, the epic, the theme of miscegenation, the quest for collective identity, regionalism, the motif of solitude, the battle between barbarism and civilization—and analyzes them by reading important texts of each tradition against each other and by placing them all in historical and aesthetic context.

Obviously such a mammoth undertaking, such an encyclopedic enterprise, is a job for a uniquely qualified researcher, someone able to digest four different artistic traditions united by a single geography and capable of understanding the continuity between the various pasts, from Alaska to the Patagonia. The role of the specialist as we know it, a researcher who knows more and more about less and less, collapses, giving way to a Renaissance-model *homme de lettres*. Fitz proves to be a capable candidate for the job. Indeed, his background may offer some clue to his personal and professional interest. It is a well-acknowledged fact that even though it is the largest, richest, and most heavily populated country of the region, Brazil, perhaps because of its linguistic isolation, remains a separate unit within the vastness of South America. Its writers, from Jorge Amado to Enrico Veríssimo, from Nélida Piñón to João Ubaldo Ribeiro, share a feeling of loneliness. They think of their works as misunderstood and unappealing to their continental companions. To combat the isolation, many of these writers are multi-lingual, perfectly fluent in Spanish and English at least. This enables them to communicate with the rest of the world. They often read large numbers of foreign books and are influenced by them. The result is a need to see the particular within the universal, and that is precisely Fitz's attitude—he expands and magnifies rather than reduces, he is always traveling to distant realities rather than staying in recognizable, comforting terrain. To put it in (mixed) figurative language, this is a global look at what the many shareholders of a condominium have in common. Rather than a sum of parts, it is the detailed description of an entire landscape.

Unfortunately it exhibits two unmistakable defects. First and perhaps more regrettably, Fitz writes a flat, unengaging prose. His paragraphs lack force and are often dry. Second, rather than dissecting a group of ideas, he often prefers to list them. Because of his ambitious scope, he seldom analyzes a specific title in detail; instead, he pinpoints some commonalities it shares with other texts of the time and investigates one or two of its dominant symbols. Consequently the conclusions are at times self-serving and plain, and the reader often stumbles through uninspired paragraphs.

Yet the book is full of passion—an invitation to further discussion. The first issue to be raised, for example, pertains to the term "New World." Although the author uses this term interchangeably with "Americanism," it is the preferred one in his pages and is even part of the title. Fitz is talking about a region struggling to understand itself by discovering its differences with Europe—that is, the Old World. Thus to employ the term is to subscribe to the division of ancient and new, a distinction that has nothing to do with the actual topographic or ecological past of Europe or the Americas, but with the supremacy of Caucasian civilization based on its lineage. Since 12 October 1492, when Columbus first set foot on Wertling Island in the Bahamas, the New World has perceived itself, and has been seen by outsiders, as a Promised Land of sorts, a paradise-on-earth ready to undermine the supremacy of the ancient motherlands. The pre-Columbian poetry and prose—epic, religious, and rhetorical in tone when Hernán Cortés and Pizarro began their conquests—dealt with the social and dynamic dimensions that related the Native Americans to Nature and the will of the gods. Their territories, according to the songs of the Texcoco king Nezahualcóyotl, the *Popol Vuh*, the *Rabinal Achí*, *The Book of Chilam Balam*, and the dramatic Inca text *Ollantay*, were created in time immemorial. The flora and fauna, the wars, the patrician hierarchy—everything in them was a design of the heavens. The very first chronicles of the discovery, written by European soldiers such as Bernal Díaz del Castillo and Gaspar de Carvajal, are a standard expression of how overwhelmed the newly arrived Spaniards and Portuguese were by so exotic a landscape, full of colors, flavors, smells, and human kindness. The aborigines were at peace with their circumstances, but that harmony was disrupted by the newly arrived foreigners. The soldiers commanded by Cortés entered Tenochtitlán in order to take control of the metropolis and make it a colony of their Spanish kings. Cortés and his followers had traveled to the Americas to accumulate fortunes and expand the boundaries of the Iberian empire. Hence Fitz's usage of the term "New World" is correct if one reads the literature written after the tragic conquest as a direct successor of Homer, Dante, and Petrarch, not of the Aztec and Inca oral traditions. The reality found in and after 1492 was "new" to old readers—that is to say, to Europeans.

The second crucial issue regarding Fitz's text is also related to the title and involves the term "rediscovery." It's clear from chapter 2, entitled "The Narratives of Discovery and Conquest," that he is not ready to take a stand in the controversy, so heated because of the Quincentennial, between those who promote the theory of the "discovery" of the Americas by Columbus and those arguing that, since one only discovers that which did not previously exist, the preferable term for the event in 1492 is an "encounter" between two civilizations. Fitz uses the term "rediscovery" to promote the idea that Americans in general, be they citizens of Quito, Québec, or Panama City, can regain control of their identity by "re-conquering" and "repossessing" their collective cultural heritage. And that heritage appears in their books, music, and pictorial art. They will recover their true self only when they perceive the entire continent as a whole—a holistic unity.

Having clarified these two terms, I can now comment on the various chapters in *Rediscovering the New World*. In his discussion of why the epic is such a favorite genre north and south of the Río Grande, the author rummages the shelves for grandiose, now-forgotten literature of the early republics. "With its conquests and its long struggles toward political and cultural autonomy," Fitz argues, "it is not surprising that American epics would have been written. What is surprising is how different these New

World epics are from each other and, often, from orthodox concepts of this ancient genre" (pp. 48–49). Fitz shows that most of the production fits the category of "art" and not "folk" epic; that is, the hero is more likely to be "collective in significance" rather than a single man or woman battling the forces of Nature. The case of Joel Barlow's *The Columbiad*, a famous-in-its-time examination of the greatness of North America, is particularly illuminating. Fitz compares him to *The Araucaniad* by Alonso de Ercilla y Zúñiga, which appeared sequentially in 1569, 1578, and 1589, and to epics by E. J. Pratt and Louis Fréchette. But Barlow's text, published in its final form in 1807, and developed from an earlier work written between 1783 and 1787, is seen as a symbol of narrative appropriation, thus becoming significant in the history of inter-American letters. A futuristic, historical revision of the newly discovered lands, the text has Columbus as its main observer and omniscient protagonist. Other figures are also at centerstage, however, including the Inca monarch Manco Capac and the first U.S. President George Washington. Barlow saturated his creation with rhetorical devices and mediocre poetry. Yet what strikes today's reader is his predictability and accommodating drive: as a solid citizen of the eighteenth century and not a visionary, Barlow refuses to perceive "America" as made of two idiosyncracies, the Brazilian/Hispanic and the Anglo-Saxon; instead, in his eyes the Genoese admiral found only one reality worth noticing: Barlow's own country. Also, as a true precursor of Walt Whitman, his epic sings to the collective spirit, to the popular North American soul. Fitz's description of this adaptative experiment is meaningful. He shows how *The Columbiad*, in an anthem of totality, celebrates the United States, its cohesive solidity, its destiny. The author's chants emerge from within the epic genre; that is, after choosing a particular genre of the European literary tradition, he adapts it to his own needs and those of his country. The result is a revamping of the epic—a renewal.

Another important theme in *Rediscovering the New World* is miscegenation. One need not forget that the Río Grande, in separating the Anglo-Saxon from the Hispanic and Brazilian realities, is also a line dividing the two opposing approaches the first settlers took when descending from their migrating boats. In Mexico and the rest of Latin America, perhaps only with the exception of the River Plate, the *conquistadores*, medieval knights thirsty for gold and power, traveled without their wives and family. Hence their relationship with the Indians involved sexual abuse: they raped and dominated the Aztec, Quechua, and Inca women, creating the *mestizo* race—a mixture, a composite. Immediately afterwards they left, creating the myth of the absent, unavailable father. With the biblical dream of finding the Promised Land in their minds, the pilgrims of the *Mayflower,* on the other hand, inhabited what was later to become the British Colonies with the hope of starting anew. They didn't mix. The scattered aboriginal tribes they found were annihilated. As a result, the purity of blood in the United States, at least in its early stages of development, managed to sustain itself, and no confusion about self-perception emerged. In Latin America, however, the collective identity has always been a question mark: "Am I Spanish or American?" the *mestizo* must ask. "Aztec or Iberian?" Miscegenation, understandably, is an obvious component of the various literatures of the region. In *La cautiva (The Female Prisoner)* by Esteban Echeverría, for example, as well as in the novels of Cirilo Villaverde, Carlos Fuentes, Jorge Amado, Darcy Ribeiro, and many others, the topic of mixed marriages, of confused devotions, is permanent and undeniable. In North America, on the other hand, the topic, never a threat to the first settlers' standards of living, appears in one way in, say, James Fenimore Cooper's *The Last of the Mohicans,* and in a very different fashion in the narratives of black twentieth-century writers such as James Baldwin and Ralph Ellison. The former offers us the view of the white man, in the eye of the author a clearly "superior" creature *vis-à-vis* the natives; the latter two examine the politics and intimate life of two races, Caucasian and African. Because of the flux of immigrants of various origins, the U.S. as a democracy is always pushed, even obsessed, with miscegenation, and the black experience, with slavery in its past, retains a special place in the nation's history. South America, never having promoted itself as a melting pot, is not concerned with the issue. Instead, the area is proud of its Catholic roots and *mestizo* background. That's why such minority literatures as Oriental, Italian, and Jewish have had a hard time emerging as valid artistic forms in Mexico, Peru, and Argentina. Fitz studies Malcolm X's *Autobiography,* two titles by Baldwin, *The Bear* and *Absalom! Absalom!* by Faulkner, Amado's *Tent of Miracles,* and Alix Renaud's *A corps joie* to prove that on both sides of the Río Bravo there are important variations to the theme. Sometimes the concern is with interracial sex, and attention is given to issues of gender and ethnic identity; at other times the author stresses political, social, and racial taboos. Conclusions are at once pessimistic and optimistic: in the U.S. and even in Canada, the author claims, there is a need to find a middle ground where ethnic and gender groups can meet; but in the American South the supremacy of the white man inevitably prevails. Literature, Fitz proves, is an instrument sensitive to any sign of sickness, a mirror reflecting the metabolism of society.

Overall, *Rediscovering the New World* tries to keep away from big, much-discussed and even abused names and texts. The strategy is always to dig in, to understand a trend instead of the shining halo of a literary star. Perhaps the best chapter is the one comparing Henry James and Machado de Assis. Fitz begins by asking why the Brazilian luminary is still very much unknown abroad, in other urban centers of the continent, as well as in Europe. The answer is brave and accurate. Like Felisberto Hernández, a Uruguayan short-story writer of the caliber of Bruno Schultz, Franz Kafka, and Danilo Kiš, born in Montevideo in 1902 and dead at age sixty-one, Machado had the bad luck to be placed, by God perhaps, "in the 'wrong country,' one not ordinarily ranked among the literary elite of Western culture." If he had "practiced his art in France, Germany, Russia, England, Italy, Spain, or even Portugal," Fitz argues, "his name would now be as familiar to students of literature as are those of Flaubert, Goethe, Dostoevsky, Dickens, Pessoa, or Cervantes" (pp. 95–96). Thus Fitz correctly implies that there are "bad" and "good" countries to be born in when it comes to the sorting out of artistic immortality.

Although there's no evidence that Machado and James ever knew of each other's work, their technically innovative, mature contribution to the modern novel is reason enough to attempt a comparison. The Brazilian was a master in tragicomedy; the North American, a genius of ambiguity, subtle statement, and psychological insight. Both authors had long careers, tried their luck in the theater, created unforgettable short fictions, used social situations to explain the internal state of their characters, and discovered the pleasures and advantages of a single-sighted, first-person narrator. *Rediscovering the New World* meditates on the various stages of their careers and aesthetic developments and examines in great detail the commonalities shared by *Epitaph of a Small Winner* and *The Portrait of a Lady*, both published in book form in 1881. Fitz then examines *The Ambassadors* and *Dom Casmurro* and ends by pointing out that, although both authors in one way or another defected from their own countries, their shared craft was a soul-searching process that helped reshape the collective identity. The value of this analysis surpasses anything else in the book.

Chapter 9, devoted to the Ur-theme of solitude, is quite engaging. The same can be said about chapter 7, "The Quest of an American Identity." The content of both is intertwined. Fitz opens the former by saying that "the evolution of solitude as a motif of New World literature is both logical and ironic: logical because one could reasonably expect it, given the cultural diversity and geographic isolation of the Americas, and ironic because one would not expect the frustration and paralysis associated with this theme to develop in cultures so consciously concerned with their own making and remaking" (p. 191). Across the Río Grande and in Europe, the United States is perceived as a nation without a past, a place that has managed to create an image of its own glory and destiny through its art and entertainment industries. With the death of the few aboriginal tribes, it seems, a sense of root, of historical continuity, was also killed and people faced the challenge of creating new, supra-historical heroes. The opposite is true for Latin America, where the Indian population, so ethnically alive in everyone's blood and skin, is a constant reminder of geographical belonging. Fitz studies the sense of cultural awareness in the Hispanic world, starting with the half-Spanish, half-Indian Garcilaso "El Inca" de la Vega, the author of the *Royal Commentaries*. Writing in 1609 and 1617, more or less at the time when Cervantes published the two parts of *Don Quixote*, this Peruvian author praised both his father's and his mother's heritage, creating a duality, a division in his identity. Yet such bifurcation generates in him a feeling of loneliness. *Rediscovering the New World* then discusses the art of Sor Juana Inés de la Cruz, about whom Octavio Paz, winner of the 1990 Nobel Prize for Literature, has written an excellent biography (Harvard University Press, 1988). Fitz also treats of João Guimarães Rosa, the author of *The Devil to Pay in the Backlands*. The argument is that as it developed, the literary quilt composed by the many Brazilian and Hispanic authors was shaped by a sensation of being cosmologically alone, unaccompanied, forgotten by all other humans. Fitz claims persuasively that the construction of the collective soul is simultaneously a cause and a consequence of literature. A nation understands itself by means of its reflective narratives, he argues, yet those very same narratives reshape its self-perception. The same can be said about the United States: from Washington Irving to Benjamin Franklin to Herman Melville, the aspects of the North American identity are a mirror, and also are mirrored in the literature.

Chapter 6, "The Five (Six?) Faces of American Modernism," addresses what I believe to be the most fundamental question of terminology the researcher is likely to find when dealing with Inter-American letters. When a literary topic treated by authors on both sides of the Río Grande is brought out, the first dilemma is how to approach the various aesthetic movements, all unique to the regional cultures they emerged from. What Spanish speakers call *Modernismo*, a poetic trend that swept all of Hispanic America between 1885 and 1915 and included writers such as José Martí from Cuba, Darío from Nicaragua, Manuel Gutiérrez Nájera from Mexico, and others from Colombia, Uruguay, and Argentina, was nothing but a revision of nineteenth-century European Romanticism, adapted and transposed to the southern hemisphere. Yet Modernism, a term used in Western letters to refer to the revolution of Luigi Pirandello, T. S. Eliot, James Joyce, Virginia Woolf, and Thomas Mann, was a completely different phenomenon: its premises were based on introspection, linguistic experimentation, the debunking of reason as a solid structure, and metafictional devices such as the introduction of the author in the piece of work or the constant reflection on the art of writing within the very same pages of a novel or the walls of a theatrical stage. Thus, from a comparative point of view, if one is to approach the narrative art of the Americas as a whole, prior to anything else the task is to differentiate, and perhaps rename, the many movements called Modernism. I say "many" because besides the two mentioned above, the immediate successors of the *modernistas* in Spanish America, sometimes also referred to as *vanguardistas*—i.e., César Vallejo, Vicente Huidobro, even Pablo Neruda and Miguel Angel Asturias—are also called modernists. And then there are the early English Canadian modernists like W.W.E. Ross and Arthur Stringer, as well as the French Canadians, and finally one has a group of early North American modernists which includes Ezra Pound and Eliot, and the later ones, including William Carlos Williams and Robert Frost. What we are talking about, then, is an essential dichotomy. During the first decades of the twentieth century, the Anglo-Saxon world underwent a literary revolution that only took hold in the Hispanic world in the fifties. Yet in cities like Buenos Aires, Montevideo, Santiago and Mexico City, a hunger for a romantic vein, absent from Hispanic American poetry and only present in Spain in kitsch authors such as Gustavo Adolfo Bécquer, materialized in a revision of the continent's narrative canon just as World War I was coming to an end. (The best essay on the topic, surprisingly unmentioned by Fitz, is by Octavio Paz: "Translation and Metaphor," in *Children of the Mire*, 1964.) Fitz ought to be congratulated for diagnosing the problem without delay.

Yet addressing this issue potentially jeopardizes Fitz's central thesis. If international literature is the sum of distinctive artistic movements, each of which is generated by specific social, political, economic, and psychological circumstances, all unique to the countries of origin, how then can one talk about Inter-American letters as a compound? Can the same attitude be applied to Europe? Could one talk about the Italian, French, Spanish, Portuguese, German, Dutch, and even British novel traditions as components of a unified whole? Each nation, or better each linguistic zone, produces and responds to a set of aesthetic stimuli that at times is influenced by foreign art and other times is not. Contemporary English prose and poetry, for instance, are very much the product of a sophisticated process that began with Chaucer and had its apotheosis in Shakespeare and Milton. Seen as a unique chain of causes and effects, the writings of these authors are different from the literature produced, say, in Luxembourg or Lisbon. And yet one could indeed talk about the "European" novel, especially from the late nineteenth century on, from Cervantes, Diderot, and Samuel Richardson on. Artistic movements such as Romanticism, Naturalism, Realism, and Surrealism did not involve one linguistic reality but swept the entire continental landscape. No one would read Emile Zola and Benito Pérez Galdós and claim they didn't share the same cultural mood, the same aesthetic concerns, although each had a different national scenario. It's possible to suggest, then, that neighboring countries, unless secluded from all world trends, fashions and events, hold similar artistic views. The fact that the various Modernist movements took place in the Americas within a margin of one to two decades is proof of the simultaneity of aesthetic trends. What Fitz is suggesting, then, is that we examine these trends against each other so that we can get a total picture. By doing so, we will not deny that the factors generating a Modernist poem such as *El espejo de agua* (*The Water Mirror*) by Huidobro in Chile are different from those influencing Eliot in writing "The Love Song of J. Alfred Prufrock." Yet these factors coexist spatially and temporally.

Some other topics discussed in *Rediscovering the New World* are regionalism and the struggle between civilization and barbarism. Both are important because, since history's early stages, the Americas have witnessed the battle between urban and provincial cultures, between chaos and order. Fitz discusses these issues in a manner that is provocative though at times dry. One compelling element he does leave out is the linguistic cross-over of some Hispanic writers in the United States and south of the Río Grande, writers who have chosen, or have been forced to accept, English as their communication vehicle. I am thinking of Oscar Hijuelos, the Cuban-North American author of *The Mambo Kings*

Play Songs of Love, the first Hispanic to receive a Pulitzer Prize for Literature; or Felipe Alfau, the Spanish-born United States creator of *Locos: A Comedy of Gestures*, a novel that when published in 1936 enchanted Mary McCarthy and was reissued in 1988 by the Dalkey Archive Press. Other names of descendants of Iberians, Mexicans, and Central and South Americans who lived or were raised in New York or California include Sandra Cisneros, Judith Ortíz Cofer, and Gary Soto. Some scholarly books and biographical dictionaries have been published on their ethnic art; Fitz might have included a section discussing their intertwining vision. But these authors are not the only Hispanics writing in English. One must think as well of Carlos Fuentes, Guillermo Cabrera Infante, José Donoso, and Manuel Puig, all Latin-American "boom" authors who gained fame in the sixties and seventies. At some point in their careers, out of sheer will or because of a need for money and visibility, they wrote books in English. The linguistic switch is fascinating: while belonging to Spanish, they target their texts for a different readership when changing into another idiom and thus must accept foreign syntactical and grammatical rules. They also deserve a room of their own in a scholarly study such as Fitz's.

The author ends his introduction by saying: "As the entire field of Inter-American literary relations continues to evolve, as I am sure it will, it is my hope that *Rediscovering the New World* will inspire other, better studies. If so, its writing will have been justified" (p. xvi). This book is a pioneering work—the door to a new understanding of a collective literary identity that honors the Latin saying: *e pluribus unum*. An invitation to a re-vision, evidence that, indeed, a frontier is inherently an artificial division.

Wallace Stevens: Toward an Erotics of Place

Milton J. Bates

Barbara M. Fisher. *Wallace Stevens: The Intensest Rendezvous.* Charlottesville: University Press of Virginia, 1990. xxviii, 186 pp.

Margaret Dickie. *Lyric Contingencies: Emily Dickinson and Wallace Stevens.* Philadelphia: University of Pennsylvania Press, 1991. xii, 198 pp.

One of the more intriguing fables in Wallace Stevens's *Collected Poems* appears in the "It Must Give Pleasure" section of "Notes toward a Supreme Fiction." It tells of a marriage between an anonymous "great captain" and a woman named Bawda. In the tradition of the fairy tale, the captain and Bawda go on to live happily ever after. Yet the course of their true love has not always run smooth, to judge from the hymn they compose for the wedding ceremony:

>   Anon
> We loved but would no marriage make. Anon
> The one refused the other one to take,
>
> Foreswore the sipping of the marriage wine.

In the remaining lines of the song, the captain and Bawda expound the lesson to be learned from their awkward courtship:

> Each must the other take not for his high,
> His puissant front nor for her subtle sound,
>
> The shoo-shoo-shoo of secret cymbals round.
> Each must the other take as sign, short sign
> To stop the whirlwind, balk the elements.[1]

As long as each regarded the other in terms of merely personal qualities, no union was possible. They could marry, we are told, only when they became "signs" to one another.

Signs of what? And in what sense might a sign be said to "stop" or "balk" the natural phenomena mentioned in the last line of their hymn? At the literal level, the captain is a military officer whose public presence ("high" and "puissant" front) bespeaks a man who is comfortable in a position of command. As "sign," he appears to be one of Stevens's solar heroes, like Hoon in his palaz or the youthful horseman "intent on the sun" in "Mrs. Alfred Uruguay." Bawda in fact loves him "as she loved the sun." Bawda's character is more equivocal. The "subtle sound" with which she is associated recalls the "shoo-shoo-shoo" of social and economic disorder in "Mozart, 1935," one of Stevens's early responses to the Great Depression. Though described as a "maiden," she bears a name associated with bawdry or illicit sexual behavior.

In this conjunction of signs, then, a powerful, transcendent, and benign force is mated with a sensual, immanent, and somewhat unsavory force. The anecdote is typical of Stevens's many allegories of male imagination and female reality, though the character of each and the nature of their relationship vary from poem to poem. Here, as so often, the mating is actually a checkmating: the time of the wedding—"At noon it was, on the midday of the year"—divides the day and the year into neatly balanced halves, and the poem leaves the captain and Bawda in a confrontational posture, "face to face." If theirs is a marriage of love, it is also one of convenience, perhaps even desperation. They need each other because any imbalance in the forces they represent would trigger the release of the "whirlwind" and other "elements," all presumably destructive.

What sets this poem apart from similar anecdotes in the *Collected Poems* is a third party, a member of the wedding whose role is difficult to specify. Catawba, the place of the marriage, is scarcely distinguishable from the bride, either as signifier (*Bawda/-tawba*) or as signified: "The great captain loved the everhill Catawba / And therefore married Bawda, whom he found there." Like the blackbird that is said to be "one" with a man and a woman in an early Stevens poem, Catawba is presented as a consolidating rather than a disruptive influence on the relationship: "They married well because the marriage-place / Was what they loved." Catawba perhaps facilitates the marriage by resolving the captain's ambivalence toward Bawda. "She" is Bawda without Bawda's disturbing sexuality.

With the introduction of Catawba, Stevens's anecdote begins to resemble an archetypal American narrative. Besides being the name of a grape native to North America, Catawba designates a river in the Carolinas and an Indian tribe that inhabited the river valley until it was decimated by smallpox and colonial warfare. By metonymy, Catawba is the New World landscape and the American Indian as first encountered by the European settlers. That encounter has been interpreted psychoanalytically by Annette Kolodny in *The Lay of the Land* and mythically by Richard Slotkin in *Regeneration through Violence*.[2] In Kolodny's Freudian account, the founding fathers initially regarded the land as a mother. When they left the oral phase behind and began to see America as a lover, they felt threatened and unmanned by her. They responded by raping and despoiling the land, a legacy that persists in today's pollution of the environment. Slotkin's version of the story likewise entails a quasi-sexual violation of the land. Daniel Boone is for him the quintessential American hero, the hunter and Indian fighter whose bloody deeds were supposed to prepare the way for an agrarian Eden.

Compared with either of these narratives, Stevens's story of the captain (John Rolfe, perhaps?) and Bawda (Pocahontas?) is relatively benign. Catawba is not ravished, though she is colonized, in keeping with the proposition the story is meant to illustrate—that "we make of what we see . . . a place dependent on ourselves." The captain and Bawda depend on one another at the end of the poem, and their love depends in turn on their relationship with Catawba. As a myth of the European conquest of the New World, the anecdote is solidly in the pastoral mode, regenerative without being violent. It becomes more troubling when one reads it as autobiography—or, more precisely, as wishful autobiography.

A decade of biographical research has produced a more or less consistent "plot" of Stevens's emotional development.[3] Growing up in eastern Pennsylvania, he felt a special attachment to the wooded hills and rivers of the region. He left home in stages, first going away to college, then launching his career in New York, and finally breaking with his father over his choice of a wife. Not the least of his reasons for marrying Elsie Kachel was his belief that this young woman from Reading would serve as *genius loci* of the land he loved. After the marriage deteriorated to mere cohabitation, he sought to reestablish the old ties to Pennsylvania through genealogical research, correspondence with relatives, and his prose and poetry. There is a sense, then, in which the story of the "great captain" is Stevens's own. The relevant lines of the fable might just as well read, "Wallace Stevens loved the ever-hill Pennsylvania / And therefore married Elsie, whom he found there." So construed, the fable represses as much as it reveals. Wallace and Elsie may have "married well," but they did not live happily ever after.

Criticism has recently undertaken the task of assigning Stevens's poems to plausible moments in the biographical narrative. The books under review are the most recent sustained efforts of this kind, and continue a project begun by Helen Vendler before much of the biographical background was available. In a 1979 essay entitled "Apollo's Harsher Songs: 'Desire without an object of desire,'" Vendler departed from the then-current view of Stevens as an "aesthetic" and "euphonious" poet whose work lacked genuine human feeling. She presented instead a poet whose desire for love and belief were baffled at every turn. Consequently, she argued, his work bears witness to "two incompatible truths—the truth of desire and the truth of the failure of desire."[4] Vendler amplified this thesis and applied it to several Stevens poems in a series of lectures delivered at the University of Tennessee and collected under the title *Wallace Stevens: Words Chosen Out of Desire*. In her introduction to the volume, she suggested that Stevens's desire did eventually attach itself to "local objects" (the title of a late poem) and places in Connecticut. He belatedly found "a place worth living for," located both in his consciousness and in the physical world.

C. Roland Wagner took up the challenge of Vendler's thesis in an essay published several years later in a special "Stevens and

Women" issue of the *Wallace Stevens Journal*. In a Freudian reading of Stevens's baffled desire, Wagner proposed that its object was union with "the ideal regressive and forbidden object," the pre-Oedipal mother.[5] Elsie may have stood in his mind for the unavailable mother, who gave him food but not love. In a poem like "Madame La Fleurie," Wagner maintained, Stevens strikes back at the inaccessible mother by representing her as a wicked and devouring witch. Concerned as he was with the Oedipal pattern of Stevens's relationships with his mother and wife, Wagner did not discuss the poet's displacement of desire onto the physical landscape.[6] But he did quote from a peculiar letter Stevens wrote to Elsie before their marriage, describing the earth on a rainy day as the face of his "dearest friend," whose company he was pleased to share with no one, not even Elsie. In fact he professed to have "enjoyed every breath of liberty" from his role as Elsie's lover.[7] Even then, however, he understood that his dearest friend was also a *femme fatale*. In a letter to Elsie a few days earlier, he had described nature as "our witch as well as our fairy god-mother."[8]

With Barbara M. Fisher's *Wallace Stevens: The Intensest Rendezvous* we have our first extended treatment of the relation between *eros* and *topos* in Stevens. Fisher pays tribute to Vendler in the introduction to the book, then specifies how her treatment of desire differs from that in *Words Chosen Out of Desire*. Where Vendler had stressed the frustration of desire in Stevens, she sets out to exhibit its positive transformations. *Transformation* is another word for *sublimation* in this case, though she finds the Freudian model inadequate to describe what happens in Stevens's poetry. To follow sublimation beyond the human psyche into the realm of the sublime, Fisher proposes that we turn to Plato at the point where Freud leaves off. Her Freudian-Platonic model of desire is filled out here and there with elements of Bergsonian vitalism, especially to explain the human impulse to make something where previously there was nothing.

The first six chapters of Fisher's book are somewhat eclectic in their subject matter, dealing with such topics as Stevensian parody and fire imagery. What links them together is the poet's search for an adequate object of desire. In the early poems,

Florida serves as his inamorata. According to Fisher, Stevens's Florida is neither a place nor a woman but an "exterior place . . . projected into a psychological interior . . . and shaped into a woman's image" (p. 61). In a poem like "The Idea of Order at Key West" the interior image is projected into the external world. Generally, however, Stevens's career can be read as an effort to interiorize, even ingest, the sybil and lover. This he succeeds in doing just once, in "Final Soliloquy of the Interior Paramour." Fisher calls this late work "the only poem in the canon that resolves in complete sufficiency" (p. 86). For once the self is a perfect trinity of male and female joined by a Dantean spirit of love.

Does this mean that Stevens's desire went otherwise unrequited? Fisher resists this conclusion, arguing that in the later poems desire is represented as a good in itself, apart from its satisfaction. Furthermore, she argues in the final three chapters of the book, most of Stevens's love poetry is directed not toward an interior world, the world of the paramour, but toward the external world of nature. Life was literally, for Stevens, the "affair of places" he once said it was. Since *place* is a slippery if ubiquitous term in literary criticism, Fisher prefaces her discussion of Stevensian *topoi* and topography with a "poetics of place" drawn from Angus Fletcher and Leonard Lutwack. Between two kinds of space, the temple and the labyrinth, there is a liminal zone which Fisher takes to be the locus of desire.

I found this scheme less helpful than another introduced later, dividing Stevens's places into *topoi* of seduction, nativity, and metaphor. It is, nevertheless, the scheme that Fisher brings to the book's concluding discussion of "The River of Rivers in Connecticut." There we glimpse Stevens as he is about to cross the threshold of desire into the templar zone, presumably to some kind of immortality or afterlife. This is an upbeat ending, especially when one compares it with Vendler and Wagner's narratives of Stevens's career. Fisher earns her conclusion, but at some cost. She must focus almost exclusively on the poems, ignoring the complications of desire in Stevens's private life.

Wallace Stevens: The Intensest Rendezvous is a rewarding study. Fisher writes with verve and wit, so she speaks authoritatively of those qualities in Stevens. Paradoxically, considering the book's concern with place, the reader is apt to feel initially dislocated. The critical ground on which the argument develops is not the familiar terrain of literary modernism or the American tradition or Romanticism. Rather, it is a place where a medieval manuscript jostles with *Star Trek,* the *Divine Comedy* with The Supremes. If this is occasionally disorienting (and to a later generation probably baffling), it is also refreshing.

Margaret Dickie invites us onto more familiar ground in *Lyric Contingencies: Emily Dickinson and Wallace Stevens*—though her aim is ultimately to defamiliarize the territory. Traditionally, she observes, the two poets have been regarded as the heirs of Emerson and his native strain of Romantic idealism. Dickie believes that they are misplaced in this tradition, and belong instead to the alternative tradition of pragmatism. Following Richard Rorty, she characterizes pragmatism as an anti-essentialist philosophy, one that defines the self and the world in terms of interaction and interrelation. Time and chance reign supreme, not some designing divinity. Gathering all these qualities under the rubric of "contingency," Dickie argues that the lyric poem is their natural medium of expression. The lyric genre allows the poet to improvise a new self with each poem; it resists the kind of closure conventionally sought in prose and other poetic forms; and it often subverts the teleological narratives of the dominant culture.

The lyric is therefore well suited to a poet like Dickinson, who was marginalized by her sex and temperament. It was also attractive to Stevens, Dickie contends, because it allowed him to try on radically different selves, including some that cross the gender barrier. In the early poetry he often projects onto female personae views he does not share or aggressively disputes. In other cases, his poems enact a masculine interest in looking at women. Nevertheless, in the early poem "Theory" he could write appreciatively of the feminine insight into contingency: "I am what is around me. / Women understand this." Like Fisher, Dickie plots Stevens's career as an effort to internalize the feminine as muse. For Dickie the quest culminates in "The Sail of Ulysses," where he arrives at "the sibyl of the self, / The self as sibyl."

Given her belief in the contingency of the lyric form, however,

Dickie must resist any neat closure to Stevens's career. "It was the nature of his desire," she says, "to be unsatisfied" (p. 103). Here she is in accord with Helen Vendler, whose *Words Chosen Out of Desire* she cites approvingly in a note. She also cites Wagner's essay and adopts his Freudian interpretation of Stevens as a man who was unable to transfer his desire from the forbidden object, the mother, to the permitted object, the lover. Therefore even as he approached complete identification with the sibyl within, often figured as mother or sister, he also grew more antagonistic toward her. According to Dickie, this ambivalence is central to his imagination and explains his deferral of desire from persons to places. Without such a deferral, she says, there would have been no poetry.

Though Dickie never gets around to examining Stevens's poetry of place, she implies that it will reflect his ambivalence toward the mother-muse. The landscape will be both his dearest friend and a devouring witch. Did he find it painful to be so deeply divided in his feelings? Dickie's answer to this question is yes—and no. She speaks not only of his "deep emotional poverty" at the end of his career, but also of his "delight in contingency" (pp. 156, 164). One wonders to what extent the delight in contingency is Dickie's rather than Stevens's. For if he was sometimes the connoisseur of chaos, he was just as often (so it seems to me) the creator of ideas of order, the poet who envisioned a "central poem" and wanted to call his *Collected Poems* "The Whole of Harmonium."

Of course, the achievement of such a grand design would have marked the end of desire. It would have been the death of the poet if not of the man. In his early poem "The Snow Man," Stevens imagines a sensibility in perfect accord with its environment, indeed made of the very same stuff. The snow man feels no desire and writes no poetry. "From this the poem springs," Stevens writes in "Notes toward a Supreme Fiction," "that we live in a place / That is not our own and, much more, not ourselves." The poem springs from displacement and dispossession because these are sources of desire. Without great violence to its meaning, the interior paramour's soliloquy might be revised to read, "Desire and the imagination are one." As a fundamentally erotic energy, desire first seeks satisfaction in the sexual other. When frustrated in that quest it seeks requital elsewhere, sometimes in a poetry of place. As Stevens puts it in "Arrival at the Waldorf," one of many such "arrivals" in his career, "the wild poem / Is a substitute for the woman one loves or ought to love."

The books by Fisher and Dickie offer contrasting yet plausible narratives of desire in Stevens. They also contribute to the larger cultural project for literary studies sketched out by Kolodny and Slotkin—what might be called an erotics of place. As we reflect on the implications of their work and look forward to other contributions in the same vein, we will want to return periodically to Stevens's fable of the captain and Bawda and their strange yet somehow typical *ménage à trois* with the ever-hill Catawba. The story gives pleasure, as it must. Beyond that, it represents an economy of pleasure we recognize as distinctly American and distinctly Stevensian.

Notes

1. *The Collected Poems of Wallace Stevens* (New York: Knopf, 1954), p. 401. This is the text for all poems cited, except for "The Sail of Ulysses," which is from *Opus Posthumous*, ed. Milton J. Bates (New York: Knopf, 1989), pp. 126–31.

2. Kolodny, *The Lay of the Land: Metaphor as Experience and History in American Life and Letters* (Chapel Hill: Univ. of North Carolina Press, 1975); and Slotkin, *Regeneration through Violence: The Mythology of the American Frontier, 1600–1860* (Middletown: Wesleyan Univ. Press, 1973).

3. The principal biographical studies are Peter Brazeau's *Parts of a World: Wallace Stevens Remembered: An Oral Biography* (New York: Random House, 1983); Milton J. Bates's *Wallace Stevens: A Mythology of Self* (Berkeley: Univ. of California Press, 1985); George S. Lensing's *Wallace Stevens: A Poet's Growth* (Baton Rouge: Louisiana State Univ. Press, 1986); and Joan Richardson's *Wallace Stevens: The Early Years, 1879–1923* (New York: Morrow, 1986) and *Wallace Stevens: The Later Years, 1923–1955* (New York: Morrow, 1988).

4. Vendler, *Wallace Stevens: Words Chosen Out of Desire* (1984; rpt. Cambridge: Harvard Univ. Press, 1986), p. 28. The phrase quoted in the last sentence of this paragraph is from p. 9.

5. Wagner, "Wallace Stevens: The Concealed Self," *Wallace Stevens Journal*, 12 (1988), 85.

6. In a recent essay, Wagner considers Elsie as a potential lover rather than

mother, and says that for Stevens Florida "was both an escape from his cold wife and an embodiment of her imagined sexuality." See "The Cataleptic Moment: Sweet Substitutes in Stevens and Proust," *Wallace Stevens Journal*, 15 (1991), 13.

7. *Letters of Wallace Stevens*, ed. Holly Stevens (New York: Knopf, 1966), p. 99.

8. Unpublished letter of 18 March 1907, quoted with the permission of the Huntington Library.

The Cambridge Conrad

James M. Haule

Joseph Conrad. *The Secret Agent: A Simple Tale,* eds. Bruce Harkness and S. W. Reid. The Cambridge Edition of the Works of Joseph Conrad. Cambridge: Cambridge University Press, 1990. xli, 429 pp.

"Solidarity with an extremest form of action is one thing, and silly recklessness is another. . . ." The words of Ossipon, spoken with "a sort of moody brutality" near the end of part IV of *The Secret Agent,* could well serve as a cautionary motto for those determined to produce reliable texts of modern authors:

I don't know what came to Verloc. There's some mystery there. However, he's gone. You may take it as you like, but under the circumstances the only policy for the militant revolutionary group is to disclaim all connection with this damned freak of yours. How to make the disclaimer convincing enough is what bothers me. [p. 63]

Substitute "Joyce" for "Verloc" and Ossipon could well be talking of the Gabler "synoptic" *Ulysses.* The tortured path of that edition, wherever it may finally lead, has unwittingly taught us many lessons about what may and what may not be done to a modern author in the quest of the authoritative critical or eclectic edition of his work. Some people associated with that enormous enterprise have indeed gone to considerable lengths to "disclaim all connection" with the result. This new version of Joyce's novel seems to many critics and readers a revolutionary outrage. Others, convinced that a little tinkering with the final product might yet produce something of merit, have published a "repair kit" that seeks to provide the tools the reader needs to negotiate safely some of its deficiencies.[1] But, like applying bondo to the dents of an old sedan, this is itself both insufficient protection from the elements and an imposing restraint on the consumer who, presumably, wishes more than anything simply to read the book.

Perhaps the most important lesson in all this is one that we should have learned long ago: know what to leave alone. The temptation to produce a text that the author himself would not recognize has been substantially increased with the advent of the computer. The difficulty of organizing, collating, comparing and then selecting from a flurry of holographs, typescripts, and proofs was daunting enough in the past to constrain the effort. But no longer. The well-armed investigator can sit with his personal computer and run a seemingly endless series of multiple-text comparisons (after, of course, some talented soul has completed the thankless task of inputting the texts to computer disk). This allows, naturally, for a level of accuracy and insanity unknown in a simpler age. It is, perhaps, another proof of the occasional usefulness of old clichés—in this case: 'If you have a hammer, you will hit something with it.' Resisting its use until there is sufficient reason is the mark both of the good craftsman and the good editor.

The first volume of The Cambridge Edition of the Works of Joseph Conrad displays many of the virtues and some of the faults associated with our current ability to consult and control multiple manuscripts and editions. By beginning with *The Secret Agent,* the editors have chosen well. This certainly is a luminous text, one of Conrad's best. The history of its publication and revision long has needed careful documentation. A truncated version of the novel appeared in serial form in the American magazine *Ridgway's: A Militant Weekly for God and Country.* Its subsequent English and American editions expanded the novel substantially, but in many ways the first editions do not agree. Subsequent reimpressions also introduced additional changes unequally. What is an editor to do?

First, the editor must examine the texts and the manuscripts, aligning each with what is known of Conrad's method and the history of his composition and with the documents relating to the publication of both the serial version and the editions of the novel. This, above all else, the editors of this volume have done with extraordinary care and resourcefulness. We learn a great deal about Conrad's method of composition, about the history of his relations with his publishers on both continents, and even about a mechanical apparatus used by a publisher that itself caused problems. We learn, for example, that the Lanston Monotype machine was used by Methuen for its first edition in 1907 and that this caused serious problems in subsequent printings. We are also given hints about other technical details that tease rather than explain. At one point at least, the editors seem to have absorbed Conrad's own ironic narrative technique when they say of the American 'Concord Edition' of 1923 that the variants it scattered throughout *The Secret Agent* were "presumably introduced in the American plates by the customary process used to repair stereos" (p. 291). To find out what this might mean, a note tells us to consult Charles W. Hackleman's *Commercial Engraving and Printing* (1924).

Of the 429 pages of the Cambridge edition, nearly half are apparatus. This is not terribly unusual for a project of this scope, but it does present a challenge even to the devoted reader. How much of this is really necessary? The question will be answered variously, but the editors had the grace to provide at the end of each section of commentary a useful summary of the major findings. It is at the end of the ninety-two-page section entitled "The Texts" that we find the short summary entitled "The Cambridge Text," and it is here that we find the best description of what has been done: "The Cambridge Edition, then, presents the modern reader deliberately eclectic texts of *The Secret Agent* and of its 'Author's Note' based on the original documents" (p. 326). Thus, the merits of this edition depend in large measure on the methods used to construct the text from multiple documents.

It is impossible to exaggerate either the scope or the detail of the textual investigation this volume provides. The essay entitled "The Texts" is certainly no simple tale. It is an admirable piece of work that is thorough in its investigation of the labyrinthian details of composition and publication. We are, at crucial points along the way, given maps of the various routes and detours to final published copy. Perhaps the most elaborate of these is found on page 291. Labeled "Chart 6" it seeks to provide the story of the first English edition, or E1. Although it is unnecessarily cryptic and, at first glance, bears an uncanny resemblance to the wiring diagram of a VCR, it is quite useful. Among other things, it helps decipher the layers and layers of revision to the text that the essay seeks to describe. It also codifies a number of decisions about the authority of each of the successive layers of revision. It is here, too, that we see the difficulties that the construction of an eclectic text can pose.

Throughout the entire essay, the editors are at some pains to separate the certain from the speculative. This is no small merit. The temptation to find certainty in a muddle that you alone have untangled is difficult to resist. But the editors have clearly marked the known from the unknown. Consequently, the essay is speckled with cautious phrases, such as "rather unlikely" and "uncertain implications." What they cannot prove beyond doubt is clearly identified.

Certainly there is no single authoritative text that the editors can simply reproduce and present. Conrad's several versions and the confusion introduced by various printings of the novel have made that impossible. Thus the editors of the Cambridge Edition felt that only an eclectic text could present Conrad's text in a reliable way. With the wealth of information they present in the introduction, there is little doubt that this is true.

The problem for the conservative reader is the rationale for the choices the editors have made, not the fact that choices were necessary. The extent of the evidence would make its full discussion here nearly as complex as the essay itself. One example, perhaps, will demonstrate the difficulty of the task: the matter of the differences between the manuscript and the serial edition:

> By no means, however, are all the differences between the manuscript and *Ridgway's* attributable to the serial's editors. The first half of the serial text contains alterations that were carried into the later book editions and must have been introduced by Conrad in the typescript, now lost, which was made from the manuscript (TS1). Some of these alterations (represented as C1a on Chart I) are additions that go quite contrary to *Ridgway's* editorial tendencies and exhibit the author's hand. The new phrase 'quasi-maternal' more precisely defines Winnie's 'affec-

tion' (13.1b), and 'by the Press' (11.30) adumbrates her concern with sports sheets and newspaper execution reports; both help prepare for the end of the novel. Others elaborate or clarify a point of reference . . . or add an ironic touch (33.1-2). There are numerous additions of this sort throughout the first half of the serial version of the novel (pp. 1–175 in E1) that Conrad must have introduced in his typescript. [p. 253]

What the editors describe is a possibility based on rather interesting evidence. They may be right. Since, as they readily admit, the typescript is "lost," there is no way to be certain. There is also a complete list of variants in this edition, so that the interested reader can see clearly where each choice was made and what alternatives were possible. In this excerpt from the introduction, we can see much of the rationale the editors used. The additions seem to them "contrary to *Ridgway's* editorial tendencies"; therefore, the additions are evidence of "the author's hand." This puts a heavy burden on the editor, however. Real authority for these changes rests not upon the evidence of a manuscript or an edition, but upon the judgment of the editors.

The next statement amounts to an argument based on felicitous phrasing. What the editors have chosen to do is to read the novel and then emend it based on what they feel best helps "prepare for the end of the novel" or adds another "ironic touch" to a work of art that they interpret as intentionally ironic. This gives them authority to conclude that all of these changes "Conrad must have introduced in his typescript." It also allows them to issue an edition of the novel that Conrad never lived to see, based on "corrections" that he *might* have made if he had been able.

In the last third of the novel, the editors feel they must correct "a number of infelicities and lapses" (p. 299). They tell us that "circumstances encouraged Conrad to lapse into numerous stylistic faults that he later failed to correct and that sometimes are not readily differentiated from compositional error" (p. 300). These are difficult distinctions to make. The production an eclectic text, however, requires choices, even if Conrad's intentions are unknown. Thus the editors attempt "to retain the authorial infelicities of these pages while correcting ascertainable transmissional errors" (p. 300).

This is straightforward enough, but it is hard indeed to draw a line between "transmissional" errors and the "infelicities" of the author. Where one draws a line here, another may draw it there. It might be more "felicitous" simply to identify the doubts the editors may have about the nature of the composition and then leave the text at those points entirely alone. While it is certainly useful to present an educated guess in an essay about the nature of the text, to introduce changes to it based on even the most informed supposition is to introduce uncertainty. The editors have been scrupulous to separate clear evidence from conjecture. However, they have decided that the nature of the project and the unreliability of any of the existing texts require synoptic emendations that are, by their own admission, far from certain.

This editorial process is controversial and encourages opinions that can appear judgmental. We learn on page 304, for example, that although Conrad "had difficulty maintaining consistency between the simple past and the past perfect, especially when writing in the 'narrative present', Conrad's tenses are by and large satisfactory." If Conrad had not proven "satisfactory," one wonders if the editors would have corrected him. This leads to a discussion of other lapses in language, notably Conrad's "Gallicisms and Polonisms." The editors are willing to allow these quirks into their edition, however, as long as "they seem to be authorial instead of transmissional" (p. 305). How they "seem" to the editors makes all the difference, and it is on that basis that many readers will judge the merits of their work. Just how the Cambridge editors distinguish between the two is most important.

We are told that, as a general rule, "this edition eschews 'correction' if an abnormality seems to have been created by Conrad" (p. 305). There is an immediate exception to this rule, however, on the next page, where we learn that the "Cambridge Edition makes a limited number of substantive emendations involving important details inadvertently left inconsistent in E1." The extent to which the editors feel compelled to make corrections that were apparently "inconsistent" extends to the "correction" of

Conrad himself, for they have altered the first English edition's "reference to the Professor's 'right' hand, despite the concurrence of the manuscript" (p. 306).

The decisions that every editor abhors, those dealing with irregular hyphenation and "word-division," the editors make on similar grounds. In many of the instances they cite, they have made judicious decisions. While it might be possible to fault them on grounds that this or that principle might have better served, they were compelled to select among methods (preponderance of occurrences and analogy with similar words, for example), and they have done so. What is noticeable, however, is the conclusion that it is possible to separate the vagaries of the author's style from the accidents of the editor's pen. Even with the evidence of computer collations of editions and manuscripts and the assumed evidence represented in their conclusions about the "tendencies" of a particular press, the Cambridge editors are compelled to make decisions based on what "seems" appropriate.

This sort of intervention, though traditionally a part of an eclectic edition, necessarily opens the text to question. Even so, this is a valuable contribution to Conrad studies. The essay portion of the edition, which establishes the history of composition and publication, is a brilliant example of what thorough investigative scholarship can reveal. The text itself is admirably free of all apparatus, aside from helpful line numbers that appear in the margin of the text.

Thus the Cambridge editors attempt to produce an edition of the novel that is better than Conrad was able to make it. While this is may not be the "revolutionary outrage" that Conrad describes in his tale or that others have found in the "new" *Ulysses*, it is nonetheless a bold attempt to wrestle with the difficult problems that Conrad's text presents. Eclectic editing is most often justified in the reconstruction of texts far older than those published in our own century. To use this approach with a modern author, when the evidence for authority is often uncertain and judgments are most open to question, is an approach that will be watched closely as further volumes appear.

Note

1. See Philip Gaskell and Clive Hart, *Ulysses: A Review of Three Texts* (Gerrards Cross: Colin Smythe, 1989). Gaskell and Hart felt the need to "repair" the three extant editions of *Ulysses,* including the Gabler "synoptic" edition of 1984. The publisher announced that "what is offered here, in fact, is not a new edition of *Ulysses,* but a kit for repairing the major faults of existing editions." See also "The Repair Kit," ed. Bernard Benstock, in the *James Joyce Literary Supplement,* 3–4 (Fall 1989), 15. In fact, this entire issue is devoted to the debates of the "Miami J'yce Conference" which focused on the 1984 Gabler edition.

Science Fiction in the Nineteenth Century

John R. Pfeiffer

Mary Shelley. *The Mary Shelley Reader, containing* Frankenstein, Mathilda, *Tales and Stories, Essays and Reviews, and Letters,* eds. Betty T. Bennett and Charles E. Robinson. New York: Oxford University Press, 1990. xx, 420 pp.

Anthony Trollope. *The Fixed Period,* ed. R. H. Super. Ann Arbor: University of Michigan Press, 1990. xviii, 183 pp.

Andrew Martin. *The Mask of the Prophet, The Extraordinary Fictions of Jules Verne.* Oxford: Clarendon Press, 1990. xiv, 222 pp.

Lyman Tower Sargent. *British and American Utopian Literature, 1516–1985, An Annotated, Chronological Bibliography.* [Second edition] New York: Garland Publishing, Inc., 1988. xxi, 559 pp.

Everett F. Bleiler, with the assistance of Richard J. Bleiler. *Science-Fiction, The Early Years: A Full Description of More Than 3000 Science-Fiction Stories from Earliest Times to the Appearance of the Genre Magazines in 1930. With Author, Title, and Motif Indexes.* Kent, Ohio: Kent State University Press, 1990. xxvi, 998 pp.

Each of the five works reviewed here is important to some significant degree to the study of nineteenth-century science fiction. Mary Shelley's *Frankenstein* is perhaps the most famous novel of the nineteenth century, and it is identified by literary historians as the first science fiction novel. *The Fixed Period* is the only work of science fiction by Anthony Trollope. Today, only specialists have heard of it, much less read it, but it belongs to the group of major nineteenth-century British science fiction works that includes Edward Bulwer-Lytton's *The Coming Race* (1871), George

Tomkyns Chesney's "The Battle of Dorking" (1871), and Samuel Butler's *Erewhon* (1872). Andrew Martin's study of Jules Verne, *The Masked Prophet*, is an arabesque of deconstructive literary analysis, part of a recent attempt by English-speaking critics who read French to reckon with the paradox of Verne's stature as one of the preeminent founders of that embarrassing genre, science fiction, whose works must be reconciled as part of the canon of major French literature. From works like Martin's we learn not merely about new meanings of Verne, but, more fundamentally, that the readers of Verne in English translations have been reading a very different Verne than the one his countrymen read in French. Lyman Sargent's *British and American Utopias* is here for the achievement it represents in presenting a progressively definitive bibliography of utopian writing, and as an honor guard for a work by the most important and venerable of all the bibliographers of science fiction, Everett Bleiler, whose *Science Fiction, The Early Years* at once establishes a new standard for accretive annotated bibliography with the intention to be exhaustive, and which, in its magisterial assemblage of thousands of works, includes, of course, the famous work by Shelley, the obscure one by Trollope, and the numerous titles of the *Voyages extraordinaires* by Verne. The great achievement of Sargent and Bleiler is to assure us finally that we know what the nineteenth-century titles to be studied are.

At least six other works, not to be reviewed here, which advance analyses of nineteenth-century science fiction, have appeared in the 1980s. They are Darko Suvin's *Victorian Science Fiction: The Discourses of Knowledge and Power* (1983); Everett Bleiler's *The Guide to Supernatural Fiction, A Full Description of 1,775 Books from 1759 to 1960, Including Ghost Stories, Weird Fiction, Supernatural Horror, Fantasy, Gothic Novels, Occult Fiction and Similar Literature* (1983); Thomas Clareson's *Science Fiction in America, 1870s–1930s, An Annotated Bibliography of Primary Sources* (1984), and *Some Kind of Paradise, The Emergence of American Science Fiction* (1985); Neil Barron's two editions of *Anatomy of Wonder: A Critical Guide to Science Fiction* (1981, 1987); and Karl S. Guthke's *The Last Frontier, Imagining Other Worlds, from the Copernican Revolution to Modern Science Fiction,* translated by Helen Atkins (1990). The publication of this register and configuration of works marks the

Science Fiction in the Nineteenth Century

attainment of a dramatically greater precision with which the history and analysis of science fiction, especially in the nineteenth century, may be written.

The Mary Shelley Reader includes the original text of the 1818 first edition of *Frankenstein,* Mary Shelley's introduction to the 1831 edition of *Frankenstein,* the novella *Mathilda,* and five of her twenty-six known stories: "Recollections of Italy" (1824), "The Bride of Modern Italy" (1824), "Roger Dodsworth: The Reanimated Englishman" (1830), "The Dream" (1831), and "The Mortal Immortal: A Tale" (1833). It also includes seven essays and reviews (a very tiny sample of what might be called her scholarly writing), eleven of the approximately 1,600 known letters, and a "Selected Bibliography" of works by and about her. Among the eleven illustrations included are the two most famous pictures of Mary Shelley.

The editors of this collection are among the best Mary Shelley scholars. Betty Bennett is editor of the three-volume *The Letters of Mary Wollstonecraft Shelley* (1980, 1983, and 1988), and Charles Robinson is editor of *Mary Shelley: Collected Tales and Stories* (1976). The selection of materials they have made for this reader could not be better—with one not quite trifling exception. Among the illustrations they could and should have included photocopies of the 1818 and 1823 *Frankenstein* title pages. Conspicuously, the 1818 edition omits the author's name, a matter of some importance in Mary Shelley's later fortunes; the 1823 edition includes her name for the first time. At least six items in the *Reader* are particularly interesting: (1) Here for just the second time since 1823, with a minimum of editorial apparatus, is the 1818 edition text of *Frankenstein.* The first was a 1983, 1984 edition by Pennyroyal Press. (James Rieger recently produced a version of it, but Bennett and Robinson's version is best. Rieger's is distracting because he has idiosyncratically chosen to publish as a critical text a combination of the texts of the published 1818 novel, Mary's working drafts [edited by Shelley], and a portion of fair copy manuscript that survives in the Arbinger Shelley archive. It is in effect a scholar's copybook of parallel and variant texts, a nuisance to the ordinary reader, as well as to the reader who wants to experience simply the original published version of the novel.) (2) Mary Shelley's introduction to the 1831 edition of

Frankenstein, is the principal source of the ghost story competition account. There are no independently substantial or informative comments about the competition in any of Mary's letters or journals. (*Frankenstein* is noticed briefly about a dozen times in the journals—not enough to make inclusion of an excerpt meaningful in this *Reader.*) The 9–11 September 1823 letter to Leigh Hunt included, containing Mary's reaction to the theatrical performance of *Frankenstein,* is the most substantial of her comments, independent of her 1831 introduction, in any form that survives. (3) *Mathilda,* finished in 1819, but not published until 1859, has prospectively major significance for its father-daughter incest subject matter. (4) "Roger Dodsworth," "Transformation," and "The Mortal Immortal" are the three stories closest to the *Frankenstein* material that Mary Shelley wrote, (5) The "Essays and Reviews" remind us that, beyond her considerable erudition, genius for languages, and critical acumen, Mary Shelley, singlehandedly, is responsible for setting out Shelley's works so that his reputation as a literary giant could emerge. (6) The "Selected Bibliography" misses nothing of basic importance, and includes in its fifty-nine entries, eleven from the 1970s and ten from the 1980s, representing a very strong current interest in Mary Shelley.

Turning to the other end of the century, there is considerable pleasure for the specialist and afficianado of Victoriana in R. W. Super's new edition of Anthony Trollope's *The Fixed Period.* Its art is of indifferent quality, but it is made of the dear old British narrative wood of the period. One is tempted to engage in the amusing exercise of speculating upon how many readers it has had since its first chapter was published in October 1881 in *Blackwood's Edinburgh Magazine.* Complete in the March 1882 number of *Blackwood's,* it was published as a two-volume novel in England and a one-volume issue in Leipzig and New York. And it was reissued in a 1981 Arno Press printing as part of N. John Hall's edition of the *Selected Works of Anthony Trollope* (62 volumes). One wonders if the number of its readers in its 110 years has reached much over ten thousand. Are there as many as a hundred people living who have read it? What justifies this edition? The most persuasive answer simply may be that Trollope is a major Victorian novelist for whom a critically edited collected edition of works has not yet been published. And, based as it is on the collation of manuscript, magazine serialization, and first novel publication, Super's edition is clearly the best we've had.

The Fixed Period is set in 1980 in the fictional south Pacific island republic of Britannula, an ex-colony of Britain, where President John Neverbend has spearheaded the enactment of a law requiring the killing—by anesthesia and draining of blood—of everyone who reaches the age of sixty-seven. The first citizen to be "deposed" under the law is Neverbend's old friend Gabriel Crasweller. But a popular resistance to the law asks for Britain to intervene, nullify the law, and take back the country. A huge gunboat with a "250-ton swiveller"—a gun that can destroy a city with one shot—arrives and Neverbend is arrested and taken back to England—during which voyage he writes the story, a first-person account, that we are reading. Left behind is Neverbend's wife, a loose end, and his son Jack, whom we have come to know via a long narrative digression describing an interminable international cricket match played with a steam-driven bowling machine. Jack also has a love relationship with Crasweller's daughter Eva.

The two most useful discussions of *The Fixed Period*, by R. H. Super in his *The Chronicles of Barsetshire, A Life of Anthony Trollope* (1988), and David Skilton in "*The Fixed Period:* Anthony Trollope's Novel of 1980" (*Studies in the Literary Imagination,* 6 [Fall 1973] 39–50), find the novel relatively weak in meaning as well as structure. Though Skilton is probably right when he speculates that Trollope hadn't "worked out the technical implications of this sort of narrative" (p. 41), Skilton analyzes Neverbend as an "unreliable narrator," a proposition that is patently untenable. John Neverbend is perfectly "reliable," even pathologically reliable, if this apparent contradiction in terms is not too distracting. Certainly he is the story's sole narrator, thus making the reader a prisoner of whatever universe he erects. But the universe Neverbend erects turns out to be a real one. He tells things as they occur, factually, truthfully, even though they occur diametrically opposite to his stated desires: his euthanasian law is revoked; the heroic stature of Galileo and Newton he has coveted eludes him; indeed, he is arrested and transported, losing family, property and country. But he is not "unreliable." Rather, he is stupidly tragic, we see finally, just because he is uncompromisingly true to the strange self that he is. His account reminds us of the inexorable, objectively real horror of Kafka's Gregor becoming a beetle in "Metamorphosis." Neither Super nor Skilton addresses the question of how Neverbend's preposterously Malthusian law got passed in the first place—coming in the story, as it does, as a *fait accompli*. This allows us to argue that perhaps the novel is for Trollope not so much about Malthusian enterprises in particular as it is about the grotesque and irresistable fates of individuals, each of which may actually be as strange as Neverbend's.

In *The Masked Prophet*, Andrew Martin touches on a major problem in Jules Verne studies, the absence of good translations of his works into English. Bad translations account for Verne's modest reputation outside of France. They also accounted, until recently, for the paucity of analyses in English of Verne's works. Martin insists that Verne belongs to the canon of major authors in the history of French literature, and he interprets the political meanings of the "extraordinary fictions" of Verne. His discussion is flamboyant and engaging, but sometimes it presumes upon the reader's critical good nature. After all, he has written a whole book on the "Masked Prophet" in Verne although Verne never mentions a masked prophet in all the many volumes he wrote. There are other presumptions as well, but one can indulge them because Martin's exposition is clever and one wants to share in the wonderful time he has reading Verne. *Prophet* includes nine chapters. Each begins with quotations from Napoleon and Jorge Luis Borges, who did write stories on the historical subject of a prophet or false prophet who wore a silver mask or veil and unsuccessfully sought to overthrow the Islamic Empire in the reign of Caliph Mahadi. Thus, Martin constructs his interpretation of Verne, not only with attention to a character, a Masked Prophet, that Verne never used, but also with reference to one author who post-dates Verne historically. In chapter 2, "The Beginning of the End," we are told simplistically, "Verne's narrative . . . looks forward from the very beginning to the end of the adventure." For Verne "end," definitively, means the "dominion of silence" (p. 53). Even so, Verne's practice is to keep "balloons" of adventure in the air. In chapter 3, "The One and the Many," we learn that "narrative, discursively imperialist, shapes heterogeneous discourses, over-riding their heterogeneity, imposing on them a fictional beginning and end, and thus threatening the anarchy of differenda with the tyranny of order" (pp. 76–77). Chapter 6, "Law and Disorder," explains that the "dialectic of expansion and contraction, power and subversion [which] informs [Verne's novels] constitutes the incessant pulse of the Vernian text, the narrative of empire and revolt" (p. 151). Finally, in chapter 9, "The Prophet of the Mask," Martin tells us he has set out not to

> discover any hidden depths but only some insufficiently noticed surfaces: the art of concealment in Verne, as in Poe's 'Purloined Letter,' consists in putting what is to escape scrutiny on open display.... Equally, my business is not to remove but rather restore the mask and examine it in closer detail, to take a rigorously superficial view of the text. Fame is a form of incomprehension. Verne is already too familiar; my task is to defamiliarize him. [pp. 13–14]

There is, as in much of the discourse of the deconstructionist critic, a lot of flourish here.

Verne's extraordinary fictions persistently tell and retell, in multifarious forms, the story of a masked prophet who promises to reveal what is concealed. It is this recurrence that provides one of the many justifications for the seemingly arbitrary act of linking Verne with the names of Napoleon and [Jorge Luis] Borges.... The fictions of Verne constitute a sequence of meditations on the ramifications of imperialism and its metaphorical counterparts. [pp. 14, 16–17]

In order to make his thesis seem cogent, Martin has had to be a verbal alchemist:

> In fact, Verne, more historian than prophet, records and reflects on the ceaseless process of annexation, colonization, and insurrection which characterized the nineteenth century. The *Voyages* are thus in one aspect a chronicle of the vices of the age. But Verne *cannot tolerate raw*

historical data in his fictional texts: his material is displaced, transfigured, configured (my italics). [p. 19]

With this incantation Martin has given himself license to find whatever he likes in the Verne texts. Sometimes Martin is carried away and concocts a word: "narratorial" stance (p. 28), or is clumsily redundant: "a positive utopia [eutopia?]" (p. 42), or is melodramatic: "The category of the unknown in Verne is precarious, always at the risk of extinction" (p. 32), or pseudoprofound: "This is Verne's trauma, his obsession, and his pretext: the discovery that any whole is always at least the sum of a number of parts" (p. 78). Even so, Martin's wit is refreshing: "It is a law of fiction that 'peace' is destined to be 'disturbed' " (p. 80). And I finished Martin's book with admiration for his dazzling verbal agility. I am grateful, too, that he chose to put his notes at the bottom of the pages.

Conspicuously absent from the edition of Lyman Sargent's bibliography of *British and American Utopian Literature, 1516–1985* is the bibliography of bibliographies and other studies of utopian writing he included in his 1979 edition. He calls this 1988 edition "a very different version" without saying exactly how it is different. Especially, he does not refer readers to the secondary bibliography in the earlier edition. This is not a minor oversight. A bibliography on utopian studies by Sargent is authoritative. The failure to advertise the existence of the 1979 list in this most likely forum, a second edition, is very unfortunate. He does not call the 1988 volume a second edition; perhaps he judged the omission of the secondary bibliography a difference great enough to nullify such a designation. Meanwhile, a predictable major difference from the 1979 volume is in number of titles listed. In 1979 there were in the neighborhood of 1,900 titles. In the 1988 list there are well over 3,000—even as he has dropped titles he discovered were not written originally in English, or that he has judged subsequently do not meet his definition of utopia. He has seen every work he lists. He laments the fact, furthermore, that his list will never be complete—especially since he discovers new titles for possible inclusion at an average of one a day.

The 1988 volume also provides an introduction which greatly abbreviates the 1979 version. In it Sargent repeats his explanation of the meanings of the words "utopia, eutopia, dystopia and utopian satire" which he has tried to use consistently in the bibliography to mean the following:

Utopia—a non-existent society described in considerable detail.
Eutopia—a non-existent society described in considerable detail that the author intended a contemporaneous reader to view as considerably better than the society in which that reader lived.
Dystopia—a non-existent society described in considerable detail that the author intended a contemporaneous reader to view as considerably worse than the society in which that reader lived.
Utopian satire—a non-existent society described in considerable detail that the author intended a contemporaneous reader to view as a criticism of contemporary society. [p. xii]

The chronological main list is restricted to utopias originally published in English between 1516 and 1985. Entries show first edition information and list some additional editions Sargent has seen. Library locations are given for at least one of the editions—more than one if the work is hard to find. Some information seems not to be given consistently or clearly. For example, some of the works are located in Sargent's personal collection and are so coded. Most others *without any code* are also in Sargent's collection, he tells us. Next, the nationality of authors is not given directly; we are instructed that it is usually to be inferred from the publication data, except that where Sargent "knows it isn't," he has said so. This is frustrating. A better practice would be simply to note author nationality explicitly when it is known, indicating with perhaps a question mark when it is not. Surely Sargent knows the nationality of a high percentage of these writers. In any case, the list is usefully accessible through excellent author and title indexes. Each has complementary title, author, and year of publication information in the listing so that we can get a quick-list from the index itself of all the titles and their dates, of works by, for example, James Blish (p. 9) just by looking up "Blish, James." Checking one of Blish's titles in the main list gives the full bibliographical information, an annotation describing its contents, a library collection location code, and, very usefully, on adjoining pages, the historical context of other works and authors writing and so listed in the same year and, of course, boundary years.

Sargent believes that the "social dreaming that we call utopianism exists in every form of human expression" (p. xiii). Certainly, of all the topics that comprise the agenda of speculative literature, none is more interesting to late twentieth-century cultures than utopianism. Moreover, common sense allows the surmise that almost no culturally important person in history has failed to indulge utopian imaginings. Therefore, a roll call of famous British and American writers who produced utopian discourses is fascinating, and easy to extract from Sargent's list—limiting it to only the most famous writers, and arresting the count at the beginning of the twentieth century. Beginning with Thomas More, Sargent lists works for Sidney, Shakespeare, Ben Jonson, Defoe, Swift, Hume, Goldsmith, Samuel Johnson, Charles Brockdon Brown, Shelley, Edward Bulwer-Lytton, Samuel Butler, Trollope, William Morris, Wells, James Fenimore Cooper, Melville, Hawthorne, Twain, Edward Bellamy, Howells, Henry James, and Shaw.

No single scholar or even group of scholars has made a more complete bibliography of the primary works of fantasy and science fiction than Everett Bleiler. Evidence of this lies in the works available for Bleiler to build on for the volume reviewed here. They are primarily his own, in the form of the almost prescient *The Checklist of Fantastic Literature, A Bibliography of Fantasy, Weird and Science-Fiction Books Published in the English Language* (1948, 1972) and *The Checklist of Science-Fiction and Supernatural Fiction* (1978). Remarkably, of the fifty-six specialized works he lists in his bibliography in *Science-Fiction, The Early Years*, virtually all of the title-accretive ones have in some measure a debt to Bleiler's 1948 and 1978 works. To go beyond the information already provided in the extended title of *Early Years*, it covers magazines except for *Amazing Stories, Wonder Stories* and *Astounding Stories*. It makes "borderline" judgments against including some "semifictional" works, some types of fantasy of history, some stories of imaginary wars, most utopias (though more about these), nonrational "weird" stories, and "self-contradicting" stories that end as it-was-all-a-dream. But, best of all, Bleiler has read each of the stories described—over 3,000 titles included in 2,475 numbered entries—and who knows how many others that he disqualified.

The problematic status of any "definition" of science fiction notwithstanding, Bleiler must perforce enunciate one or not. He chooses to do so, and I convey it here out of respect for a person who has undoubtedly read, with a scholarly consciousness engaged, more science fiction than anyone else. His definition of science fiction may be extracted from his introduction:

Put briefly: Science-fiction is not a unitary genre or form, hence cannot be encompassed in a single definition. It is an assemblage of genres and subgenres that are not intrinsically closely related, but are generally accepted as an area of publication by a marketplace. Science-fiction is thus only a commercial term. And since English usage normally hyphenates compound words that mean other than their components, of the two forms that are met, "science-fiction" and "science fiction," the hyphenated form is to be preferred. . . . [The] three major components of science-fiction are the quasi-scientific story, the lost-race story, and the future story. The first of these . . . contains . . . pretended science of technology. . . . The lost-race story [is] a highly schematized story based on the survival of otherwise extinct people. . . . The third major component . . . may be called future fiction. In this case futurity, perhaps with a few gimmicks or props, has traditionally been considered sufficient to classify a story [as science-fiction]. [pp. xi, xii]

The introduction also provides "The Motifs of Science-Fiction" and—not to be taken lightly—five pages presenting "A Brief History of Early Science-Fiction in Terms of Story Clusters." The heart of the volume, "Book and Story Descriptions," occupies 848 8-1/2 x 11 pages. Author entries are alphabetized, followed by chronologically listed titles. Where known, life dates, nationality, and basic professional identities of authors are given. For each work, first publication information, an extremely detailed plot summary, and brief remarks about historical importance and literary reputation are provided. Ancillary sections to Bleiler's volume include "Background Books" (extensively summarized), a "Motif and Theme Index," a very useful "Date Index," which facilitates locating all listed works published in a given year, a "Magazine Index," a "Title Index," an "Author Index," and the "Bibliography."

Though it seems almost boorish to bring them up at all, there are a number of niggling problems with the entries in *The Early Years*. In the Defoe entry a line on the importance of Robinson Crusoe to the history of science fiction would be appropriate. Next, some confusion develops from Bleiler's practices for reporting nationality of authors. Commonly, nationalities of many authors are given. Sometimes a nationality is given with a question mark: "English?" Sometimes: "Presumably British." Sometimes: "No information." Sometimes no comment on nationality is offered, as for Russell Holman and Frank Wall. I ran across another problem, an anomaly of indexing: "Seestern (pseud. of Ferdinand H. Grautoff) biographical information is provided under the author's name," is alphabetized in the "S's." But there is no listing for "Grautoff" in the "G's." "Seestern" in the author index simply returns the reader to the "S's" in the main list. Only when we find "Grautoff" in the author index are we directed to a not-before-mentioned second pseudonym, "Parabellum." It is under "Parabellum" in the main list that we finally discover the "biographical information" for "Ferdinand Heinrich Grautoff." In another puzzling practice, sixty-four pages are devoted to a wonderfully analytical "Motif and Theme Index," which omits entries for "prophets" (there is one for "prophecies"), "magician" (there is one for "magic, supernatural"), "bomb," and, remarkably, "scientist" (there is one for "mad scientist" with about 125 references). In a corpus of summarized science fiction as representative as this one the omission of "scientist" from the index denies the reader the convenience of a vastly interesting and important socio-literary datum, though it would seem to have been relatively easily within Bleiler's power to supply it. His discussion of his motif index does not address this matter.

Turning to the virtues of *The Early Years* is a pleasure. I have no quibbles about omissions; I can't think of any. The breadth of the coverage is breathtakingly great. Everything of Wells, Verne, Stratemeyer (Tom Swift), and Burroughs (John Carter, Pellucidar, Tarzan) bearing a stamp of science fiction is included.

Science Fiction in the Nineteenth Century

Another way in which Bleiler's coverage is impressive is in his listing of utopian works. He "excluded utopias, or ideal societies, unless they had fantastic elements that fitted within the general definition of science-fiction: futurity, inventions, interplanetary matters, . . ." (p. viii). Yet his protocols for inclusion remained so generous that a comparison of just the "A" and "B" sections of the title indexes of *The Early Years* and Lyman Sargent's approaching exhaustive *British and American Utopian Literature* shows that, of the 194 titles listed by Sargent, Bleiler has included the amazingly large number of 86 of them. The summaries are detailed. Bleiler made them so because hundreds of the stories he includes are extremely rare—perhaps only a few copies in existence, and those in private collections. And the summaries are, I am convinced, highly accurate. I read Trollope's *The Fixed Period* for the first time for this review. Bleiler's extended summary of it is correct, presented as exactly as if it were *Frankenstein*.

Edith Wharton's Network

Elizabeth Ammons

Candace Waid. *Edith Wharton's Letters from the Underworld: Fictions of Women and Writing*. Chapel Hill: University of North Carolina Press, 1991. x, 237 pp.

Susan Goodman. *Edith Wharton's Women: Friends and Rivals*. Hanover: University Press of New England, 1990. ix, 208 pp.

Contemporary Wharton studies began about twenty-five years ago when the author's papers at the Beinecke Library were opened to scholars and the most recent wave of the women's movement in the United States kindled serious interest in women in literature and women writers. Susan Goodman and Candace Waid's books make important contributions to this current criticism.

Goodman's *Edith Wharton's Women* takes up the tricky question of the author's feelings about other women and the ways in which her attitudes shaped her fiction and can be read in it. Most existing scholarship has emphasized Wharton's distance from other women, beginning with her mother, from whom, by her own accounts, she never felt sufficient love, support, or guidance. It is therefore not surprising, according to the standard view, that women receive hostile treatment in her fiction and repeatedly display destructive, competitive behaviors toward each other. Challenging this argument, Goodman holds that Wharton felt much more ambivalent about her mother than is usually acknowledged, with the result that she sought both to "embrace and deny" her (p. 26). Moreover, Goodman emphasizes that the relationship Wharton enjoyed with Sara Norton, the daughter of the famous Harvard professor Charles Eliot Norton, was warm and egalitarian; their friendship contradicts representations of Wharton as a woman alienated from women and from her own femaleness. The result, Goodman says, is bonding between women in the fiction that is complex, often supportive, and frequently positive.

As Goodman phrases it, most Wharton critics, feminists included, "tend to see her women in isolation and as primarily competitive. In contrast, I see her heroines struggling to define themselves through connections with other women" (p. 3). Goodman agrees that the tension for Wharton between her ambition to be a writer and her sexual identity made "her relationships with other women and with women writers difficult." Nevertheless, Wharton was not "so much a woman among men as a woman who sought value for her life and her work in relationships with women" (p. 6). We see this in the fiction in Wharton's repeatedly "pairing her heroines and making them rivals for the same man. Sorority flourishes under the women's competition, as they become allies in the process of reshaping themselves" (p. 3). Goodman summarizes the positive effect of this female competition-turned-alliance:

Women who seem to be opposites are in reality more similar than dissimilar. Each begins to see from the other's perspective, and their expanded consciousness is both painful and enriching. The supposed rivals become the means for each other's moral growth, as they realize that being true to another woman means being true to oneself. What appears to be a sacrifice is in reality a touchstone that imbues life with meaning. [p. 7]

Goodman's departure from the usual critical line produces many valuable insights about Edith Wharton and about her fiction. Among the best things in this book are the abundant quotations from Wharton's letters to Sara Norton from 1899 to 1922, most of which have not appeared in print, and Goodman's emphasis on the warmth and depth of the friendship that this long correspondence with Norton maintained. Wharton's affection for Sara Norton was strong. All simplistic portraits of the author as a woman-hater are roundly contradicted by the letters Goodman quotes.

Likewise, Goodman's thesis yields some perceptive readings of

Wharton's fiction. She observes, for instance, that *The Custom of the Country* (1913), widely regarded as a criticism of American marriage, should also be thought about as "an indictment of irresponsibly permissive child-rearing practices" (p. 62). Discussing *Ethan Frome* (1911), she comments that the book "demonstrates that the failure to gain independence results in death—or worse, maiming. That realization may have been a literal lifesaver for Wharton" (p. 77), who two years after the publication of the short novel sued for divorce and thus ended her long, unhappy marriage of thirty years. Most provocative is the observation that the incestuous relationship at the center of *Summer* (1917), while clearly unhealthy, also "has its unconscious fascination" (p. 80). Indeed, Wharton's ambiguity about the incest, Goodman argues, probably explains her inability to resolve crucial issues in the book and critics' consequent division over its conclusion. Similarly original and stimulating is Goodman's idea that the writer Vance Weston in Wharton's last published novels, *Hudson River Bracketed* (1929) and *The Gods Arrive* (1932), not only stands in for the author but also, and paradoxically, figures as "a parody of the male writer who has little distinction" (p. 129).

Some weaknesses do keep *Edith Wharton's Women* from being as uniformly strong and useful as it might be. Certain generalizations do not hold up. For example: "After Lily [in *The House of Mirth* (1905)], Wharton's heroines are less male-identified, and they more readily recognize their connection and responsibility to others of their gender" (p. 50). But what about Undine Spragg? Or Zeena Frome? Also, vagueness on occasion makes meaning difficult or impossible to grasp. For instance: "In later novels, such as *The Mother's Recompense* (1925) and *the Buccaneers* (1938), Wharton defines mothers and daughters more by gender than by role as each tries to fashion an identity that is consistent with societal definitions of womanhood" (p. 25). The difference between definition by "gender" and definition by "role" here needs explanation.

Most open to question in *Edith Wharton's Women*, however, is the degree to which Goodman proves her thesis that Wharton enjoyed significant positive relationships with women and that the ties between women in her fiction can be read positively. On the first point the argument that Wharton shunned women who might truly be her equal, selecting maids and, later in life, much younger women as her closest friends, is not really contradicted by Goodman's portrait of her friendship with Sara Norton. What was it, one might object, but a relationship between a rich, famous, public figure and a relatively unknown, dutiful daughter conducted long-distance and (most convenient for preserving control) by correspondence? Similarly, there is truth in the claim that bonds between women in the fiction at times turn from hostility to support; but this study would be stronger if it also dealt more fully with the undeniable anger and envy of women toward each other, the fear of female friendship in Wharton's work, and the egotism and mania for control of women's sacrificing themselves for each other. Comparison here with Wharton's contemporaries who could imagine women openly befriending and supporting one another—writers such as Sarah Orne Jewett or Kate Chopin or Pauline Hopkins or Sui Sin Far—would be helpful.

Candace Waid, drawing her title—*Edith Wharton's Letters from the Underworld: Fictions of Women and Writing*—from the Persephone-Demeter myth that fascinated the author, defines her subject as "Wharton's attempts to imagine the place of the woman writer" (p. 3). As Waid explains, while her book pays some attention to Wharton as the successful publishing author, it is more concerned with the "recurrence throughout Wharton's work of failed artists, unfinished texts, and anxieties about silence, inarticulateness, and suffocation" (p. 3). For Edith Wharton the eating of the pomegranate in the Greek myth represented sexual knowledge—entrance into the dark underworld of male erotic power and sexual union. Also and more generally, however, the myth evoked the whole underworld of experience that the serious writer must enter and engage to create art, the dangerous realm of adult experience that Wharton, like many women of her time and class, associated with the masculine. In light of the deep conflicts that the author felt between being a woman and an artist, Waid examines "two major areas of emphasis in Wharton's work: a self-conscious attention to writing and the conditions of art and a deeply ambivalent preoccupation with women and the conditions of female identity" (pp. 3–4). Studying these interrelated topics, Waid focuses on selected works to explore and unravel Wharton's complicated attitudes toward and inscription of her identity as a woman writer.

Many of Waid's readings are nothing short of brilliant. She argues of *The House of Mirth,* for example, that we need to understand Bertha Dorset—the literal writer of letters in the book—as a type for the woman writer, an idea that is so startling yet so obvious that it immediately registers as completely accurate. One wonders why Bertha's role as writer has not been studied in detail before—a measure, of course, of how sharp the perception is. As Waid explains: "Although Bertha is often on the margins of the narrative, she is crucial to any understanding of Lily Bart and the place of writing in the novel" (p. 21). Bertha's writing controls the plot. She is "not just the author of well-placed stories that frame Lily as a disreputable woman, she is also the powerful scripter of scenes in which Lily Bart is cast as a character" (p. 23). Thus a major narrative line in *The House of Mirth* derives from Bertha's writing, including the question of what result her writing will produce and the issue of whether another woman, Lily Bart, whom we also see writing throughout the novel (frequently her job consists of writing for other women), will participate in or resist the kind of writing that Bertha represents. As Waid succinctly puts it: "In the end, the dramatic tension of the novel turns on the question of whether Lily will play the role of the writer" (p. 26). Also Bertha, associated with the underworld, embodies many of Wharton's fears and conflicts about being a woman writer. On the one hand, the character is sexual, powerful, and able to write copiously and with abandon. On the other, however, she is ruthless, totally self-centered, and profoundly alienated from other women, whom she treats either as flunkies or rivals.

Waid's investigation of the broad topic of writing and gender in Wharton's work leads her to many valuable, provocative insights. She says of *Ethan Frome* that it "is at once Wharton's most intimate and distanced story of estrangement; it is a personal meditation on what it means to write books as bridges across the abyss of her greatest fears" (p. 62), primary among them the fear of inarticulateness, muteness. *Frome,* filled as it is with images of infertility and crippling, is "profoundly concerned with the problem of an interior story that cannot be told, a story that lies in the gaps of a series of stories" (p. 63). Also extremely useful is Waid's argument that Wharton's ghost stories contain the repressed story of women who become, as she puts it, "unquiet ghosts" because they cannot speak. The idea is especially welcome in providing an appropriately rich way of thinking about work that is usually overlooked in critical books about Wharton.

Saturating Waid's study is the issue of how gender and the creation of art interacted for Wharton, an interaction that was, Waid maintains, often terrifying. Wharton carried with her throughout her life a "vision of the monstrous and murderous feminine" (p. 184). At the same time, she vigorously aligned herself against the kind of soft, comforting femininity that she associated with popular women writers. Complicating this further, she aimed to be a woman who wrote within a cultural context that defined the elite writer as male. Capturing some of this turmoil in one brief statement, Waid reminds us that "Wharton's novels recurrently picture characters who sit at their writing desks and then choose suicide" (p. 14). For Wald, female figures are not the only representatives of the woman writer in Wharton's work, and therefore she succeeds in pushing interpretation forward in some surprising ways. She builds, for example, on the established idea that *The Custom of the Country* tells the story of a writer's destruction by a false muse (Undine Spragg) by bringing to the surface gender issues. Discussing Ralph Marvell's seduction by Undine, she theorizes Undine's relationship to gender and writing:

> As the embodiment of a superficial beauty and a dangerous artifice that conceals an interior emptiness, Undine represents a fatally alluring surface language; she is a devouring muse who feeds on the language of description. I will claim that Undine is Wharton's emblem for American culture; but more specifically, I will argue that in her attention to and embodiment of a language and aesthetic based on ornamentation, decorative color, and deceptive surface, she represents the aesthetic Wharton identified with the feminine. [p. 131]

Edith Wharton's Network

In this reading Ralph—a covert type for the woman artist—is destroyed by his fatal attraction to feminine art, surface art: decorative, pretty, shallow creation.

This fear of being classed with women writers and therefore dismissed as second-rate—soft, trivial, minor—led Edith Wharton, as many critics have noted, to dissociate herself from other women writers. Chief among them were Sarah Orne Jewett and Mary Wilkins Freeman, whose visions of New England, Wharton pronounced with scorn in a much-quoted phrase, were produced through "rose-colored glasses." Jewett and Freeman, Edith Wharton was saying, were feminine writers, and she was not. She was tough and truth-telling, a genuine artist. Given this well-known contempt of Edith Wharton for her supposedly inferior feminine peers, certainly one of the most exciting things that Waid does in *Edith Wharton's Letters from the Underworld* is to challenge Wharton's insistence that no one link her with the likes of Jewett or Freeman. Specifically, Waid demonstrates a strong, close connection between the fiction of Freeman and Wharton—an idea, like so many in this book, that startles with its immediate ring of truth. (If nothing else, Wharton's vigorous warnings against grouping her and Freeman should have tipped us off.) Supplying abundant, persuasive, textual and extratextual evidence, Waid maintains that "in reading Mary Wilkins, Wharton would have found resonances, even striking echoes, of her own fiction" and then argues a palpable connection between Wilkins's stories and *Summer*. "In particular," Waid says, "I will argue that *Summer* is a revision and rewriting of Wilkins's important story, 'Old Woman Magoun.' . . . The story Wharton tells in *Summer* of the burial of a mother named Mary is also written as a rejection of the women's stories represented by Mary Wilkins" (p. 91). In a superb chapter, "Wharton and Wilkins: Rereading the Mother (*Summer*)," Waid carefully constructs the historical possibility, indeed probability, that Mary Wilkins Freeman had an important influence on Wharton. This chapter not only opens up a major area for Wharton scholars—the relationship between Edith Wharton and writers such as Mary Wilkins Freeman—but it also serves as a prod to methodology. Waid's refusal to rest with the received truism that Wharton differed radically from the women regionalists she turned her nose up at should serve as a model for future scholars. Her determination to think through from the beginning what others have tended to circulate in a closed circuit as established and known results in a book full of exciting new angles of vision.

Indeed, this determination not simply to accept but rather to question and challenge truisms in the existing scholarship is what distinguishes both Goodman's and Waid's studies. Goodman takes seriously the outrageous idea that Edith Wharton might actually have liked women, that she might have had positive feelings and relationships as well as negative ones and that those affirmative bonds might have affected her work in important ways that have generally been ignored because the theme of Wharton's misogyny has been so overdetermined in the criticism. Likewise, Waid disturbs many critical commonplaces, arguing that the ghost stories deserve serious sustained study, that Wharton's famous scorn for Mary Wilkins Freeman masks a deep, complex attraction to the other writer, that we need to be very supple and imaginative in our readings of the figure of the writer in Wharton's fiction, and that no one simple paradigm of "woman writer" can begin adequately to open up the many levels of struggle that Edith Wharton found herself engaged in as a creative woman. Books such as these launch an exciting new period in modern scholarship on Wharton. They represent a new generation of works which acknowledge and draw on former works but genuinely move Wharton's studies forward in provocative ways.

The Magic Hand of Chance: Keats's Poetry in Facsimile

Susan J. Wolfson

John Keats: Poetry Manuscripts at Harvard, A Facsimile Edition. ed. Jack Stillinger. With an Essay on the Manuscripts by Helen Vendler. Cambridge: Harvard University Press, 1990. xxii, 266 pp.

> "It has been said that the Character of a Man
> may be known by his hand writing."
> —Keats to Charles Dilke, 4 March 1820[1]

In the Keats collection of the Houghton Library at Harvard is a manuscript of *The Cap and the Bells; or, The Jealousies*, on one leaf of which (showing stanza 51) appears upside down a mysterious fragment from Keats's handwriting; the manuscript is the only authoritative source of this text, in fact. With the *r*'s, which Keats habitually dropped in the speed of writing, interpolated, it reads:

> This living hand, now wa[r]m and capable
> Of ea[r]nest grasping, would, if it were cold
> and in the icy silence of the tomb,
> So haunt thy days and chill thy dreaming nights
>   hea[r]t
> That thou would wish thine ∧ own dry of blood
> So in my veins red life might stream again,
> and thou be conscience–calm'd—see here it is Ӏ
> I hold it towards you.

Here is what might be taken to be an uncanny prediction in the nineteenth century of "The Death of the Author" notoriously announced by Roland Barthes in our own: the text, rather than representing the author as a presence, represents him in another sense, as a substitution "at the cost of the death of the Author." Keats's intuition of this economy may account for the decidedly Keatsian actors that play in Barthes' allegorical scene: the "modern" notion which replaces "the Author" is called a "scriptor," a figure for whom the "hand, cut off from any voice, borne by a pure gesture of inscription (and not of expression), traces a field without origin—or which, at least has no other origin than language itself, language which ceaselessly calls into question all origins."[2]

And yet, as much as the fragmentariness of Keats's lines handily allegorizes Barthes' meditation, their rhetorical force has a peculiarly revivifying effect against the death so reported. It is true that the voice Keats scripts is one that imagines, and asks its listener to imagine, a hand cut off from the voice which speaks—and as readers, we have only this gesture of inscription with which to contend. Yet the figure of origin is not so much effaced by these lines as perversely doubled and re-doubled. Reversing what he had described in a verse that he wrote out in a letter to his (by now, dead) brother Tom as a sense of the "warm . . . nerve of a welcoming hand" (*Letters*, 1:304), this scripted voice, I think for all its readers, exerts a power beyond the merely nervous, grasping the imagination in a haunting poetics of presence.

This effect is intensified for readers who know Keats's writing by the way these fragmentary lines evoke more than the verse to Tom. In fact, they summon a whole Keatsian discourse of hands as the expressive agent of poetic potency and the synecdoche of authorial presence. This is especially marked in the idealism of temper and temperature in early poems. To one friend Keats remarks, again in verse, "as my hand was warm, I thought I'd better/Trust to my feelings and write you a letter" (*Letters*, 1:112). On another occasion, a poet asks for "a golden pen" and "hand of hymning angel" to "write down a line of glorious tone" ("On Leaving Some Friends"). The initiate of "Sleep and Poetry" exclaims, "O Poesy! for thee I hold my pen . . . for thee I grasp my pen!" (ll. 47, 53), prefiguring his intent to "seize" events "Like a strong giant" (ll. 81–82).

The hand as a signifier of poetic capacity is so frequent a trope in Keats's verse, both serious and light, that it begins to acquire the character of a Keatsian signature. Playfully prophesying that his other brother George's child will be a poet, Keats imagines how, even now, this babe

> lifts its little hand into the flame
> Unharm'd, and on the strings
>   sings
> Paddles a little tune and ⟨signs⟩
> With dumb endeavour sweetly!
> Bard art thou completely!   [*Letters*, 1:399]

Keats's transcriptive superimposition of the verb of voice, "sings," over the hand's gesture of figuring, "signs," is a suggestive icon in itself. In another light verse, Keats represents himself in a more parodic register as "a naughty boy" with nothing to do

> But scribble poetry—
>   He took
>   An inkstand
>   In his hand
>   And a Pen
>   Big as ten
>   In the other.   [*Letters*, 1:313]

This last comparison, cartooning the eroticism which often infuses these gestures, belies some more ambiguous handlings of power in Keats's networks of passion, handlings which become ghoulishly aggressive in "This living hand." The poet of "Time's Sea" tells a woman of having been "tangled in thy beauty's web, /And snared by the ungloving of thy hand." "You say you love," complains the poet on another occasion,

> but then your hand
> No soft squeeze for squeeze returneth;
> It is like a statue's, dead,—
> While mine for passion burneth—
>   ["You say you love," ll. 16–19]

When Endymion clutches at his fading Indian Maid, a figuring of hands spells the solipsism that motivates all this shepherd's visionary romances:

> he seiz'd her wrist;
> It melted from his grasp: her hand he kiss'd,
> And, horror! kiss'd his own—he was alone.
> [4.508–10]

No wonder that the poet who speaks an "Ode on Melancholy" advises the man vexed by his mistress to "Imprison her soft hand."

If hands link lovers to each other and potency to poetry, the urgency of several of these gestures is shadowed by apprehensions of failure, of opportunities that elude grasping. The poet of an early sonnet fears that he "may never live to trace ... with the magic hand of Chance" all the visions by which he is inspired ("When I Have Fears"). With George about to emigrate, Keats says that he "cannot write"—not just for want of inspiration but for a physical sensation of incapacity: "I am now so depressed that I have not an Idea to put to paper—my hand feels like lead—and yet it is [an] unpleasant numbness it does not take away the pain of existence—I don't know what to write" (*Letters,* 1:287). He tells George in the letter that reports Tom's death, "I have not the Shadow of an idea of a book in my head, and my pen seems to have grown too goutty for verse" (2:5). In "Hyperion," the poem on which he was working at the time of Tom's death, Saturn's loss of power is spelled by an "old right hand [that] lay nerveless, listless, dead, / Unsceptred" (1.18–19), while the narrator of his torment fears that the sorrow "and such like woe" of this subject will prove "Too huge for mortal tongue or pen of scribe" (ll. 159–60). We are not surprised to discover that Keats has the poet of his attempted revision of this poem, "The Fall of Hyperion," begin by deferring judgment of his dream to the time "When this warm scribe my hand is in the grave" (1.18). The dream itself recounts a prophetic agony on the steps of Moneta's temple: "When I clasped my hands," the poet reports, "I felt them not. / One minute before death ..." (1.131–32). In addition to this company of poetic figures, there are also a set of well-known anecdotes about Keats's hand that have become incorporated into the Keats story. Leigh Hunt recalls how Keats "would look at his hand, which was faded, and swollen in the veins, and say it was the hand of a man of fifty"; Coleridge reports that after first meeting Keats, who shook his hand eagerly, he remarked, "There is death in his hand."[3]

All this swirls strangely around the spectral animations of "This living hand," enhancing its already evocative power. As Jonathan Culler describes his experience of this effect, "we can believe that the hand is really present and perpetually held toward us through the poem. The poem predicts this mystification, dares us to resist it, and shows that its power is irresistible."[4] Part of this queerly arresting power is created by the verse form itself, the suspense of syntax across lines—or in Milton's famous phrase for the play of blank verse, "the sense variously drawn out": through apposition and subordination, Keats's first sentence dilates, displays, and defers the completion of its sense, slowly but relentlessly releasing a subjunctive contingency into a daunting consequence. The terse exhortation and declaratives that follow the dash after "conscience-calm'd" "—see here it is— / I hold it towards you"—sharpen the assault, seeming, in their epigrammatic summary, almost to parody the Shakespearean sonnet as they enforce an abrupt turn from the dilated subjunctive proposition ("would, if it were . . . that thou would") to concentrated actuality and immediacy, from a stagey eloquence of tone to a sudden colloquialism, from an expansive iambic rhythm to a set of spare monosyllables.

That the conjuration of warm life into icy death is, in the rhetoric of these lines, both hypothetical in the present and prophetic of a future gives this fragment a peculiar enough intensity—and a shock-affect at stark variance to the final effect proposed with bitter irony: being "conscience-calm'd." But Keats's fragment is more powerful yet for an accidental effect: that of leaving its readers uncertain about their proper relation to the speaker's verbal gesture. If we were sure of a dramatic context, in which "I" and "you" signify characters whom we watch and with whose rhetorical position we do not coincide, we might marvel at the effect (think, as Keats may have, of young Lucius' cry to Titus' corpse: "O grandsire, grandsire, ev'n with all my heart / Would I were dead, so you did live again!" [*Titus Andronicus*, 5.3.172–73]). But since the context of Keats's lines can be only a matter of conjecture, and in any event must remain forever unknowable, most of us, affected by the sensationalism of the gesture, take its proposal personally: lacking any reference to a visual stage or other dramatic frame, we feel operating a dynamics of reading similar to that produced by a personal letter or lyric poem whose author is absent, and with whose unspecified addressee, in the rhetoric of reading, we effectively, and affectively, identify. We take these lines as the trace of an absent speaker, its voice begging for admission to, or imposing itself upon, the present consciousness of the reader they project.

Even in this orientation, however, a reader may be unsettled, for the parting lines, "see here it is— / I hold it towards you," activate the question of reference by suspending the declaratives between a present moment, in which the speaker invites earnest grasping, and a manipulated event of imagination, in which a cold hand, as promised, assaults the conscience. Do the two "it"s refer to a living hand or a dead one? The whole rhetorical thrust of the utterance not only confuses the question but makes it supererogatory. For what it provokes in the reader is an act of imagination that conceives the present as past, the sensation of earnest grasping as the chilling grip of a nightmare, the actual as spectral and the spectral as actual.

The peculiar power of this solicitation has received some fine attention from Lawrence Lipking and Timothy Bahti, both of whom confront the question of interpretation and both of whom wind up writing allegories of interpretive occlusion.[5] For Lipking, the undecidability of reference—are we to imagine a living hand as dead, or an absent one as present?—provokes "two fully coherent yet mutually exclusive" readings. Taking note of Lipking's offhand remark that "the very act of writing might be thought to confirm that a warm and capable hand is moving toward a reader," Bahti figures out a way to coordinate these "radically contradictory" possibilities. He proposes that the poem's final lines represent the living hand turned dead, written as dead in the poem's proleptic narrative, and "it"—the two letters of the neuter pronoun—is the *handwriting*, or "hand," of the "living hand": "it," and the whole text of "This living hand...." This dead or written hand, then, comes before us declaring itself "living" in the first line, and from our necessity of reading it as living it enacts its proleptic wish: that the reader(s) pour life into the "entombed" tomb of text so that it might live "again," as meaningful representation.

In different ways, Bahti and Lipking take the indeterminacy of the poem's manuscript as an event to be manipulated into meaning. Lipking sentimentalizes the fragment's parting gesture as signifying Keats's investment of "hope in the reader's conscience, not in his own imperishable work"; indeed, for Lipking, this is what makes the fragment fit "so snugly at the end of Keats's poems: . . . the process of his work can never be completed save by our own responsive acts of attention." Bahti's point, essentially the same but conscripted into a rigorously deconstructive case, is that any poetics of reciprocity has to engage a reading of the living hand "as an entombed script or text that is 'living' only to the extent that it is animated by readers' understanding [our "earnest grasping" or comprehension], in accordance with the poem's narrative." The poet's "I" has to be reanimated, revived as living and capable of writing "This living hand...," and fated, in the sequence already generated, to write itself back into the silence of the grave, thence to emerge again. This ceaseless involution of cause and effect, Bahti argues, renders the poem less a fragment than a textual moebius strip, a figure of "ongoing completion beyond which any continuation of the text would only cancel the meaningfulness at which it has arrived." Or, as Lipking writes succinctly but with a similar sense of impasse: "In his presence [the poet] enforces a sense of absence, in his absence presence."

Lipking's and Bahti's efforts to ascribe a rhetorical integrity to these lines demonstrate a longing, in the presence of this mysterious holograph and in the absence of sure protocols for interpretation, for some plan of action, some principle by which to assimilate these lines to a Keatsian or a critical canon. The more dramatic effect, however, is the way Keats's fragment produces—

in fact, demands—a dialectical interplay of two intelligences, author and reader, both of whom must surrender to some uncertainty. Faced with a suspense of verse in mid-line, the reader is left in uneasy complicity with the fragment's last word, "you," and forced to surrender imagination to the writer; at the same time, the writer, whose language remains suspended in a gesture of petition, must surrender final authority to the reader.

Or a reader who is also an editor. The last plate in Jack Stillinger's *John Keats: Poetry Manuscripts at Harvard, A Facsimile Edition* is a photolithograph of this fragment, along with two transcriptions (about the nature of which, more later). Here is the best typographical approximation I can offer of what Keats's living hand wrote:

>   This living hand, now wam and capable
>   Of eanest grasping, would, if it were cold
>   and in the icy silence of the tomb,
>   So haunt thy days and chill thy dreaming nights
>   heat
>   That thou would wish thine ∧ own dry of blood
>   So in my veins red life might stream again,
>   and thou be conscience-calm'd–see here it is Ƴ
>   I hold it towards you.

Every editor I know of regularizes the margins, capitalizes the first words of these lines, supplies the *r*'s Keats obviously dropped from "wam," "eanest," and "heat," adds some clarifying punctuation, and helps Keats out further by guessing that he meant "hea[r]t" to be inserted between *own* and *dry* rather than between *thine* and *own* and emending accordingly. This is all routine: it is a standard editorial practice in preparing an edition of almost any writer—even for a scholarly market—not only to emend such errors of spelling and syntax but also to regularize other "accidental" features (as opposed to the "substantive" ones: variants of wording, word order, or wholesale revisions that would have more than an accidental effect on the sense of a passage). Some editors, such as W. J. B. Owen in his edition of *The Fourteen-Book PRELUDE by William Wordsworth* (Cornell, 1985) and Stillinger himself in his edition of *The Poems of John Keats*

(Harvard, 1978), supply a full list of these variants, just in case readers want to know what the manuscript evidence is, or beyond this knowledge, may want to consider the significance of a variant they deem as other than "accidental." The use of capital letters, for instance, is subject to this kind of scrutiny, for what is mere typography to some conveys a symbolizing intention to others; and on the presence or absence of punctuation, as numerous instances in both literature and law confirm, hangs more than a tale or two. In the interests of efficiency and of holding down publication costs, however, many editors apply emendations of accidental elements "silently," that is, without annotation.

In his full-scale editing of Keats's poetical works, *The Poems of John Keats,* Stillinger made a conscious decision to edit "according to the ideal of 'final authorial intentions,'" by which he means that the texts he supplies represent, "as exactly as can be determined, the form that Keats himself would have sanctioned and preferred over all others."[6] Stillinger was then, and still is, very attuned to the whole issue of "intention"—what constitutes it, whether it is recoverable—in no small part because such questions are more than matter for theoretical discussion for editors; they have a direct, practical bearing on the presentation of the text. Unless one has world enough and time, as well as a rich publisher, to produce all versions in which a text is available, an editor has to decide on a base text, the most authoritative version against which variants are collated. In all these decisions, the evidence of a holograph—an autograph draft or fair copy manuscript—is given a primary claim; the only texts usually accorded a rival claim are the versions published while an author was alive and which were therefore, presumably, subject to his or her supervision. But even on the path to publication, as Stillinger has shown in a suggestive and richly detailed recent study, *Multiple Authorship and the Myth of Solitary Genius* (Oxford, 1991), texts can be subject to substantial interference, even corruption. The "purity" of hand attributed to a holograph is why one major theory of editing, originally put forth by W. W. Greg and subsequently elaborated by Fredson Bowers, insists on crediting an author's fair copy manuscript over printed texts in matters of determining authority.[7] As Bowers puts the case baldly, "When an author's manuscript is preserved, this has paramount authority, of course."[8] Stillinger himself has intelligent reservations about this principle (again, see his discussion in *Multiple Authors*), but he has the utmost respect for the evidence, even if the chief value of studying holograph texts turns out not to be that of establishing an authoritative text, but only the line of textual genetics, the process by which a text develops into the form credited authoritative.

For anyone interested in the case of Keats, the Harvard Library holds a major archive of autograph manuscripts, to which Stillinger's *Facsimile Edition,* in effect, gives us access, along with some valuable interpretive help. It includes 140 photographs covering thirty-eight separate documents (sometimes, one work in more than one version)—all in all, fifty-two items, presented on 129 pages; all that are excluded are poems in holograph letters (some of which I quoted in the first part of this essay). On the recto pages are the photolithographs, and on facing pages Stillinger provides two transcriptions. In italic script, on the left side of the page, is an edited reading text drawn from Stillinger's *Poems* and reflecting the preferred reading of the draft, along with the introduction of some helpful punctuation and with other elements regularized. Closer to the plate, on the right side of the page and in roman type, is an exact transcription of all of the elements of Keats's script, regularized, as far as I could tell, only to straighten the margins where no indentation was indicated, and occasionally to supply a capital letter. In many cases, where the manuscript is a fair copy, a reader can do without this help and read Keats straight. But there are other cases—emphatically, for example, the pages of "The Eve of St. Agnes," which are not only rough drafts in themselves but are further obscured by the smudge of ink from obverse pages—where Stillinger's expert interpretation of text, insertions, cancellations, subscripts, superscripts, and so forth, is generous and necessary. Even Stillinger isn't sure, on some occasions, of the validity of his readings and so represents his transcriptions as only "closely *approximate*" (see "Editor's Introduction," pp. xii–xiii).

This caution noted, the general reader as well as the textual scholar are now afforded an unmediated vision of Keats's hand in the pressure of its composition—its true and false starts, its cancellations and revisions, its interlineations and marginal addenda (we see, for example, Keats lining up and blocking out the quatrain rhymes of "On first looking into Chapman's Homer")—and, not the least, in its assurance. What is perhaps most astonishing to discover in perusing this visual record is the rush of inspiration and fullness of conception with which Keats composed, even in such demanding forms as the sonnet, Spenserian stanza, ottava rima. We see a sonnet later titled "Written in Disgust of Vulgar Superstition" confidently written out with few revisions and improvements, boldly signed "J Keats," and inscribed, just as boldly, "Written in 15 minutes." To encounter these manuscripts is to feel the attraction of an oft-debated term, namely "genius." Whetting our anticipation for this encounter, Helen Vendler provides an appreciative introductory essay, aptly titled "The Living Hand of Keats" (pp. xiv–xxii), in which she reports her own "experience in the presence of these literary relics" by discussing the subtle signifyings of Keats's handwriting—the semantic value of its supposedly accidental compressions, contractions, expansions. Studying the manuscripts tends to solicit our visual attention in ways that reanimate the perplexities of composition in Keats's scripting: what, for instance, of the intimate relation to be sensed in the "heat" that Keats first wrote, suggestively, for the "heart" of the person addressed by "this living hand"? In the gesture of such scrutiny, we find ourselves with Keats, tracing the magic hand of chance that shadows his books of charactery.

Notes

1. *The Letters of John Keats, 1814–1821*, ed. Hyder E. Rollins, 2 vols. (Cambridge: Harvard Univ. Press, 1958), 2:272.
2. Barthes, "The Death of the Author" ("La mort de l'auteur", 1968), trans. Stephen Heath, *Image-Music-Text* (London: Fontana, 1977), pp. 142–48; I quote from pages 148 and 146.
3. Hunt, "Mr. Keats, With a Criticism on His Writings," *Lord Byron and Some of*

His Contemporaries; With Recollections of the Author's Life, and of His Visit to Italy (London: Henry Colburn, 1828; rpt. Philadelphia: Carey, Lea & Carey, 1828), pp. 213–35; I quote from page 213. Coleridge, *Table Talk* (recorded by Henry Nelson Coleridge and John Taylor Coleridge), 2 vols., ed. Carl Woodring (Princeton: Princeton Univ. Press, 1990), 1:325, 11 Aug. 1832.

4. Culler, "Apostrophe" (1977; rpt. *The Pursuit of Signs: Semiotics, Literature, Deconstruction* [Ithaca: Cornell Univ. Press, 1981], pp. 135–54), I quote from page 154.

5. Bahti, "Ambiguity and Indeterminacy: The Juncture," *Comparative Literature*, 38 (1986), 209–23; Lipking, "This Living Hand," *The Life of the Poet: Beginning and Ending Poetic Careers* (Chicago: Univ. of Chicago Press, 1981), pp. 180–84.

6. *The Poems of John Keats*, ed. Jack Stillinger (Cambridge: Harvard Univ. Press, Belknap Press, 1978), p. 1.

7. This case was first put forth by Greg in "The Rationale of Copy-Text," *Studies in Bibliography*, 3 (1950–51), 19–36, first presented to the English Institute in 1949; and by Bowers, first in "Current Theories of Copy-Text," *Modern Philology*, 48 (1950), 12–20, and elaborated in many subsequent publications.

8. "The editor must choose the manuscript as his major authority, correcting from the first edition only what are positive errors in the accidentals of the manuscript." Bowers, "Some Principles for Scholarly Editions of Nineteenth-Century American Authors," *Studies in Bibliography*, 17 (1964), 223–28; I quote from page 226.

A Defense of Thomas More against Modern Revisionism

Philip C. Dust

Louis L. Martz. *Thomas More: The Search for the Inner Man*. New Haven: Yale University Press, 1990. xi, 112 pp.

Anyone as complex as was Thomas More cannot be neatly categorized under psychological commonplaces from undergraduate textbooks. In *Thomas More: The Search for the Inner Man,* Louis Martz instructs his readers in what I hope will become a fuller, more positive, and more helpful approach to More. Martz's evidence is largely drawn from More's writings themselves and from his own non-polemical, patient inquiry into what they reveal of More's thinking. The first chapter defends More as a man who, however much he transcended his age, was still a part of it and subject to its limitations. The second chapter concentrates on one of the polemical works, *The Confutation of Tyndale's Answer*. The third and fourth treat the final works, *The Dialogue of Comfort* and the *De Tristia Christi*.[1]

More's great classics of world literature, the *Epigrams* and the *Utopia*, are not discussed as such. For students of literature, they are far more important than all the rest. But perhaps Martz felt that they have already received such intensive investigation that we might learn more about More the man from the others. The fact is that in the literary works, More, like Shakespeare after him, does tend to conceal himself under the guises of differing *personae*. In the other works we hear his own voice more directly.

The brunt of recent scholarly attacks on More has been directed at his attitude and role in persecuting heretics. Martz answers this criticism thoroughly and in its historical context. When he says that More's approval of the burning of heretics was "a judge's grim approval of the well-deserved punishment of a criminal who has committed what More calls the worst of crimes—the crime of leading other souls to eternal perdition" (p. 4), he is placing that attitude in the setting of a century where practically everyone on either side, Protestant or Catholic, thought as More did. Even in our own century it has taken the World Council of Churches and then, somewhat belatedly, Vatican Two to counteract that attitude.

Martz makes a great deal of the Holbein portrait of More and his family at Nostell Priory as revealing More the inner man (see pp. 9–14). In the context of More's desire for fame and fortune, another key item on the agenda of those who impune More's integrity and his motives, what strikes me as especially significant is the fact that he did not sit alone for such a painting but rather with his family. Even when he was deservedly famous, he thought of himself primarily as a husband and father. And Martz argues against the notion that More had an unbridled desire for power, quoting from Harpsfield: "But his father minded that he should tread after his steps, and settle his whole mind and study upon the laws of the Realm. And so being plucked from the universities of studies and learnings, he was sent to the studies of the laws only of this Realm" (p. 15). John Guy adds that More's father was so adamantly opposed to his son's humanistic and religious interests that he cut his son off from allowance until he towed under.[2] Pursuing a political career, then, and possessing the abilities he did, there is really nothing to blame him for, if he distinguished himself in office after office until he rose to the position of Chancellor of the realm. He simply did extremely well what he had been forced to do. And, then, when faced with his original and never-waning devotion to his religious principles, at a salary of over £820 a year, he gave it all up.

Martz places More's polemical writings and his acrid style squarely in the tradition of such writing throughout the Renaissance (see pp. 19–27). He cites another great practitioner of that style, John Milton, and says that to charge "that such vituperative violence in writing represents the real Thomas More, the inner man, seems to me as wrong as if we were to say that Milton's prose propaganda presents the real Milton, the inner man, rather than

A Defense of Thomas More

Paradise Lost" (p. 21). For my own part, I wish that both More and Milton had devoted all the energies they used in their vast polemical works to other literary efforts. But I speak only as a student and teacher of literature, not as one who can turn the clock around and change history. Both More and Milton were caught up in the necessities of their times, both were actively engaged in them, and both were very capable in the political and religious arenas. Fortunately, they did leave us better things. The *Utopia* and *Paradise Lost* will long outlive the polemical works and, as products of the profound inquiring spirit of man's most serious questions and deepest longings, remain as evidence of their authors' commitments to brilliant expressions of human comedy and tragedy.

Of all the works More has left us, it is the controversial works which have drawn the most critical fire. But Martz goes directly to the heart of the matter here by showing that More's *Confutation of Tyndale's Answer*, while it is undeniably polemical, fits Jaques Martitain's comment on the Augustinian order of the heart rather than that of the intellect (pp. 34–35). The method as described by Maritain "consiste principalement à la degression sur chaque point qu'on rapporte à la fin, pur la montrer toujours" (p. 35). Martz's book also follows this order. He concludes this section with a discussion of More's meditation on the passion, much as he will conclude his book with More's final meditation on the passion in the *De Tristia Christi* (pp. 50–51).

But we must not forget the critics. Martz dedicates his book to the "community of editors who for thirty years have worked together to create the Yale Edition of More's works" (p. xi). Following a Renaissance method of proving a position for More, I have gathered together the conclusions of many of these editors against those who are as guilty of being overly polemical as they accuse More of being. The testimony is from those who have worked closest with the works and is, I think, impressive enough to make a strong case.

Louis A. Schuster says in his summary of the polemical environment of *The Confutation of Tyndale's Answer* that "Even Tyndale, More reasons, is worth addressing and praying for. Like the old heretic Berengarius, he might some day revoke his position and die a virtuous man."[3] Richard Marius in this work concludes that "More chose the church of the apostles, fathers, and martyrs," and that "he lived himself as part of that universal body which stretched the tabernacle of its faith over history, this present earthly life, purgatory, and paradise itself."[4] John M. Headley puts More's *Responsio Ad Lutherum* in the polemical tradition in this fashion: "The response to Luther required a master of dialogue and dispute, a man who was both fully informed and religiously concerned and yet, in order not to inhibit his language, one who was not of spiritual estate. Whether Thomas More proffered his own services or was simply assigned the job of refuting Luther remains unknown. At any rate, More was to prove eminently suitable in his new office."[5]

Germain Marc'hadour deftly places the setting of *A Dialogue Concerning Heresies* in More's own house at Chelsea. He concludes that More the "*paterfamilias,* especially during the months while his *Dialogue* was in the making, would certainly on occasion play the heretic's advocate, and champion some novel exegesis he had brought home from the trial scene, or from perusing a pamphlet. Just as he was later to prepare his family for his imprisonment, he was now giving them small injections of heresy, while he sat in their midst, to provide them with a measure of immunity."[6] In his edition of *The Apology,* J. B. Trapp concludes: "The Apology is Thomas More's defense not only of his and the church's position, but of his own integrity." And he adds of More: "On the other hand, he had never been corrupt or pettily cruel, as he was accused of being. It is the vice he abhors, not the persons of those who practice it."[7]

Most recently we have the testimony of Germain Marc'hadour in his introduction to *The Supplication of Souls* that "More is readier than most Catholic controversialists of his day to confront the reformers on their own chosen ground, the Bible."[8] And in his edition of *The Letter To Bugenhogen,* Frank Manley takes issue with recent judgments of "fanaticism" on More's part when he concludes: "Seen from this distance, More and Luther are both larger than life, heroic figures. They stand out from all other men of their age in their purity of heart, the fervor of their faith, their love of God, and their willingness to follow the dic-

A Defense of Thomas More

tates of conscience despite the opposition of the entire world. What they did then exemplifies what the human spirit is capable of and thus consoles us all and gives us hope."[9]

Perhaps the best clues to More's inner self are found in the Tower Works. Martz devotes well over one-half of his defense of More to the Tower Works, the last letters, *The Dialogue of Comfort*, and the *De Tristia Christi*. He is more concerned to show, as he carefully does, More's artistic structurings as revealing a saint than to deal with well-preserved archaeological evidence of heroism. More elucidates the relationship between More's last letters and *The Dialogue of Comfort* for the first time and leads to the conclusion that they are "the preparation of More's mind to meet his death, if God so wishes" (see pp. 55–64). Here too, Martz presents an astute analysis of *The Dialogue of Comfort* as a model of the repetitive process of composition, an example of the art of meditation, and a preparation for More's own death in his meditation on Christ's agony in the Garden of Gethsemane. More was afraid to die. *The Dialogue of Comfort* was his way of coping with that fear. Again Martz offers a careful study of the Latin style and structure of the work and concludes: "Thomas More writes here nothing less than a small classical oration, a Philippic, or a Catilinian oration, exactly the kind of formal speech that he had long ago imagined for his speaker in the humanistic history of *Richard III*." (p. 98) Finally, the *De Tristia* is a preparation for the soul to cast "off the body to escape the earth and reach eternity" (p. 101).

Notes

1. Recent debate about More was ignited in part by G. R. Elton's "Thomas More, Councillor," in *St. Thomas More: Action and Contemplation*, ed. R. S. Sylvester (New Haven: Yale Univ. Press, 1972), pp. 87–122, and Richard Marius' *Thomas More* (New York: Knopf, 1984).

2. John Guy, *The Public Career of Sir Thomas More* (Brighton: Harvester Press, 1980), p. 4.

3. *Complete Works of St. Thomas More* (New Haven: Yale Univ. Press, 1973), vol. 8, pts. 1, 2, 3, p. 1268. Hereafter cited *Works* with volume number, date, and pages.

4. *Works*, vol. 8 (1973), p. 1363.

5. *Works,* vol. 5, pt. 2 (1969), p. 731.
6. *Works,* vol. 6, pt. 2 (1981), p. 494.
7. *Works,* vol. 9 (1979), p. xx.
8. *Works,* vol. 7 (1990), p. lxxiv.
9. *Works,* vol. 7 (1990), p. lxiv.

True Fairy Tales

Alan Richardson

Jeanie Watson. *Risking Enchantment: Coleridge's Symbolic World of Faery.* Lincoln: University of Nebraska Press, 1990. xiv, 235 pp.

Recording his early fascination with fairy tales in a letter to Thomas Poole, Coleridge goes on to frame a defense of the child's reading of fantasy literature quite uncharacteristic of his era: "Should children be permitted to read Romances, & Relations of Giants & Magicians, & Genii? I know all that has been said against it; but I have formed my faith in the affirmative.—I know no other way of giving the mind a love of 'the Great,' & 'the Whole'" (p. 8). All that had been said included the attacks of rationalists like Locke—"I would not have children troubled whilst young with Notions of *Spirits*"—as well as of Christian moralists like Sarah Trimmer, for whom fairy tales were "only fit to fill the heads of children with confused notions of wonderful and supernatural events, brought about by the agency of imaginary beings."[1] Either fairy tales were deemed too unnatural (Locke thought children should be kept innocent of most Christian dogma for the same reason) or supernatural in the wrong way (Trimmer held that early education should be grounded in catechism and Bible reading). Coleridge found a means of answering both objections with a single formula. An early exposure to the fantastic would free children from the "microscopic acuteness" and imaginative poverty marking the too "rationally educated," opening their infant minds to the mysteries of both religion *and* science:

I remember, that at eight years old I walked with [my father] one winter evening from a farmer's house, a mile from Ottery—& he told me the names of the stars—and how Jupiter was a thousand times larger than our world—and that the other twinkling stars were Suns that had worlds rolling around them—& . . . I heard him with a profound delight and admiration; but without the least mixture of wonder or incredulity. For from my early reading of Faery Tales, & Genii &c &c— my mind had been habituated *to the Vast*—& I never regarded *my senses* in any way as the criteria of my belief. [p. 8]

Coleridge's pioneering defense of fairy tales has become, along with comparable remarks by Wordsworth and Lamb, a *de rigueur* inclusion in histories of British children's literature, in which the first-generation Romantics figure as prophetic heralds of the "golden age" of Victorian children's fantasy. (It is less often remarked that the early fairy tale collections—the *Arabian Nights,* Tabart's *Popular Fairy Tales,* Edgar Taylor's translation of the Grimms—made their way in England without help from the Romantics, whose comments on fairy tales were limited mainly to private letters and unpublished works). What has been lacking, until the recent appearance of Jeanie Watson's thoughtful study *Risking Enchantment,* is a consideration, not of Coleridge's role in the domestication of fairy tales, but of the role of fairy tales in Coleridge's poetic development.

The fairy tale meant a great deal more to the Romantics—in Germany as well as in England—than a traditional form ideal for children despite its bad reputation. As a "folk" genre, the fairy tale, like the popular ballad, represented one remnant of a seemingly organic oral culture, an authentically popular form rooted in the experience and wishes of common men and women. As a fantastic genre, it offered (along with the romance and the Gothic or ghost story) a model for prose and verse narratives which could reclaim the supernatural for modern literature. Through its associations with medievalism (most fairy tales were thought to date from a feudal past), with Orientalism (via the immensely popular *Arabian Nights*), and with childhood, the fairy tale could be seen as the primitivist form par excellence, redolent of the primal and elemental, its appeal to children part and parcel of its associations with the pure childhood of culture. As such, the fairy tale seemed in addition to open a path into unconscious experience, that largely unexplored area of the psyche in which childhood remained a living presence, in which superstition and the magical or marvelous had found a last refuge from the searching critiques of the Enlightenment.

For all of these reasons, not to mention its associations with a lost "national" culture, the fairy tale became a potent literary force in late eighteenth- and early nineteenth-century Germany. The Grimms, whose *Kinder- und Hausmärchen* began appearing in 1812, were relative latecomers to the scene: Musaüs had published his *Volksmährchen der Deutschen* in 1782, a collection which played a role in Germany similar to that of Percy's *Reliques of Ancient English Poetry* in England. Goethe had already celebrated the fairy tale in *Die Leiden des Jungen Werthers* (1774), in which Werther, that connoisseur of the elemental, tells fairy stories to Lotte's younger siblings when not reading Homer and Ossian or cultivating the society of peasants and madmen. Perhaps more importantly, Goethe helped establish the literary fairy tale (or *kunstmärchen*) as a full-fledged adult form in his densely symbolic "Märchen" (1795), a work which inspired Novalis to include the equally demanding *kunstmärchen* of Klingsohr in *Heinrich von Ofterdingen* (1802). The form was also exploited to great effect by Tieck, von Eichendorff, Brentano, Morike, and Hoffmann, among others, a collective outpouring which finds no analogue in British Romantic writing. The rise of the symbolic fairy tale in England would have to wait on Victorian writers like Ruskin (whose "King of the Golden River" appeared in 1851) and George MacDonald; and even MacDonald's difficult tales remained, for the most part, tied to the dictates of the children's book industry as the German *kunstmärchen* did not. The failure of the literary fairy tale to emerge in nineteenth-century England as a viable form for adults—the only major example that comes to mind is Christina Rossetti's *Goblin Market,* and even that proved commodifiable by the children's trade—is one of several problems which Watson's study, for all its felicities, fails to address.

What Watson does show, conclusively, is that Coleridge's interest in the fairy tale was much more than incidental. Watson argues that for Coleridge, fairy tales (and the related realm of "Faery") remain a prime signifier of "the Whole" and "the Vast."

If he does not actually write fairy tales (with the exception, Watson claims, of "Christabel"), Coleridge does produce a number of "tales of Faery": that is, Coleridge draws on traditional fairy tales, and related forms like the folk ballad, for a "language and a set of genre conventions" which he employs to construct "symbolic metaphors" and (often fragmentary) symbolic narratives throughout his poetry (pp. 2, 12). "Faery" (Watson's key term) is an intentionally capacious and flexible concept, standing for a certain literary use of folk materials, for a "consubstantial" vision of the world (which is itself "symbolic" of what Watson calls the "Reality of Spirit"), and for a mythic "Other World" emblematizing a "mental space" hospitable to the magical, marvelous, or suprarational (pp. 2–3). Faery is ultimately, however, a secular term with sacred import, a metaphor for what Watson (whose fondness for capitalized abstractions rivals that of Coleridge) calls "God-Spirit-Love" or "Spirit/God/Wholeness/Love" or "Spirit/Truth/God" (pp. 29, 45). Fairy tales, it turns out—or at least tales of Faery—come true: Coleridge transforms the traditional genre into a vehicle for conveying the "sacred story of Spirit," a map for reading "the Word behind the words" (pp. 2, 31).

Watson further associates Faery with a related "cluster of symbols of Spirit": music, androgyny, nature, the soul, poetry and poetic genius (pp. 45–46). Obviously, Watson is casting a rather wide net, one that can take in almost any poem by Coleridge, as can her meta-genre "tale of Faery," which embraces dream vision, tragic ballad, dramatic fragment, and any poem about love, whether fairies or supernatural elements of any sort feature in it or not. At times, the flexibility of her categories serves Watson surprisingly well—her readings of individual poems tend to be much sharper than her loose critical model might imply. Her juxtapositions of texts rarely considered together, like "Kubla Khan" and the "Songs of the Pixies," or "The Destiny of Nations" and "The Rime of the Ancient Mariner," work well both to provide refreshingly original readings of the canonical poems and to bring neglected, worthwhile texts into consideration. Moreover, Watson's "cluster" of faery and related symbols, however generously defined, is often justified in critical application, particularly when used to bring out the significance of terms like "Fairy-Land" in "The Eolian Harp" or "elfish light" in "The Rime of the Ancient Mariner," images which might seem merely ornamental but play an important role in the symbolic systems of the poems they embellish. Watson's association of faery, poetic genius, and the bower of Romance produces a strong reading of Coleridge's late "The Garden of Boccaccio," which is convincingly presented as his "last great poem" (p. 202). And her reading of "Christabel" underscores the ambivalence of Coleridge's characterization of Geraldine by stressing this figure's usually unnoted sympathetic and even Christ-like aspects, although Geraldine's sinister side is not adequately accounted for.

The more pressing questions which one must address to this study, however, are: did Coleridge consider fairy tales as vehicles for "Truth," and should we in turn read Coleridge's "tales of Faery" in the light of the Truth they are said to convey? Coleridge certainly felt that fairy tales prepared the child auditor or reader to later accept religious teachings, much as he argued (in "The Destiny of Nations") that in the presumed childhood of culture "Superstition" paved the way for the spread of Christian teachings. But nowhere, to my knowledge, does Coleridge suggest that traditional fairy tales, or literary tales modelled on them, should themselves be read as symbolic, quasi-sacred narratives. In one of his few public comments on fairy tales—from a lecture given in 1818—Coleridge declared that the *Arabian Nights* tales "cause no deep feeling of a moral kind—whether of religion or love; but an impulse of motion is communicated to the mind without excitement, and this is the reason of their being so generally read and admired."[2] In his famous rejoinder to Anna Barbauld on the lack of a "moral" in the "Rime of the Ancient Mariner," Coleridge praises one of the Arabian tales for what a folklorist would call its "a-morality": "It ought to have had no more moral than the Arabian Night's tale of the merchant's son sitting down to eat dates by the side of a well, and throwing the shells aside, and lo! a genie starts up, and says he *must* kill the aforesaid merchant, *because* one of the dates had, it seems, put out the eye of the genie's son."[3] For Coleridge, a work of "such pure imagination" conveys an aesthetic power fundamentally unrelated to religious or moral truth, however much it may exercise the mind's capacity to suspend disbelief.

It is not the Arabian tale, however, but the "Rime of the Ancient Mariner" that Coleridge explicitly describes as a work of "pure imagination," leading one to wonder whether Coleridge would indeed have endorsed the kind of reading practiced in *Risking Enchantment*. Watson grounds her "symbolic" approach in an appeal to Coleridge's own critical practice, specifically his approach to Scriptural narratives as "living *educts* of the Imagination," forming a "system of symbols, harmonious in themselves, and consubstantial with the truths, of which they are the *conductors*" (p. 33). For Watson, Coleridge's poems are also such "*educts*," his symbols comparably "consubstantial" with transcendent truths. The entire corpus of "Faery" poems is read as luminous, immanent with transcendent meaning, gesturing toward Wholeness even when fragmentary, gesturing toward Love even when bitterly despairing. This is certainly not the way Coleridge read the poetry of his contemporaries, whose intentions might overshoot their performance, whose images or symbols might prove weak or inappropriate, whose works were altogether fair game for critical scrutiny. Although Scott, for example, (as Watson points out) worked the same poetic vein of "ballad and romance," with a fair sprinkling of fairies and other folk beliefs (p. 22), he won no points on this ground from Coleridge, who harshly dismissed Scott's poetry for its facileness (an "unspurred yet unpinioned Pegasus"), its sloppiness, and its derivative language.[4] Perhaps more to the point, Coleridge did not read Wordsworth's "Immortality" ode as gospel truth, for all its praise of the child's intimations of the "the Vast" and "the Whole." Rather, Coleridge looked sharply at Wordsworth's comparison of the child to a "philosopher" and "Mighty Prophet" and asked, "What does all this mean?" For Coleridge, Wordsworth's attribution to the child of philosophical and religious wisdom illustrated one of the characteristic defects of his poetry, "thoughts and images too great for the subject," or, more trenchantly, "*mental* bombast."[5] Perhaps it was in order to avoid just such a disjunction between the infantile and the profound that Coleridge, unlike Goethe or Novalis, chose not to write symbolic fairy tales, despite his early defense of fairy tales as reading for children, and his use of "faery" as a prime signifier of imaginative power.

A more critical, less celebratory account of Coleridge's interest in fairy tales and "faery" images might well begin with his failure to write a literary fairy tale that we would recognize as such, as opposed to, say, a hybrid of ballad, romance, and Gothic with some reference to traditional fairy tales such as one finds in "Christabel." It might also ask why, given the central position of "Wholeness" in both his philosophical and critical writings, so many of Coleridge's poems—"Kubla Khan," "Christabel," "The Ballad of the Dark Ladie," "The Three Graves"—should prove fragmentary and open-ended. Particularly given the significance of androgyny in Coleridge's poetry—a significance which Watson establishes quite convincingly—why are female figures in Coleridge's poems of "faery" so often associated with the demonic: the "Nightmare" Life-in-Death in "The Ancient Mariner," the "woman wailing for her demon lover" in "Kubla Khan," Geraldine in "Christabel"? Such questions are broached in Watson's study but not really answered: incompleteness and dissonance are accounted for by the fact that we live, and Coleridge writes, in a "fallen" world. "But the Garden also held the Snake and the Forbidden Fruit—possibilities for disorder, division, irrationality" (p. 24). This strikes me as having it both ways: Coleridge's poems either embody Wholeness or evoke it negatively in their very fragmentariness; his bleak, tragic poems of love attest to the power of Agape by illustrating the limitations of Eros; a figure like Geraldine is "necessarily *both* ambiguous *and* good" (p. 180; my italics). Ironically, in a book entitled *Risking Enchantment,* the poet never really risks anything, since he cannot fail: Coleridge either attains his poetic object directly, or gets it across despite a poem's tragic (or missing) ending, "teaching the desirability of wholeness and Love" by confronting us with their absence (p. 158).

That Coleridge might (like Scott) write a bad poem, or (like Wordsworth) come up with an inappropriate image or metaphor, is not a possibility in this study, which takes its cue from Coleridge's reading of Scripture and not from his reading of fellow poets. Not that Watson herself avoids risks: she celebrates wholeness and presence in a critical climate that favors the fragmentary and absent; she advances a frankly Christian interpretation of Coleridge at a time when secular (especially historicist) approaches are ascendant; she elucidates works of "high" culture with insights drawn from fairy tale criticism and scholarship. For all this, and for the flashes of interpretive brilliance that emerge throughout *Risking Enchantment,* one can only admire the author, even if one ends by wishing she had approached her subject less in a spirit of piety and more in a spirit of inquiry.

Notes

1. John Locke, *The Educational Writings of John Locke: A Critical Edition with Introduction and Notes,* ed. James L. Axtell (Cambridge: Cambridge Univ. Press, 1968), p. 302; Sarah Trimmer, *The Guardian of Education,* 5 vols. (London: Hatchard, 1802–06) 2:185.

2. Coleridge, *Lectures 1808–1819 On Literature,* ed. R. A. Foakes, 2 vols. (Princeton: Princeton Univ. Press, 1987) 2:191.

3. Coleridge, *Coleridge's Miscellaneous Criticism,* ed. Thomas Middleton Raysor (Cambridge: Harvard Univ. Press, 1936) p. 405.

4. Coleridge, letter to Wordsworth (early October 1810), in *Scott: The Critical Heritage,* ed. John O. Hayden (London: Routledge & Kegan Paul, 1970) p. 56.

5. Coleridge, *Biographia Literaria, or Biographical Sketches of My Literary Life and Opinions,* 2 vols., ed. James Engell and Walter Jackson Bate (Princeton: Princeton Univ. Press, 1988) 2:136–38.

The Body-Soul Topos in English Literature: The Evolution of a Literary Motif

Mona Logarbo

Rosalie Osmond. *Mutual Accusation: Seventeenth-Century Body and Soul Dialogues in Their Literary and Theological Context.* Toronto: University of Toronto Press, 1990. xiii, 284 pp.

Riddle 41 in Williamson's edition of the *Exeter Book* riddles ends as so many of the Old English riddles do, with a direct challenge to the reader or listener, whom the riddler exhorts, "Cyþe cynewordum hu se cuma hatte/eðþa se esne þe ic her ymb sprice" (ll. 15–16). The "cuma," referred to earlier in the riddle, is a noble guest in the courts, who cannot be harmed by the ravages of hunger, old age, or disease; his "esne," if he serve this lord well on their "siðfate" together, will bring about their prosperity. But if this servant attends his master badly, we are told, both will reap only sorrow, or in the riddler's metaphorical language, "cnosles unrim care," the countless offspring of sorrow. The nature of the "siðfate" which the two have undertaken, briefly alluded to at the beginning of the riddle, becomes mysterious when the riddler discloses that

> Ne wile forht wesan
> broþor oþrum. Him þæt both sceðeð
> þonne hy from bearme begen hweorfað
> anre magan ellorfuse
> moddor ond sweoster. [lines 10–14]

Is this "siðfate" literal or metaphorical? Who is the sole kinswoman, both mother and sister to the travellers who are brothers? The riddler deliberately poses these ambiguous questions but tells his audience finally that the solution does exist indeed: the reader or listener can declare it with "cynewordum," apt words. The riddler asks that we suspend our literal grasp of the subject and share his perception, and thus, we must creatively arrange our ideas to perceive the riddle's meaning.

What the Anglo-Saxon audience construed from this riddle remains unknown to us, but in 1859, Franz Dietrich proposed the solution "der Geist und der Leib" (p. 473), and this interpretation has been accepted by critics and editors since then. Using the language of kinship metaphorically, the riddler draws the distinction between body and soul, describing them as brothers and fellow travellers in this life. The bond of kinship unites them not only on their earthly pilgrimage, but throughout eternity. The riddle thus attempts to describe the nature of the body-soul relationship, and the reader infers that the riddle's ultimate concerns are death and the afterlife.

The nature of the body-soul relationship imaginatively delineated in Riddle 41 is one of the earliest European poetic expressions of an inquiry which has ancient roots and a long history, and whose main implications in Western literature have been philosophical and theological. Rosalie Osmond draws upon this tradition of body-soul literature in her work, tracing the philosophical understanding of the nature of the body-soul relationship from antiquity to the seventeenth century. Her survey of the philosophical speculation concerning the nature of the soul from the time of the pre-Socratics through the Middle Ages provides a comprehensive and enlightening overview of the development of the ideas and attitudes which shaped the body-soul genre in Western literature. By pointing out the successive stages in the amplification of the medieval literary dialogue and debate between body and soul, she provides the basis for the crux of her work: a detailed study of the seventeenth-century understanding of the nature of the body-soul relationship and its influence on the form and content of English literature of that period.

The work contains an inclusive bibliography of both primary and secondary sources, as well as many relevant explanatory footnotes which point out pertinent texts for further reference;

the well-organized index is indispensible for locating various subjects easily in the text. The appendix, which includes only William Crashaw's translation of "St. Bernard's Vision" and two later ballad versions of this work (ultimately derived from Crashaw's), would benefit a larger audience if it incorporated as well a selection from the medieval English body-soul literature which the author discusses. It would, for example, be particularly useful for the reader to have the complete *Vercelli Book* "Soul and Body I" since it (and the *Exeter Book* version) are the earliest English poetic expressions of the body-soul theme. All subsequent Insular (as well as Continental) body-soul literature has its basis in these particular works found in tenth-century English manuscripts. This appeal for extension, however, is not a criticism of a deficiency but a suggestion for widening the broad spectrum of literary sources supporting the introductory chapters. As Osmond indicates, Crashaw's translation furnishes a significant thematic and formal link between fourteenth- and seventeenth-century versions of the body-soul debate (p. 85); as the antecedent work, the Old English poem provides an extant and substantial foundation for a study of the body-soul genre in English literature.

The organization of the text of *Mutual Accusation* elucidates the development of the philosophy underlying body-soul dualism, delineates appropriate medieval sources of body-soul literature, and builds to the crescendo: a study of the body-soul theme in seventeenth-century English literature, from its traditional expression in dialogue and debate to its subtle yet pervasive poetic and dramatic representation. Osmond's purpose is not to provide an in-depth, detailed source study of the history and development of English body-soul literature, but to trace the evolution of a literary motif, highlighting the significant philosophical, theological, scientific, and literary lines of progression. She has succeeded in evoking the complexity and richness of the inquiry about self-perception, which, despite its various cultural inflections through time, reflects the universal mystery concerning the nature of the human being. As Osmond's preliminary chapters disclose, our Western philosophical inheritance of the particulars of this inquiry manifests the continuous transmission, distillation, and integration of ideas from ancient times. In part one of the book, Osmond provides the necessary philosophical and theological background on the nature of the body-soul relationship by giving a survey of the major Classical and Christian influences which conditioned the development of sixteenth- and seventeenth-century thought and shaped the contemporary literature, which is treated in part three of the book.

The development of medieval English body-soul dialogues and debates provides the connection between the purely philosophical aspects of the nature of their relationship and the literary appropriation of this theme in seventeenth-century English literature. Part two of *Mutual Accusation* sets forth a specifically literary analysis, tracing the evolution of the medieval debate genre to its embodiment in seventeenth-century body-soul dialogues. The distinctive categories of these dialogues reveal the transitional aspect of this genre during that time: the didactic dialogues, which are close in form and content to their medieval prototypes; the discursory dialogues, which convey contemporary belief and speculation concerning the nature of the soul; and the philosophical dialogues, which tend to be more abstract and speculative than the aforementioned (p. 84). This particular section of the work treats the most immediate literary background for the seventeenth-century poetry and drama, and, on the whole, it establishes an ample cadre within which to unfold the variety of seventeenth-century literary forms.

I have focused my critique on the background material in parts one and two in order to amplify certain issues and details which Osmond has brought to the foreground; I will emphasize particularly the inherent connections between the secular and religious treatment of the body-soul theme in medieval English literature. In this way, the concerns of *Mutual Accusation* will benefit a larger academic audience, particularly scholars of medieval English literature, as well as those whose inclinations are more philosophical or historical.

While in chapter 1 Osmond has traced carefully both the Classical and Christian perceptions of the body-soul relationship, she has not elaborated on the link between the ancient philosophical ideas as they are synthesized in the works of the early

Christian Fathers and the transmission of these ideas to the West. She provides an outline of the significant contributions of the Church Fathers to the growth of body-soul theology, but does not stress the importance of the link between the Church in Alexandria and that in Rome as the means by which the repository of ancient, pre-Christian ideas on the nature of the body-soul relationship make their way finally into Western literature. Body-soul theology ultimately has its roots in early Egyptian Christian literature, although the body-soul narrative itself does not arise from Christian origins.

As Osmond emphasizes in the text, certain details of the narrative, such as the dualism itself, are derived from much more primitive sources whose concerns were transmitted through the influence of Christianity: the legend, bound to the religion of ancient Egypt, was adopted by the Egyptian Fathers to further their own Christian preaching. In this manner, pagan elements found their way into homilies, saints' lives, and other forms of popular expression during the early Christian era, particularly in Alexandria where the Church was formed by Clement, Origen, and Athanasius. From the time of these early Fathers, we have certain apocryphal books, apocalypses, and saints' lives which undoubtedly were disseminated in Western Europe through Rome. The narrative may have been intentionally brought to Rome, or perhaps had a more subtle and less deliberate introduction there. Yet the close connections between the Church in Rome and the Church in Alexandria ultimately ensured this narrative's appearance in Rome (Dudley, p. 9).

As the center of the Christian Church in Egypt and as a cultural cross-roads, Alexandria was a sort of forcing-house of ideas on the nature of the soul culled from such diverse sources as Egyptian religion (both non-Christian and Christian) and the ancient mythologies at the heart of Orphism, Gnosticism, and Manicheism (these last three contributing significantly to the intellectual formation of St. Augustine). The Alexandrian Church's role, both in integrating the pieces of ancient mythological narrative with theological speculation and in introducing this material to the West in various narrative forms, reflects part of a larger pattern in the development and transmission of body-soul literature: in tracing its evolution from ancient mythologies, there appears to be a general movement from narrative (as expressed by the myths) to a more abstract, philosophical presentation (as expressed in the speculative theology on the nature of the soul), which provides substance for further narrative development. Old English body-soul literature reflects the different facets of this cyclical pattern, and the material assumes a variety of forms. The "Soul and Body" poems, the versions of the *Three Utterances of the Soul,* certain Old English homilies, and Bede's stories describing the death of holy men in the *Historia Ecclesiastica* and the *Historia Abbatum* indicate that by the tenth century, the English body-soul narrative had become a flexible literary vehicle which served primarily the needs of a popular audience. This narrative eschews the purely philosophical concerns involving the metaphysical nature of the body-soul relationship, and with its vivid visual imagery appeals strongly to the imagination.

Earlier Coptic sources such as the Macarius legend and the *Visio Pauli* provide much of the detail which colors these Old English narratives. The *Visio* itself is a seminal work in the development of the body-soul tradition in the West. As Osmond points out, much of the detail associated with the damnation of the soul—its torment by demons, the righteous soul's salvation, and the judgement meted out for suffering or bliss in the afterlife—arises from the *Visio Pauli* (p. 57). This work was written originally in Greek no later than the middle of the third century (Silverstein, p. 3), although some scholars place it in the late fourth century (Himmelfarb, pp. 16–19). The immediate sources for this apocalypse, namely the apocalypses of Peter, Elias, and Zephaniah, point to a Coptic origin (Healey, p. 19, nn. 2, 3); some of the homiletic material of Origen, Macarius, and other Egyptian Fathers on the judgement of the soul after death has been embroidered into the fabric of the *Visio Pauli* as well (Silverstein, p. 3). The *Visio* provided three significant themes around which the various elements of body-soul literature crystallized: the narrative itself, in which the departing soul is admonished to look back on its body; the respite of the damned, during which time the soul actually returned to its body to vilify or praise it;

and the punishment of the wicked, which further emphasized the alienation of soul from body.

The *Visio* was translated from Greek into Latin, and from there found expression in various European vernacular languages, particularly the Romance languages. The *Visio* also passed into English in the tenth-eleventh century, derived from a Latin version (Healey, p. 27, n. 31). The Old English body-soul narrative which evolves from this version is composed basically of two significant elements: the separation and departure of the soul from the body and the soul's address to the body, which develops specifically from the address of the sinful soul to its body, although neither the Greek and Latin sources of the *Visio* nor the Old English translation of this work contains such an address. T. D. Batiouchkof suggests that the address is a late development which evolves from the scene in the *Visio* in which the soul, after departing from its body, is admonished to look back and recognize it (pp. 23–25). This momentary glance at the body, which will share the rewards or punishments of the soul, provided the literary framework for the soul's speech of praise or blame.

Osmond, however, indicates that St. Paul's intercession on behalf of the tormented souls in Hell is the origin of the address of the damned soul to its body (p. 57); moved by the suffering of the sinful souls in Hell, St. Paul asks a respite of God for them, which he obtains. Regarding the soul's address to its body, it seems that both the admonishment to the soul to look back on its body and the respite contribute to the actual development of the address of the soul: the former provides the original impetus and the latter the occasion for the address to occur. In an eighth-century Latin version of the *Visio* (from which the Old English *Visio* is derived), God grants the suffering souls a temporary cessation on Easter of their punishment, one day and one night for eternity, and not the weekly respite from Saturday evening until Sunday night which Osmond indicates (p. 57). In terms of literary evolution, the Easter respite develops first; the weekly respite and the sporadic reprieve evolve from the significance of Sunday itself as the memorial of Christ's Resurrection.

The various recensions and translations of the Latin versions of the *Visio* provide many variants in the length of this respite, revealing the Western shift in focus from the Easter respite to a weekly one: the Urûmiah and Vatican Syriac texts give no respite; in an Armenian version, Hell is destroyed and all the sinners pardoned; in the Coptic story, the sinners are exonerated from Easter to the Ascension; in the Ethiopic, only one night's respite is granted; in the Harvard Syriac text, reprieve is given for one day and night on Sunday for all eternity (Casey, pp. 1–5). Yet in the later, shorter Latin redactions, the freedom is to be given each Sunday and its duration is stated concisely: "Nocte dominice diei et refrigerium usque in perpetuum de hora nona sabbati usque ad secundam feriam [hore prime]" (Willard, p. 968, n. 21). Thus, sometime between the long Latin versions of the eighth century and the later, pre-twelfth-century shorter redactions of the *Visio*, the nature of the respite changed from an annual to a weekly one with a clearly defined duration from the ninth hour of Saturday to the first hour of Monday.

In the Old English versions of the *Visio*, there are four durations of the respite which evolve from this tradition: annually; weekly, on Sunday; weekly, unspecified day; and sporadically. The tradition of the weekly Sunday respite links the secular literary motifs with ecclesiastical concerns: the custom of the weekly Sunday respite in the Old English versions of the body-soul narrative evolved from formal legislation which promulgated the sanctity of Sunday since it was the day of Christ's Resurrection (Levy, pp. 54–69). In the earlier versions of the *Visio*, the granting of the respite is the end of St. Paul's journey to Hell and receives less attention than the depiction of the joys of the righteous and the torments of the damned; in the later versions, the granting of the reprieve becomes the focal point of the narrative, giving the *Visio* a Sabbatarian emphasis. Because of this emphasis on Sunday, the *Visio* has been transformed into a sort of admonitory homily, and its influence on both Old English secular and religious literature is extensive.

As mentioned before, the earliest Old English poetic expression of the body-soul narrative dates from the tenth century and is found in the *Vercelli Book* "Soul and Body I" and the *Exeter Book* "Soul and Body II." These two works are the immediate predecessors of the later Middle English soul and body debates, and Osmond has done an excellent analysis of the development of the debate from these works, demonstrating the elements the two have in common, particularly the notion of the responsibility for sin. Although this specific issue implies philosophical and theological concerns, the medieval debates are not an academic exercise extolling the virtues of logical argument, but take advantage of the inherently didactic nature of the debate to address a popular audience. This literature appears to be an attempt to satisfy the popular understanding of the nature of the body-soul relationship and the responsibility for sin. On the whole, the Vercelli and Exeter poems and the contemporary literature thematically related to them reflect the appeal of penitential literature, which stressed the necessity of repentance for human salvation. The "Soul and Body" poems resemble other Old English poems such as "Christ III" and "Judgement Day II" in which the body serves as the image of the soul: the physical decay of the grave-sound body is a reflection of moral deterioration. As Allen Frantzen has pointed out, these particular poems are rooted in the penitential tradition; they echo a leitmotif which runs through the penitentials: sin through the body requires repentance through the body (pp. 187–88). The "Soul and Body" poems thus are linked intimately with both the penitential and homiletic traditions in Anglo-Saxon England.

Osmond recognizes the compatability of the various elements of the body-soul narrative with the homiletic tradition, but states that the Exeter and Vercelli poems exist "independently of any such context" (p. 58). But clearly the subject matter and details of these poems—the return of the sinful soul to excoriate its body for self-indulgence during life, the gruesome description of bodily decay, and the threat of eternal damnation and suffering—cannot be abstracted from a parenetic context. Two Old English homilies in particular bear comparison with the Exeter and Vercelli poems, namely Blickling Homily X ("Þisses Middangeardes Ende Neah Is") and Vercelli Homily IV. The theme of the Blickling homily is the inevitability of Doomsday, and the homilist employs a *memento mori* device from a third-century Latin homily of Caesarius of Arles, a warning from the bones of an entombed body to their living kinsman to clarify the abstraction that all earthly joys end in the grave (Cross, pp. 435–36). Likewise, the Vercelli homily is an appeal for repentance and righteous living and contains a passage which describes a blessed soul entreating God and the angels to return it to its body since this body had lived so ascetically; immediately following this passage, a condemned soul vilifies its body for having had to endure its excesses.

The contents and arrangement of the Exeter and Vercelli manuscripts also support the idea of the mutual connection between the homiletic and poetic material: the *Vercelli Book,* a sort of homiliary, has six poems interspersed randomly among the homilies—"Soul and Body I" is interpolated between Homily XVIII and Homiletic Fragment I. Notwithstanding its homilies, this particular codex was not meant for liturgical use (Gatch, p. 142). In the *Exeter Book* "Soul and Body II" is one of a group of didactic poems, mostly religious in nature, which convey homiletic concerns. The compiler evidently meant to underscore the homiletic affinity of this group of poems by juxtaposing them: they occur on folios 76b–100a.

The form of the Old English address conveys well the need for repentance, particularly the "Soul and Body II," which contains only the address of the sinful soul to its body (Krapp and Dobbie, *Exeter Book,* pp. 174–78). The very language of the lines describing the worm Gifer's attack on the body after death indicates that the single address of the soul to its body is consciously employed and is not just a truncated debate as Mary Ferguson has stated (p. 72). One of the first things that Gifer does is to tear the corpse's tongue into ten parts, thereby ensuring that the claims of the soul will go uncontested by the body. This action also intensifies the dramatic effect: the rotting body would not seem so grisly if it could answer the soul; the devastation of death and damnation would not be so stark. While the emphasis on the vanity of earthly pleasures in these early poems is, as Osmond notes, "a ubiquitous medieval concern" (p. 61), the poems are uniquely Anglo-Saxon in expression: the vividness and concreteness of the imagery of bodily decay reflect the understanding of a materialistic culture which grasped well the abstract in terms of the concrete. Thus is there emphasis in secular poems such as "The Seafarer" upon rewarding valor and loyalty with gold and castigating betrayal by deprivation and exile. In an analogous fashion, the penitentials and related popular literature dramatize the idea of punishment for sins through the body.

Although neither the Exeter nor the Vercelli poem exhibits the sophistication and subtlety in form or content of the seventeenth-century body-soul debates, they do reveal the unique treatment of the body-soul theme in Old English literature: body and soul here are explicitly described as kinsmen, as they are in Riddle 41. Since the pagan Germanic socio-cultural institution of kinship formed the basis for all relations in Anglo-Saxon England, this metaphor provided a vehicle for the development of medieval English body-soul literature. The reference in the poetry to the body and soul as kinsmen is a vestige of a pre-Migration Germanic concept. Henry Mayr-Harting has detailed concisely the complexity of the christianization of Anglo-Saxon England, emphasizing the various social and cultural traditions which shaped its Christianity: originally a Celtic nation conquered by Rome, Britain was invaded by Germans and Scandinavians and then converted back into the Roman sphere. The use of the kinsmen analogy in both the Exeter and Vercelli poems discloses a primitive Anglo-Saxon spirituality and reveals how a culture whose literary tradition originated in pre-Conversion oral poetry grasped the Christian conception of the proper relationship between body and soul in terms of the implications of a familiar social institution.

The Exeter and Vercelli "Soul and Body" poems are virtually identical, except that the Exeter poem does not contain the address of the righteous soul as Osmond indicates (p. 104); this address is found only in the Vercelli poem. In the first fourteen lines of this poem, a sort of prologue, the poet speaks directly to the audience, exhorting it to consider the fate of the soul after death separates it from the body, when "asyndreð þa sybbe þe ær samod wæron,/lic ond sawle" (Krapp, pp. 4–5). This separation finds dramatic expression in the case of the sinful soul, which has no formal introduction: it is abruptly introduced, described as "geohðum hremig" (line 9). From this point on, the condemned soul rebukes the body for their damnation and graphically suggests its proximity to the body during life by speaking of their union, an ironic counterpoint to the kinship which they supposedly share:

> "Eardode ic þe on innan. Ne meahte ic ðe of cuman
> flæsce befangen, on me fyrenlustas
> þine geþrungon." [ll. 33–35]

During life, the body is literally the soul's dwelling, yet their kinship is oppressively circumscribed by the body's sinful desires. This relationship continues even after death: condemned to "hellegrund" (line 104), the soul reveals that death only physically liberates soul from body; the two are still bound spiritually, although this type of kinship is perverse for them now.

Having related the consequences of physical separation and spiritual estrangement from its body, the soul incisively states that for the body, all bonds of human relationship have been severed:

> "Ne eart ðu þon leofra nænigum lifigendra
> men to gemæccan, ne meder ne fæder
> ne nænigum gesybban, þonne se swearta hrefn
> syððan ic ana of ðe ut siðode
> þurh þæs sylfes hand þe ic ær onsended wæs." [ll. 52–56]

God brings about the separation of body and soul at death: God sends the soul to the body because of his power; thus, God alone has the right to recall the soul at death through the same power. Death literally severs bonds of human relationship: the body is no longer connected to its "meder" or "fæder," who in effect represent all other relations through kinship since they are at the head of the relational structure; this configuration of kinship according to the degrees of closeness or distance involved the *sybbe,* or all of a person's cognates within a certain degree (Lancaster, p. 232). The soul also suffers here: it is beyond any type of communion with life; the body's sins have removed it from even the memory of the living. Consigned to oblivion, the soul suffers a fate comparable to that of the body.

The Body-Soul Topos in English Literature 251

In "Soul and Body I," the Judgement Day theme complements the body and soul as kinsmen theme. The soul admonishes its body that on Judgement Day

> "þonne ne bið nan na to þæs lytel lið on lime aweaxan,
> þæt ðu ne scyle for anra gehwylcum onsundrum
> riht agildan, þonne reðe bið
> dryhten æt þam dome." [ll. 97–100]

This reference to the punishment of every joint in the body does not occur elsewhere in Old English literature (except for the *Exeter Book* "Soul and Body II"); Thomas Hill thinks its appearance here as a specific corporal punishment reveals the influence of the penitential tradition on body-soul literature. Yet this allusion need not be interpreted only as a reference to that particular tradition. One of the most common ways for the Anglo-Saxons to represent the different degrees of kinship was to arrange the *sybbe* according to the joints (*glied*) of the body.[1] If the relationship between the "sybbe" mentioned at the beginning of the poem no longer exists, then figuratively, the punishment of all the joints of the body (literally "any little limb grown onto a limb") represents this dissolution. The body's punishment, the physical wrenching apart of its joints on Doomsday, is a literalization of the soul's physical separation from its body and its spiritual alienation from God. The ensuing grisly catalogue of bodily decay fulfills the soul's warning to the body concerning corporal punishment: there *is* no joint so small that it will not suffer for the body's sins. The body's impotence after death parallels the soul's powerlessness during life; their separation after death and the body's subsequent corruption in the grave accentuate the dramatic irony of their union as "sybbe" during life.

It is no doubt the forcefulness and uniqueness of the Old English "Soul and Body" poems which helped to foster the survival and development of such literature in the sixteenth and seventeenth centuries. As Osmond astutely reveals in her treatment of later English body-soul literature, the medieval content and form underwent a variety of transformations to satisfy the religious, social, and philosophical needs of the age (pp. 115–

84). It is impossible to abstract body-soul literature from its historical context, and although Osmond integrates significant historical material with the text when appropriate to highlight or explain the examples she uses, a brief historical overview at the beginning of chapter 4 ("Survivals of Body and Soul Literature in the English Renaissance") would convey some comprehensive sense of the radical political, social, and religious transformations of the period, as well as the subsequent reflection of these changes in body-soul literature.

The Tudor sovereigns, who ruled England from 1458–1603, presided over an age of phenomenal novelties: religious reform and the spirit of scientific inquiry are but two manifestations of the revolt against the transcendent orientation of medieval religion and philosophy. Thus, the humanists have a predilection for examining and analyzing original sources rather than accepting what they believed to be the tenuous authority of medieval commentators. Yet, as Osmond remarks concerning body-soul literature, "Translations from ancient sources were . . . still secondary as an influence to the survivals of the medieval period" (p. 71). Also, the medieval iconographic tradition continues to form an integral part of this literature until the late sixteenth century. Both of the foregoing issues raise the single query: precisely why did body-soul literature, so patently grounded in medieval religion, maintain its medieval tenor well into the sixteenth century in England?

The prevailing historical atmosphere provides an answer: during the dawning of an age of progress and speculation, the human mind may look backward as well as forward. Thus it is that attitudes characteristic of the fourteenth and fifteenth centuries endured well into the age of the Reformation in the literature. The variety in English Renaissance literature bears this out: Caxton introduces printed books, yet his publications consisted of translations of French prose romances and Malory's *Morte Darthur*—works whose substance was more medieval than contemporary; the Dance of Death remained a powerful image for the Elizabethan imagination; even Elizabethan lyric poetry embodies the sentiment of the transitory nature of earthly endeavors.

Another explanation for the persistence of medieval attitudes in the body-soul literature of this period lies in the conservatism of orthodox homiletic literature, whose leitmotif in the Middle Ages was the vanity and evanescence of earthly possessions and achievements against the permanence of eternal beatitude. As in the Middle Ages, this caveat voiced perfectly the ideas in the later body-soul literature. This literature did not suffer any immediate and drastic changes in the sixteenth century simply because the appeal of its subject was so universal. Even Puritanism, with its "excessive contempt for the medieval past, its insensitivity toward sacramental values" (Dickens, p. 320), embraced the *contemptus mundi* aspect of body-soul literature, as Osmond illustrates (p. 85).

The theological and philosophical complexities inherent in the body-soul dialectic find renewed expression and adaptation in seventeenth-century English literature, as Osmond's exposition in part three of *Mutual Accusation* amply illustrates. While her aim is not to set forth an exhaustive treatment of this body of literature, her analyses are comprehensive and insightful: her explication of Donne, Marvell, Milton, and Shakespeare, among others, provides a touchstone with which one may measure and interpret the contemporary literature. During the seventeenth century, the body-soul theme proliferates in secular poetry and drama, and the protean imagery of the Metaphysical Poets heralds a true metamorphosis of form and content in the body-soul genre. Challenged by the prevailing intellectual spirit of their age, poets such as Donne strove, according to Osmond, "to produce startling effects of irony and paradox" in their works (p. 115).

Obsessed by the relationship between physical and spiritual love, Donne attempts to reconcile them in much of his poetry. Osmond rightly indicates that this particular predilection originates in the "Aristotelian concept of the body as the instrument of the soul, enabling the soul to exercise its faculties" (p. 116). Yet the body-soul theme in the metaphysical poetry has not been impressed into the service of purely philosophical speculation: while these poets may have been predisposed to abstract interests in their contemplation of problems of ultimate reality, they are more the inheritors (although at several removes) of the Provençal troubadours, who glorified *amor,* or personal love, as a religious experience. Thus, Donne avers the primacy of men and women as living personalities and not just abstract ideas. In the unity of both body and soul, the self is fulfilled, as Osmond emphasizes in her analysis of Donne's "Aire and Angels" (pp. 117–18).

The Metaphysical Poets endow the reciprocal experience of love with profound dimension in their quest: how can the spirit function through the flesh, which encumbers its activity; how does love concerned with the fragility of the flesh assume an aspect of divinity? When the poet attempts to express these problems, he yields to paradox and incongruity, using imagery which suggests the fundamental conflict at the heart of the problem itself. The clash of terms is for the poet the spark which illuminates reality. In Donne's poetry, this reality is especially complex and powerful. His appeal to concrete, individual experience and his justification of love as a natural passion of the human heart in which both body and soul participate transform the body-soul theme to adumbrate the modern sexual ethic.

To accommodate the demands of metaphor in poetry and drama, seventeenth-century authors expanded and exploited the body-soul analogies which have colored the narrative from ancient times. Osmond's explication of these analogies in chapter 7 constitutes an appropriate prelude to the book's coda, a study of these analogies as an integral motif in Jacobean drama. Her treatment of this issue extends further than identification of superficial narrative patterns in the drama. In her analyses of certain characters in *The Atheists Tragedy, The White Devil,* and *The Malcontent,* she proves that the variety of uses of the body-soul topos "does not mean that it functions randomly as an extraneous piece of decoration" (p. 165), but often may be integral to an implied comparison between internal and external corruption. In *The Dutch Courtesan,* for example, whores who sell their bodies (and souls) are likened to politicians who sell "honor, justice, faith" (p. 165). In this one image, private, individual corruption is inextricably bound to public depravity.

Osmond's brief analysis of Shakespeare's *Othello* and *Measure for Measure* brings her survey of seventeenth-century English body-soul literature to an appropriate end. The general movement in this genre in English literature from the Middle Ages to the seventeenth century has been from a straightforward, literal treatment of the body-soul theme to a figurative presentation. This progression is manifested clearly in the literature: the medieval body-soul dialectic functions as a sort of conscience, as an admonition to set the errant faithful on the path of an ascetic life. The reproductions in the text from the Cambridge University library manuscript depicting Philibert's vision of Soul and Body debating are an iconographic literalization which epitomizes the medieval understanding of body-soul dualism. While the later poetry and drama may not belong under the formal rubric of body-soul literature, it provides a reified presentation of the body-soul motif to lay bare the complexity, often the perversity, at the heart of human relationships.

Osmond's fine interpretation of Iago as the evil, controlling soul, Desdemona as the unwitting, powerless body, and Othello, then, as "the battleground of soul and body" (p. 183) who cannot distinguish the two, illuminates a neglected aspect of seventeenth-century literature. But the proper study of the body-soul conflict does not end here: Osmond asseverates in her work that the modern focus of such literature has shifted from a moral to a psychological orientation as we seek a satisfactory manner of expressing "the dualistic experience of the self" (p. 187). This quest, it seems, is a manifestation of an integral, vital part of human nature; *Mutual Accusation* attests to its primacy.

Note

1. Arranging the *sybbe* according to the joints of the body put the father and mother at the head; brothers and sisters at the neck; first cousins at the shoulders; second cousins at the elbow; third cousins at the wrists; and fourth, fifth, and sixth cousins at the joints of the fingers (Lancaster, pp. 232–33). The Anglo-Saxon laws contain few references to this sort of classification: an eleventh-century Northumbrian Priests' Law uses "cneowe" ("knee") to designate the degree of kinship (Whitelock, p. 438, no. 61.1), but as Lancaster

suggests, perhaps the paucity of direct references concerned with ordering the kindred this way indicates that these terms were common knowledge (p. 233).

Works Cited

Batiouchkof, T. D. "Le débat de l'âme et du corps." *Romania*, 20 (1891), 1–55, 513–78.

Casey, R. "The Apocalypse of Paul." *Journal of Theological Studies*, 34 (1933), 1–32.

Cross, J. E. "The Dry Bones Speak—A Theme in Some Old English Homilies." *JEGP*, 56 (1957), 434–39.

Dickens, A. G. *The English Reformation*. New York: Schocken Books, 1976.

Dietrich, Franz. "Die Rätsel des Exeterbuchs: Würdigung, Lösung and Herstellung." *Zeitschrift fur deutsches Altertum*, 11 (1859), 448–90.

Dudley, Louise. *Egyptian Elements in the Legend of the Dead*. Baltimore: Furst, 1911.

Ferguson, Mary H. "The Structure of the Soul's Address to the Body in Old English." *JEGP*, 69 (1970), 72–80.

Frantzen, Allen. *The Literature of Penance in Anglo-Saxon England*. New Brunswick: Rutgers Univ. Press, 1983.

Gatch, Milton. "Eschatology in the Anonymous Old English Homilies." *Traditio*, 21 (1965), 117–65.

Healey, Antonette D., ed. *The Old English Vision of St. Paul*. Speculum Anniversary Monographs 2. Cambridge: Mediaeval Acad., 1978.

Hill, Thomas. "Punishment According to the Joints of the Body in the Old English 'Soul and Body II.'" *Notes and Queries*, 214 (1969), 246.

Himmelfarb, Martha. *Tours of Hell: An Apocalyptic Form in Jewish and Christian Literature*. Philadelphia: Univ. of Pennsylvania Press, 1983.

Krapp, George P. *The Vercelli Book*. Vol. 2 of *Anglo-Saxon Poetic Records*. 6 vols. New York: Columbia Univ. Press, 1931–53.

Krapp, George P., and Elliott V. Dobbie, eds. *The Exeter Book*. Vol. 3 of *Anglo-Saxon Poetic Records*. 6 vols. New York: Columbia Univ. Press, 1931–53.

Lancaster, Lorraine. "Kinship in Anglo-Saxon Society." *British Journal of Sociology*, 9 (1958), 230–50, 359–77.

Levy, Max. *Der Sabbath in England: Wesen und Entwicklung des englischen Sonntags*. Leipzig: Tauchnitz, 1933.

Mayr-Harting, Henry. *The Coming of Christianity to England*. New York: Schocken, 1972.

Silverstein, Theodore, ed. *Visio Sancti Pauli: The History of the Apocalypse in Latin, Together with Nine Texts*. Studies and Documents 4. London: Christopher's, 1935.

Whitelock, Dorothy, ed. *English Historical Documents c. 500–1042*. Vol. 1 of *English Historical Documents*. 12 vols. New York: Oxford Univ. Press, 1955.

Willard, Rudolph. "The Address of the Soul to the Body." *PMLA*, 50 (1935), 957–83.

Williamson, Craig, ed. *The Old English Riddles of the Exeter Book*. Chapel Hill: Univ. of North Carolina Press, 1977.

A New Dreiser Biography—
For Our Time

Frederick C. Stern

Richard Lingeman. *Theodore Dreiser: At the Gates of the City, 1871–1907.* Vol. 1. New York: G. P. Putnam's Sons, 1986. 478 pp.

Richard Lingeman. *Theodore Dreiser: An American Journey, 1908–1945.* Vol. 2. New York: G. P. Putnam's Sons, 1990. 544 pp.

The frontispiece of volume 1 of Richard Lingeman's 1022-page, two-volume Dreiser biography shows us the young subject of the work, "circa 1893," in four-in-hand tie and stiff stand-up collar, with burning eyes and full, jutting lips, looking youthfully intense and arresting. The frontispiece for volume 2 shows us the Dreiser of 1928, wrapped in a winter coat and scarf, a fancy walking stick in hand, hair much thinner, eyes looking sideways, but still intense, still arresting. In 1893 the young Dreiser was working as a reporter for the St. Louis *Globe-Democrat,* edited by the able Joseph McCullagh, who saw in the young man from Terre Haute abilities as a reporter. By 1928 the young reporter had become, by turns, editor of "ladies' fashion magazines," essayist, subject of and participant in controversy, and from the publication of *Sister Carrie* on always novelist. By 1928 he was the author of the novel some think of as his most important, certainly his most famous work, *An American Tragedy,* published at the very end of 1925. Richard Lingeman's biography charts the journey from one frontispiece to the other, and from before the first one and beyond the second one to the novelist's death, in a biography that I find a pleasure to read and believe to be a major contribution to Dreiser scholarship.

There have been several quite good biographies of Dreiser, in particular Robert H. Elias's *Theodore Dreiser: Apostle of Nature,* which most critics have heretofore found the most compelling, but also W. A. Swanberg's good *Dreiser,* and others.[1] I enjoyed Lingeman's books very much. Yet I wondered why, and indeed if, we need a new biography of a major literary figure every few decades. In a telephone interview (17 September 1991) with Lingeman at his office at *The Nation*—he is the journal's Executive Editor—I asked him why he had decided to write a new biography of Dreiser. "I felt the others were good," he replied, "but there is new information, and the earlier books had the faults of their times." In regard to Elias's work, Lingeman pointed out that Elias did not have sufficient space to cover all aspects of Dreiser's life. Even in the 1970 revision that corrects "my errors that had escaped my final check" and rewrites "passages that subsequent research by me and others showed to be in need of modification" (p. vii) of the original 1948 edition, Elias's book is only 435 pages long. Furthermore, Lingeman pointed out, "Helen was alive [when Elias was writing] and sensitive." The remark refers to Helen Dreiser, the novelist's second wife. Dreiser met Helen Patges Richardson in 1919. He fell in love with her, lived with her, fought with her, neglected her, pained her with his many affairs, depended on her, and eventually, in 1943, after the death of his first wife, married her. It was a tempestuous relationship that Elias—who knew the Dreisers—could not have presented as fully and absorbingly as Lingeman does and still have spared Helen's feelings about what was, perhaps, the single most important relationship in Dreiser's life, other than that with his mother. In regard to Swanberg's biography, Lingeman said: "He tries to be fair, but he disliked Dreiser. He focused too much on his faults." That seems to me an accurate description of Swanberg's book, which in many other ways is quite fine.

"I also tried to write a more spacious biography," Lingeman went on, "and I was trying to do more, given the time that has passed, with the relationship of the works to the times in which they were written. I was trying to tie the works to the times more completely." It seems to me that Lingeman succeeds admirably in this regard. Lingeman told me that he believed he had more contact with what he called "the old left community" that meant a

A New Dreiser Biography

good deal in Dreiser's life, than did the earlier biographers. "We should look back on the political aspects of the life with more sympathy, more understanding," he said. He was referring, I presume, to Dreiser's joining the American Communist Party near the end of his life and his long-standing sympathy for and defense of the Soviet Union and Stalin himself, to his early objections, later overcome, to the entry of the Allies into World War II, and to other political stands that may now seem idiosyncratic, if not foolish. "In a reverse way," Lingeman also told me, his biography was written in support of and in the furthering of "the realistic social novel. We have gotten away from that more than we should. We need more books like Updike's *Rabbit* books or Russel Banks's novels. That neglect, I think, is pointed up indirectly by my biography of Dreiser." I will return to this comment.

Dreiser is certainly a major figure in the fiction of the United States, and one whose work, even now, nearly half a century after his death, continues to be controversial. I will permit myself the reporting of a personal experience, to illustrate this briefly. When I published my *F. O. Matthiessen, Christian Socialist as Critic* a decade ago, surprisingly much attention was directed to the chapter dealing with Matthiessen's book *Theodore Dreiser*.[2] Some accused me of speciously defending Matthiessen's defense of Dreiser. Others thought it was the best thing in my book *because* it defended both Matthiessen *and* Dreiser. The argument then, and, though perhaps to a lesser degree now, turns on the importance of a writer whose style is so cumbersome, whose interest in the "belletristic" is so slight, and whose books are so determinedly, to use Lingeman's phrase, "realistic social novels." The post-modern—oh, that much used and abused phrase—has given us a fiction which really makes very little effort to render "reality" in any direct way. Contemporary theory has convinced us that to do so is impossible, that it is in the very nature of language to hide, and to some degree to obfuscate whatever the relationship may be between an "outside" and an "inside" the text, if we can establish a relationship at all. The "realistic social novel," therefore, is much in disrepute in some quarters. This is not to say that there are not fictional efforts, and important, richly intriguing ones, to put the reader in touch with something *like* the reality a Dreiser, an Updike, attempt to offer us. Whether it is DeLillo or Carver, Dorfman, Allende, Cortazar or, above all, the master of the genre, Gabriel Garcia Marquez, post-modern writers whose concerns are, in some sense, socio-political—like Dreiser's—have found devices other than efforts to render reality in seemingly unmediated, direct ways, and found these devices more effective than they find those of that school of realism and "naturalism" that Dreiser most richly represents. Compared to "magic realism," or other such post-modern devices, Dreiser does seem hopelessly old-fashioned in his ponderous way. Whether it is the frequent intervention in the narratives of some unidentified authorial voice, or the circumlocutious descriptive passages that festoon his works, we find in Dreiser—even those of us who continue to admire him—much that is clumsy, out-of-date, awkward.

Nevertheless, Dreiser is not just historically important. It is not only his battles against the "puritans"—often in tandem with his friend, defender, and, at times, most severe critic H. L. Mencken—that make him significant, nor is he only an interesting "datum" in the history of the letters of the U.S. He is a writer of enormous sympathy for the disadvantaged, of enormous understanding for the mind of that peculiar American character, "the capitalist," "the financier," of profound and sympathetic insight into the mind of the murderer driven not by sheer brutality but by the untrammeled desire for place, money, and power. Long before the advent of feminism, he created an "American girl" that makes Henry James's version seem a peculiarity of class rather than a product of "typicality." Dreiser is, in these ways—if not in felicity of language or grace of execution—the closest thing the United States has ever produced to a Balzac, a writer of "the human comedy." Few critics, I think, will dispute this from the point of view of his subject matter, or the range of his interests. The dispute centers on the value *qua* art of his fiction as literary product rather than as social reportage.

Lingeman's biography re-emphasizes the degree to which Dreiser saw himself as a defender of "truths" that the "puritans" attempted to cover up and keep him from telling. They were not

A New Dreiser Biography

truths very friendly to the culture in which the novelist lived. He saw deeply into its consumerism and other false values. Though he understood both the negatives and the positives that drive the financier or the poor-boy-turned-murderer, or the putative "genius" artist, he made no apologies for them. Instead he connected them to the culture in which they waxed and condemned not the individuals, not the Carrie Meebers, Jennie Gerharts, Cowperwoods, Eugene Witlas, or Clyde Griffiths—but the values they acquired from the society that spawned and shaped them. "As he admired the strong and sympathized with the weak," writes Matthiessen, "he became deeply involved with both. As he kept groping to find more significance in their lives than any his mind could discover, he dwelt on the mystery of the inexplicable as no rigorous mechanist would have done."[3] That is accurate, I believe, and I believe Lingeman's biography, better than any hitherto written, helps us to understand the wellsprings for these ideas and feelings in Dreiser. Lingeman gives a full-length "portrait of the artist" that does much to help us understand his art.

He does not hide Dreiser's many wens and warts and makes no apologies for Dreiser's many follies, peculiarities and idiosyncracies; he does let us understand how, from the brooding depths of the man's own suffering, despite his sometime vainglorious self-seeking, despite the foibles of his sexual life and his other personal relations, he retained a monumental integrity in the fiction he wrote. That is a good deal, and, in part perhaps, it is this sense of the novelist's sources in his own life and sympathies that give warrant to Lingeman's stated aim to promote a greater emphasis on the "realistic social novel." Lingeman repeatedly points to sources in Dreiser's own experience for the qualities of the characters he created in the novels. Time and again, and beyond anything Elias or Swanberg have been able to do, Lingeman demonstrates that Dreiser looked to his *experience*, often to his searching investigations, not unlike those of the contemporary "investigative reporter," to arrive at his characters' qualities. The term "realistic" is here given a very particular meaning, not just the usual "imitating reality from the writer's imagination" but something like "imitating reality from the writer's imagination *as formed by her or his examination of particular models which we can identify.*" It is this last phrase that makes, I think, a difference. If one considers here the Lukacian notion of "typicality" in character, one can see that, though Dreiser was no Marxist—not even when he almost simultaneously joined the Communist Party and started going to church—he did attempt, as a "realist," if not as a "naturalist," to give us characters that exemplified the culture about which he was trying to tell the truth. In his penultimate paragraph in volume 2, Lingeman writes:

> He was the most "American" of novelists. His hungry curiosity probed the nooks and crannies of the national life, as he sought to perform what he saw as his mission—understanding a large, youthful, dynamic country that had no deep roots in the past and that was in a perpetual state of change and becoming. He retained a deep compassion for the voiceless mass of individuals in this land; their tawdry dreams and desires had for him the beauty of prayers. [v.2, p. 482]

Does Lingeman offer us new materials about Dreiser? Certainly he does. For example, there is Donald Pizer's important book *The Novels of Theodore Dreiser* to draw upon, and the same critic's edition of *Theodore Dreiser: A Selection of Uncollected Prose*.[4] These books were not available to either Elias or Swanberg, though, of course, the raw data were available in several crucial Dreiser repositories. There is the extensive work of Thomas P. Riggio in his edition of *Dreiser's American Diaries, 1902–1906* and the *Dreiser-Mencken Letters,* both published in the '80s, the latter especially frequently drawn upon by Lingeman.[5] There are also some Lingeman interviews that Elias and others did not have. Most interesting among these are the interviews with the Englishman Cedric Belfrage, founding editor of the left-wing weekly newspaper *The National Guardian,* expelled from the United States during the worst of the McCarthy era—and in his younger days, in 1940, Dreiser's assistant. There is much more as well, material added to the Dreiser archives, especially at the University of Pennsylvania's Van Pelt Library. It seems clear that Lingeman did have new materials to draw upon, and that these materials amplified and explained a good deal.

Was much of it new, however, in another sense, in the sense

that it lets us see Dreiser in a new way, or permits us to interpret his works differently than had been the case, or enables us to understand them better? I am not so sure of such a claim. Certainly Lingeman's more ample, more richly documented work gives us a good deal more to go on than we had before, but by and large his and Elias's conclusions are similar. This is not to say that Lingeman's use of the new materials is not valuable, and will not prove invaluable for future Dreiser scholarship and criticism. Sometimes the amplifications, whether based on new materials or ingenious use of existing materials, are such that they extend and solidify what we already knew. For one example, I found the episode in Dreiser's life, after the first abortive publication of *Sister Carrie* but before he was to go on to a prosperous stint of magazine editing, when he was really down and out, close to suicide, left with "one dollar and fifty-six cents" (v. 1, p. 369) after paying his rent, interesting in Elias, but deeply moving in Lingeman, who—Dreiser-like—piles detail on detail, drawing extensively on Paul Dresser's *The Songs of Paul Dresser* for his sources. I think it fair to say that, in this instance as in others, it is Lingeman's style—his journalist's, magazine-writer's style, that compares favorably with Elias's more scholarly writing, and that Lingeman has used his resources very well.

Another issue these volumes raise has to do with Dreiser's place in "the canon." In light of the on-going effort to rethink "the canon" in the literature of the United States, one wonders if Lingeman's biography will not help create a somewhat more prestigious place for Dreiser's work than it now occupies. The reshaping of the canon has many elements and aspects, only one of which is a reconsideration of the notion of "the beautiful" in literature. If we are no longer so sure that standards of literary excellence can derive only from the criteria which several generations learned from the New Critics, or, in a direct line of descent, from Matthew Arnold; if we are no longer so certain that there is only one standard for "the best that has been thought or said," then perhaps the attack on Dreiser which has, all too often, relegated him to the place of literary pioneer without much intrinsic merit will be rethought. If so, then Lingeman's biography will be a primary document in any such rethinking.

Finally, I want to add one more to the many merits I find in Lingeman's work. I find important the biographer's great sympathy—not unlike the novelist's for the characters he created—for his subject. It is not an uncritical sympathy. Lingeman is of our time, and he is a writer who makes no effort to hide his political sympathies, those of the Executive Editor of one of the country's most important left journals, and he judges Dreiser accordingly. He does help us to understand, even more fully than Elias or Matthiessen did, how Dreiser could have made the political choices he did make. Lingeman also makes us feel sympathetic toward the writer's enormous struggles to complete his work—perhaps more so in regard to the embattled and long-delayed *The Bulwark* than any other book. He makes us understand the importance in Dreiser's life of financial insecurity, whether real, as at times it was, or only imagined, as it sometimes was. But he is by no means uncritical of his subject, even when he is sympathetic. We see Dreiser's vaingloriousness, his frequent self-deceptions, his incessant, callous using of women, his at times venomous anti-Semitism, his political naivete, anglophobia, jealousies, occasional dishonesties and frequent streaks of overblown ego and egotism. But these flaws, serious as they are, do not erode Lingeman's fundamental sympathy, nor ours. Even in considering the novels, Lingeman makes no excuses for the gaucheries of *The "Genius"* or the weaknesses of *The Bulwark* or *The Stoic*. But he also sees their essential importance, their essential quality. As he relates the stories of the novels' creation, reports to us Dreiser's sources, he also tries, usually successfully, to explore the novels' meanings, to give us thoughtful "readings" of the works, to evaluate them and to judge them. That is all to the good, especially because it comes from a biographer both so sympathetic to—and so aware of the flaws of—his subject's creative history.

Two things do trouble me about these volumes, despite my general admiration for them. The first is a matter of substance, the second a matter of form. The substantial matter has to do with what I will call Lingeman's occasionally unwarranted psychologizing of his subject in relation to the fictions he wrote. I do not mean that I distrust Lingeman when he presents psychological reasons for Dreiser's choices of subject matter, nor do I find his notations of similarities between Dreiser and his characters unwarranted. Indeed, often these moments are illuminating, as when he writes of Dreiser's state as comparable to Cowperwood's while he was completing *The Stoic*.

> Dreiser and Cowperwood were at the same stage in their respective life cycles; fiction and reality rubbed uncomfortably close. Cowperwood's greatest triumphs were behind him; he was engaged in one final grand project, which he would not live to complete. Dreiser's greatest novel was behind him. Although he would tell an interviewer that his best work was still to come, he sometimes feared he was through. Recently, gazing at a portrait of himself by Wayman Adams, which Kirah Markham said he liked because it made him look like a successful financier, he had remarked despondently to a friend, "I am not that man any more." His sense of his own physical decline is refracted through Cowperwood. [v. 2, p. 374]

Lingeman's comments are sometimes less convincing, however, when their psychoanalytic freight is heavier. In connection with *The Bulwark*, Lingeman pushes strongly the notion that Dreiser saw in Solon Barnes something of his own father. Quoting Vera Dreiser, a psychologist and the novelist's niece, Lingeman writes: "His niece Vera Dreiser thought he was 'identifying his own father with the character in his trials and tribulations'" (v. 2, p. 440). He repeats this notion later, in his own words:

> Solon still retains vestiges of the father figure that served as a model for him in the earlier version of the novel. In being humbled by tragedy he learns that discipline is not an end in itself; it must be tempered by mercy. He realizes that he had not been understanding enough with Stewart, as the Reverend McMillan was not with Clyde Griffiths, as Dreiser believed his father had not been with his children. [v.2, p. 462]

Too much is speculative here, I think, about Dreiser's motivation and feeling; too much is not supported, so far as I can tell, in any significant way. There are a number of instances like this, but they are a minor flaw in the work. More often, Lingeman supports his psychologizing pretty well, and in those instances gives us solid insights.

The problem in form has to do with the notes to the two volumes. They seem inordinately clumsy and difficult to follow. There are no indications in the text that there is a note. If one thinks that a statement, quote, or other item might be based on some source, and one wishes to check that reference, or if one suspects some explanatory comment might be available, one must turn to the back of the volume, find the appropriate chapter number, and then comb the listing of unnumbered notes, not even keyed to page numbers in the text itself, until one finds a phrase that reflects the material one wishes to check. Thus, if one is interested in the source of a particular item in the middle of a chapter, one must approximate where in the list of notes this particular item might be, attempt to figure out just what the key phrase is under which the item might be listed, and then search the chapter's notes to find it. It is not that the notes aren't plentiful; and I can vouch, to the degree that I have checked, that they are accurate. It is just that they are very hard to follow.

I asked Lingeman, in my telephone conversation with him, why he used this notation system. He told me that he thought it was unobtrusive, that he has used it in his other books, and—his honesty does him credit—that though his publishers had wanted him to use another system, he had insisted on this one. I suppose for the reader who reads purely for narrative, these notes represent no problem. For the reader, however, who wishes to follow the scholarship of the volumes, who sometimes wonders about the validity of a conclusion, or who otherwise wishes to follow the research process, they are a pain. Perhaps this is a mere quibble on my part—but I take it that every review, even of an important and otherwise much appreciated work, is entitled to one such quibble.

Do we *need* a new biography of each important literary figure for every generation? I don't know that Lingeman's fine books have answered my question, but they have suggested that we can *use* these new volumes. His sensitivity to political issues, his use of new materials, and materials of his own investigation, his boundless, nonetheless critical sympathy for his subject, his searching analysis of Dreiser's writings—all these have given us, I believe, a new "standard" biography of a writer who is of enormous importance. Will the biography help to re-emphasize the "realistic social novel," as Lingeman seems to hope? I'm not so sure of that, given the post-modern impulse that questions the ability of language to reflect reality in any direct way. But the biography will re-emphasize the importance, the richness, and the validity of Dreiser's achievement. That is the most one can ask at this moment in our cultural history. This biography will last and will be used, appreciated, debated—and, in time, replaced by another biography of Dreiser for another generation. Lingeman's biography is an indispensable work not only in Dreiser studies but also in our efforts to re-examine "the canon," to re-examine a particular moment in the United States's literary and social history, and to reassert the value of sympathy for, and the effort to understand, those who cannot speak for themselves.

Notes

1. Robert H. Elias, *Theodore Dreiser: Apostle of Nature*, Emended ed. (Ithaca: Cornell Univ. Press, 1970), Original ed. New York: Knopf, 1948; W. A. Swanberg, *Dreiser* (New York: Scribners, 1965).

2. Frederick C. Stern, *F. O. Matthiessen: Christian Socialist as Critic* (Chapel Hill: Univ. of North Carolina Press, 1981), pp. 175–218.

3. F. O. Matthiessen, *Theodore Dreiser* (New York: William Sloan Associates, 1951), p. 238.

4. Donald Pizer, *The Novels of Theodore Dreiser* (Minneapolis: Univ. of Minnesota Press, 1976); Pizer, ed., *Theodore Dreiser: A Selection of Uncollected Prose* (Detroit: Wayne State Univ. Press, 1977).

5. Theodore Dreiser, *American Diaries, 1902–1906*, ed. Thomas P. Riggio (Philadelphia: Univ. of Pennsylvania Press, 1982); *Dreiser-Mencken Letters*, ed. Thomas P. Riggio, 2 vols. (Philadelphia: Univ. of Pennsylvania Press, 1986).

Byron in Context

Malcolm Kelsall

Peter W. Graham. *"Don Juan" and Regency England*. Charlottesville: University Press of Virginia, 1990. xii, 219 pp.

In an essay for Jerome J. McGann's *Historical Studies and Literary Criticism* (1985), Marilyn Butler suggested that "the writings of the past ask for an educated reading, as far as possible from within their own discourse or code or cultural system" (p. 1). Peter Graham's *"Don Juan" and Regency England* offers just such an "educated reading" of Byron's cosmopolitan and English comic epic. The aim is to examine the poem "as part of a literary discourse and as a picture of the culture that frames it" (p. 7). This is a study, therefore, of the way contexts shape textual meanings. But they are not the contexts which might most obviously come to the educated reader's mind. The book begins in "certain corners" of Regency England, deliberately away from the implied (but undefined) center. The first chapters concern the suppressed prefatory material to *Don Juan;* then Southey's *Letters from England,* which Byron perhaps never read. Next comes Regency pantomime, which, if it is "literary discourse," is discourse without words on the margin of literature. Lastly, by way of prolegomena, Professor Graham examines Lady Caroline Lamb's *Glenarvon,* a poor novel which Byron detested.

This is a boldly peripheral beginning, and highly successful. To understand why it succeeds requires setting aside the author's modesty, which is part of the attractiveness of his style and intrinsic in the Horatian and empirical methodology. For these essays, in our own cultural context, are symptomatic of a revolution in method. They may be likened to Simon Schama's *Citizens.* I choose Schama's chronicle history of the revolution of 1789 as an appropriate symbol, for the bicentennial of the revolution in

France coincided in contemporary history with the destruction of totalitarian theory and practice across half of Europe in 1989. It is not an accidental conjunction, for both the practical revolution in Europe and the intellectual revolution in critical methodology are marked by a strong opposition to *a priori* theory, and thus to practical or ideological totalitarianism. Faced with the multiplicity and multivalency of the events of 1789, Schama was driven to a descriptive typology of cultural events and artifacts— a social history of ballooning, or the preparation of Mirabeau's bier—ordering chaos by the device of consecutive narrative. There can be no explicatory theory. So too, like the fall of the Bastille, the demolition of the Berlin Wall may be "read" in our own times as a symbolic act, but a symbol uncontainable by the limitations of its ideological opposition to "totalitarianism" because the meanings of the word "freedom" which it evokes are limitlessly multivalent.

There is an obvious connection between Schama's narrative method and the intricate perplexities of *Don Juan*. So too there is a clear historic link between Byronic opposition to Congressional Europe in 1815 and the overthrow of the Marxist empire. In a lesser way (and the word "lesser" is descriptive, not pejorative) Graham's *"Don Juan" and Regency England* also shares the same liberal spirit. Because its aim is to give the intricately detailed portrait of a culture, it follows that the reader must eschew any predetermined conclusions arising from theoretical interpretations—such as those familiar critical postulates which censure or praise a writer or culture in terms of the critic's *a priori* race, class, or gender stereotypes (what is sometimes called, in a phrase which Orwell would have understood, "political correctness"). Likewise, the intricacies of the Byronic text, and its resistant individuality, cannot be collectivized into some reified abstraction, such as "Romanticism," whether that "Romanticism" is traditionally based on the usual canonical writers, or reassembled from alternative texts. If there is no Romantic canon, then there is no "Romanticism."

That is why it is ideologically important that Graham begins in "certain corners"—for there is no center to occupy. His "intricately detailed portrait of a culture" is distinguished by its "mobility" (to use a favored Byronic word), constructed from a flow of displacements and contratexts linguistic and generic, a series of textual and temporal juxtapositions, a heteroglossia of parabasistic ironies and chronotopic relativities (to allude to the two principal critics who nourish his interpretations: Friedrich Schlegel and Mikhail Bakhtin). His "educated reading," therefore, cannot be hegemonic, but must always be, as he claims, "transgressive," or, to adopt a Schlegelian term, "hovering" about the text. Thus "education" cannot be a closed (or canonical) enterprise, nor can it lead to a reading for which there are easy, *a priori* short cuts. The wider the literary culture of the critic and the more detailed and local the historical placing of the text, then the more clearly one sees its multivalency and meanings. This methodology demands of the critic the same discipline, even training, as that of a good editor. There is an open-ended play about the process, also, which sees all artifacts within a culture as potentially interrelated, so that the appearance of the latest volume of Wordsworthian metaphysics, or the marketing of diluted beer, are contemporaneously both significant indices of Regency culture, and provide ways of explicating Byron.

This is brilliantly illustrated by the equal weight given by the commentary at various times both to Byron's debate with Wordsworth and the Lakers, and to his reflections on beer-drinking. The first the literary critic might take as a common matter for analysis (more of that in a moment), but the literary significance of Regency brewing practices is less obvious. Yet the stability of the price of a pint of beer in the eighteenth century had been one of the indices of the very stability of society itself, "part of the nature of things in that limited horizon of certainty that every society takes for granted" (p. 175). One of the most obvious effects of the revolutionary wars was both to destabilize the price of a staple product (the common drink of the people), and to induce the regular practice of "beer doctoring." Thus, when Byron wrote, "And when I think upon a pot of beer—/But I won't weep . . ." beneath the flippant triviality he is reflecting upon the social degeneration of British society under the financial pressure of counter-revolutionary conflict; and when he introduces "thin potations" for John Bull into the *ubi sunt* catalogue, the local event becomes a symptom both of the transience of all things, and of Byron's Cuvieresque vision of imperial decline and fall. In this way the mobility of things is made *mobile*, for "the diminished nature of beer is a symptom of social degeneracy even the bluff common man can detect" in Regency society (p. 175). By incorporating social commonplaces (*communia*) into his epic, Byron has made the poetic sublime comprehensible to everyman, and an epic about everyman.

There is an important distinction to be drawn here (as Graham argues) between this kind of demotic (and flippant) mode in Byron, and the more flat-footed democratic politics of Wordsworth and the Lakers generally. It is a particularly teasing problem, for the cultural methodology of *"Don Juan" and Regency England* inevitably produces a conflation between Byron and his literary antitypes which is unsettling. The conflation is inevitable because the mosaic method of assembling a cultural image by juxtaposing discrete tesserae must produce unexpected conjunctions—the crucial question being whether contiguity implies connection. When connections are convincingly established, as they usually are in these essays, one becomes aware of how much Byron is seeking to define his own position by nice distinction from that of the apostate democrats he so often ridiculed, and yet resembled. This is brilliantly shown, for instance, in analysis of Byron's Scriblerian subversion of Wordsworth's preface to "The Thorn" in the preface to *Don Juan,* for Byron's own writing takes on some of the very qualities of the thing it mocks, becoming itself (in Byron's words) like Wordsworth's piece, "a preface or note (I forget which)." The issue of contiguity with difference is pursued further by Graham in a long, subtle, and widening reflection on the role of "Southey" as the fictional composer of "The Isles of Greece," and the contiguity of Byron and the Lakers is compellingly brought home in a long sleight of hand in which a description of a Byronic passage (which the reader is teased into recognizing but cannot quite place) turns out to be an account of a passage from the renegade Southey's *Letters from England*.

Although this parallel-hunting is conducted with the nicest discrimination, yet, very occasionally, the declared imperative of

"Don Juan" and Regency England to read the times "from within their own discourse or code" (p. 1) seems to falter, as if the writer, willy nilly, were taking sides with one "code." It is a Byronic prejudice in these essays, for instance, to use the word "Tory" pejoratively of Southey, as if we all agreed that Southey was indeed an apostate laureate of what we all recognize as that deplorable ideology called "Toryism." Of course that is how the "liberals" and the "radicals" would like the word to be read. But in a study of this kind one might ask from within the Tory "code" whether Southey's *Essays Moral and Political* do not have as much to argue in terms of realizable politics in their day as (say) the unfulfillable (and unfulfilled) rhetoric of Orator Hunt. It seems facile to write off a poet as a "Tory" because he was a no-good apostate like Edmund Burke, or Byron's false heir, Benjamin Disraeli. Of course, what needled Byron was the charge that really it was himself who was a "Tory" at heart and an "apostate" from revolutionary principles. This was Lady Caroline Lamb's accusation in *Glenarvon*, and Graham is at pains to show how Byron rewrote *Glenarvon* in *Don Juan* to clear himself from the taunt. But what exactly is the difference between Byron's mobility (his ambivalence, his irony) which are now terms of critical praise, and "apostasy," which is a term of critical abuse? At least the earlier generation of writers (the Lakers) had believed (for awhile, perhaps naively) in an inspirational cause. It is something which is no longer there in the wartime culture and the post-war depression of Regency England. Byron's cynical mobility is extreme—is it symptomatic of one aspect of his age? One moment he is hot for the Luddites, the next abandons all interest in the practicalities of industrial reform; he is up for Major Cartwright and parliamentary reform, then regrets that the yeomanry cavalry had not sabred Hunt at Peterloo; he admires Napoleon as a superman, then dismisses the emperor as a renegade to his own greatness; Byron the revolutionary Carbanaro ends by "spitting" on the movement as pusillanimous. In the wake of revolutionary failure he writes (of the mobility of things): "I have seen crowns worn instead of a fool's-cap," but he would be well aware that something in those words applied to himself. He wore a coronet (if not a crown), and in composing *Don Juan* ("Black letters upon

foolscap") he too had adopted the motley guise of a bard who hovered, he said, "between fool and sage." It is not surprising, therefore, that Lady Caroline Lamb's charge that he lacked fixity of principle cut to the quick and that he should turn the full power of aristocratic disdain against the apostate Lakers. Attack is the best form of defense. But he is an anti-monarchical revolutionary who sneers at his democratic opponents for marrying milliners, a "friend of the people" who is, self-admittedly, as proud as Satan of his rank.

The other major issue of contention between Byron and the Lakers which Graham considers concerns Byron's "cosmopolitanism" as preferable to their "provinciality": "I wish they would change their lakes for ocean," wrote Byron. But, as with the argument over apostasy, on close examination, within the weft and warp of Regency culture, Byron's cosmopolitanism begins to look far more provincial than his satiric dichotomy would admit. Even the foreign cantos of *Don Juan* are, essentially, about England, and provincially about Byron's domestic affairs—*domestica facta*—he punned (in a rejected epigraph), turning the cosmopolitan discourse of classical Latinity to a joke about himself and Annabella Milbanke. The very words of foreign tongues are continually appropriated by English pronunciation, so that Don Juan himself is half an Englishman (and part Byron himself) even before the poem brings him "home." Developing the argument in a passage of penetrative exposition, Graham shows how a character from "provincial" Southey's *Letters from England* is recreated in John Johnson, Juan's English, paternal *alter ego,* so that, even in the exotic Turkish seraglio, domestic connection with the "tight little island" two thousand miles away is maintained. Indeed, *"Don Juan" and Regency England* provides the most persuasive argument yet for Byron's ramshackle masterwork possessing, after all, a master plan, or, rather, an organic imperative which brings the reader and the poet inevitably to Norman Abbey—back to the provinciality from which Byron originated.

Although Norman Abbey is not provincial in quite the same way as Grasmere, yet it has none of the cosmopolitan status of a Versailles or a Vienna. It is *rus* in opposition to *urbs,* culturally carrying with it, in pedestrian satire, the Horatian/Popeian tradition of retirement away from the center of things. In moving to the country, therefore, *Don Juan*'s Horatian satire paradoxically has, deep down, much in common with Wordsworth's pastoral meditation in *The Prelude*. If I might intrude into the argument the kind of wide generalization that Graham's close analysis eschews, the Napoleonic war had cut off English society from "the continent" intellectually as much as "the Continental System" had divided Europe into two spheres of influence. Napoleon is the true cosmopolitan of the era, a Lycurgus to the civilized world, whose aim was to obliterate national divisions from the Channel to the Urals. He is the first European of the modern world, or the last Augustan. Such, at least, is the argument of his own memorials from St. Helena. "Regency society," on the other hand, becomes more and more turned in on itself, defining its Englishness (or Britishness) by a sense of place and of British history—hence the revival of Gothic architecture in the English country house, or works of literature such as *Mansfield Park, Waverley, The Prelude,* and *Don Juan*. If it be argued that Britain, at the same time, became a world empire—was not that empire the provincializing of the rest of the globe, Little England writ large in Indian or West Indian parish church and cricket club? Or, turn the mirror the other way, is not the Regent's own pleasure dome of Kubla Khan the most provincial of fantasies— a seaside pavilion at Brighton!

Byron at Ravenna, or Pisa, or even at Missolonghi, remains within the provinces even when most "cosmopolitan." Indeed, it is a sign of English provinciality that one should claim that being actually on "the continent" is taken by Byron as a sign of cosmopolitanism. But is Ravenna more than the Clacton of the Adriatic; Pisa the Aberystwyth of the western seaboard? Cosmopolitan Byron's self-congratulation adds up to very little more than that he has, like Pope's "young Aeneas," travelled "greatly daring." Compared with the intense, spiritually intellectual pilgrimage, shall one say, of even the parsonage at Haworth, how might one weigh Byron's claim to be a citizen of the world?

If there is a case to be made that the "provinciality" of *Don Juan* is informed by a true "cosmopolitanism" which distinguishes it from the Lakers, that wider dimension comes not from Byron's holidaying in foreign parts, but from the detritus of the poet's classical education—the fossilizing remains of the *communia* of a European culture. Graham is especially strong on Byron's appropriation of the classics, and *Don Juan and Regency England* in this respect is a model for the "educated reading" for which Marilyn Butler asked. It is an old argument that if you want to understand a text, you must grasp its literary context, but Byron has rarely been better analyzed from the basis of European classicism, whether that classicism is seen panoptically as part of the chronotopic structure of a poem endlessly ruminating upon change and similarity under the passage of time—*tempus edax rerum*—or whether the critical eye focuses closely on a phrase, like "Castalian tea," to tie together the story of the virgin who fled the embraces of Apollo with Byron's own loss of favor among the "fastidious literary nymphs" of London. (By the way, I wonder if Graham has missed the allusion to Oedipus's deformed foot in his analysis of Byron's retelling of the tale of Thebes at Norman Abbey.)

Perhaps the strongest "cosmopolitan" association of the poem is that which links Byron to Augustanism by way of Pope and his circle, and thus back to the *sermo pedestris* of Horace. This would be the wider "community of wit" of which Graham writes, uniting Byron's "immediate audience" of the "witty, worldly, well read, enlightened, liberal" humanists with the Scriblerians under Queen Anne, and Horace both in his "hot youth" and later reconciled (in some measure) to the new conservativism which followed Philippi (p. 25). If this is so (and Graham's case is compelling), yet does the circle of Hobhouse, Kinnaird, and Moore have the same weight as that of Harley and Bolingbroke, Pope and Swift, let alone that of the golden, but ambivalent, first Augustan age? The implication of Pope's satire is that the embattled cultural minority of which he is a part, is, none the less, both the repository of the best that has been thought and said, and close to potential centers of power. Pope's bust stands among the Worthies of the patriot opposition at Cobham's Stowe, his portrait hangs above the mantelpiece at Lyttelton's Hagley. Even at his most despairing, in *The Dunciad*, there is an immense potency in Pope, and in the power of the transformatory voice of his satire. In this, Pope is far more in possession of the magic rod of the traditional clown which, in Grimaldi's hands, reshaped the world (of which Graham writes so suggestively in his chapter on pantomime) than is Byron in the harlequin pose of *Don Juan*— "What, after all, are *all* things—but a *show?*" Pope is, ultimately, his own hero and makes his own "show." Byron's claim is that he cannot find a hero; and *Don Juan*, like Scott's *Waverley*, becomes a comedy of modern history in which the protagonist is not the maker of events, but accidental in the great tide of history. Byron's text looks forward to Auden's "all I have is a voice," whereas Pope is still truly part of a community of power in so far as he is sure of his place in European culture. Just as *Don Juan* is composed of the *bric a brac* of a decaying society, so too it is composed by the poet as part of the *bricolage* of an aimless peregrination. With Pope there is a center, both local (provincial) and cosmopolitan: the Palladian symbolism of Twickenham. Byron's Juan, like the poet, is a bird of passage at Newstead/Norman Abbey. As Graham concludes in his excellent book, there could be no conclusion to *Don Juan*, for that would be to betray the poem's "essence." Except that there is no essential center to be betrayed.

Varieties of Blasphemy: Feminism and the Brontës

Peter Allan Dale

Irene Tayler. *Holy Ghosts: The Male Muses of Emily and Charlotte Brontë.* New York: Columbia University Press, 1990. x, 342 pp.

In what surely is one of the most famous dreams in Victorian literature, Lockwood, the narrator of *Wuthering Heights*, sees himself alienated from a community of Christian worship and accused of the sin that "no Christian need pardon." This is the sin described by Matthew as blasphemy against the holy ghost: "All manner of sin shall be forgiven unto men: but the blasphemy against the Holy Ghost shall not be forgiven."[1] What makes blasphemy against the holy ghost so unredeemable is a question that has vexed theologians for centuries. For our purposes it is enough to recognize that denial of the holy ghost goes to the very essence of the Christian religion. It amounts to a rejection of that religion's claim to *comfort* (to use the key word) fallen humanity in its worldly tribulations. That Emily Brontë was acutely conscious of the consequences of transgressing the "First of the Seventy-First," as Lockwood's dreamed fundamentalist calls it, is evident in the story of Catherine and Heathcliff. Their insatiable desire for one another, which, of course, lends itself wonderfully to our most recent versions of psychoanalysis, is, in the conventional religious discourse Brontë so deliberately deploys at the outset of her narrative, the soul's pursuit of the comforting presence which has been denied. (The passive construction preserves me temporarily from specifying who is doing the denying, the characters or their creator.)

That not just Emily but all the Brontë children agonized over the unforgivable sin, and over the dangers of apostasy in general, is a fact of their writing which late twentieth-century academic readers tend to ignore, perhaps because we have come to regard apostasy, at least in religious matters, as an especially benighted occasion for anxiety. The word names, after all, the lamentable (and punishable) tendency to stray from the father of all Eurocentric canonicity. For the Brontës, however, apostasy in the traditional religious sense was the problem above all others which their art needed to engage. When *Villette*'s heroine Lucy Snowe describes what she is writing as a "heretic narrative,"[2] she means "heretic," as we will see, in the most profound imaginable sense. But no less important, her creator understands that Lucy's narrative extends and brings to a devastating conclusion a corporate project of dangerous writing embarked upon years before when she (Charlotte) and her siblings were children. They all in one degree and another wrote self-consciously heretic narratives—and worried about it in the way unforgettably enacted by Lucy's "insane inconsistency" (*Villette,* p. 495).

Some understanding of this, surely, has informed Irene Tayler's decision to announce her focus as *"Holy Ghosts."* A certain embarrassment over the excessively orthodox implications of such an announcement, as well as a desire for specificity, no doubt caused her to continue with, *"The Male Muses of Emily and Charlotte Brontë."* The addition tells us, first, that the Holy Ghost(s) may also be read in secular terms as poetic inspiration, and, second, that the gender of that inspiration is very much the issue. If we are troubled by the heterodoxy of "male" in this context (and we are meant to be), we are assured that we at least have in hand a substantial discussion of what should matter most to late twentieth-century readers of these writers: the peculiar conjunction of their religious, aesthetic, and sexual preoccupations. In this we are not disappointed, but, as I will need to indicate, neither are we entirely satisfied.

Tayler's introduction sets up two distinct theses. The first is that the Brontës' works (Emily's and Charlotte's; neither Anne's nor Branwell's is discussed) negotiate a crucial transition from Romantic visionary writing to Victorian realism, which is also a generic transition from poetry to novel as the period's dominant mode of literary production. The second is that in their works the

Varieties of Blasphemy

central thematic concern is the relation between gender and creativity.[3] There is a continuum between these two theses, but one of the problems of the book is that it takes a very long time before the continuum is articulated. What, in effect, happens is that the first thesis all but disappears from view as Tayler focuses with increasing exclusivity on the more topical problem, the place of gender in Emily's and Charlotte's conception of their muse and of what is not always the same thing, their holy ghost.

That a preoccupation with gender effectively swallows up the other critical project announced in the opening pages should not bother those who would have wished to pursue the fate of Romanticism in these sisters' poetry and fiction. This is partly because that fate is, albeit with difficulty, still discernible in the book and partly because it is, after all, a story already told by several competent hands (belated realization of which may, in fact, account for Tayler's relative loss of interest in the topic).[4] What should bother readers, however, is that Tayler has not chosen to adjust what looks like an original but bypassed rhetorical structure to accommodate what actually happens in the book. It should bother them because it is symptomatic of a problem that runs throughout the text and inevitably detracts from an original and provocative reading of the Brontës. Tayler needed to conceptualize not only her overall project but also her account of each phase of each sister's development far more sharply and to order her arguments far more economically before publishing.

The overall argument is briefly put. Drawing theoretically on D. W. Winnicott, Tayler begins with a model according to which the female or maternal element is "in effect one's ontological center," the source of one's being. The male element, which is secondary in the sense of coming after original being, is the desire to do and to relate to others, "pursuit, performance, possession" (p. 8). Applied to the Brontës, this yields the interpretation of Emily as an artist motivated, above all, by the desire to return to the maternal principle of being, Charlotte as one motivated, ambivalently but ultimately, by the desire to attach herself to the male principle of doing, and to participate in the "father world." This means that "in a sense" (the hedge is something we will need to return to), "Emily's position was more radically feminist than Charlotte's; to the end, Emily valued female being as the root and goal of her life. But it was Charlotte who insisted that women have the right to live as fully as men do, and that in order to act on this right, women must 'do' as men do, they must reach for what the world offers or represents, must move towards a God who is male in that He is not the origin but rather the destination of life's journey" (p. 10). Having established this fundamental demarcation, Tayler then divides the remainder of her book into two chapters on Emily, one on her poetry and one on *Wuthering Heights,* and four chapters on Charlotte, one on the juvenilia and poems, one on the first three novels, and, disproportionately, two on *Villette.* As Tayler argues her case through the complexity of actual texts, the "in a sense" persistently returns to disrupt the neat polarity of Emily, feminist poet of original being, *versus* Charlotte, novelist of paternalistic doing and relating, and that is a deep-seated problem with which we will have to contend.

There is a venerable critical tradition that situates Emily Brontë as a late Romantic and, in this fashion, distinguishes her from her prosaic Victorian sister. Tayler's reading of Emily is in effect a continuation of this tradition, brought up to date and transformed into an issue of gender. How this works I will come to in a moment. First, however, we need a working notion of what makes Emily so plausible a Romantic. Briefly, it is that she appears, with Blake, Wordsworth, Shelley, Hölderlin, Schelling, Fichte, et al., to be seeking to revise or re-envision Christianity as a secular mythology. She appears, that is, to be doing what M. H. Abrams has identified as characteristically Romantic. The great Romantics "measured their enterprise against the earlier revelation . . . , either as presented in the Bible itself or as represented by Milton or other Biblical poets; and they undertook . . . radically to recast, into terms appropriate to the historical and intellectual circumstances of their own age, the Christian pattern of the fall, the redemption, and the emergence of a new earth which will constitute a new paradise."[5] In these terms the principal female protagonist of *Wuthering Heights* is unquestionably a descendant of the Romantics. When we hear initially of the first Catherine, she is a child spontaneously appropriating the texts of the past, including the Bible, by writing her name and her story in their margins, trying, in effect, to displace them "not altogether for a legitimate purpose" (*Wuthering Heights*, p. 62). The first part of that story, one recalls, is of revolution against the rituals of "awful Sunday," and its visionary center is her dream, recounted by Nelly, of being cast Satan-like out of heaven and liking it: "The angels were so angry that they flung me out, into the middle of the heath on the top of Wuthering Heights, where I woke sobbing for joy" (*Wuthering Heights*, p. 121). From at least this moment on it should be apparent to the reader that the novel's title announces not simply a geographical space but a spiritual space as well, a sort of heretic New Jerusalem. As Sandra Gilbert and Susan Gubar have concluded, Catherine's creator is a female Blake, "that powerful son of a powerful father, in reversing the terms of Milton's Christian cosmogony."[6]

Tayler makes a still more appropriate connection. Emily, she says, is closest to Shelley among the Romantics. Shelley is the preeminently Platonic Romantic, seeking his earthly paradise ultimately in a love that takes us back again to the originary oneness or completeness that predates the disruptive division of humankind into male and female. Love, as he puts it,

is that powerful attraction towards all that we conceive or fear or hope beyond ourselves when we find within our own thought the chasm of an insufficient void. . . . We are born into the world and there is something within us which . . . thirsts after its likeness. . . . We dimly seem within our intellectual nature a miniature as it were of our *entire self,* yet deprived of all that we condemn or despise, the ideal prototype of everything excellent or lovely that we are capable of conceiving as belonging to the nature of man.[7]

And so on. The particular passage and the ancient concept it rearticulates in the Romantic era are familiar enough. Tayler's point, with which I agree, is that what Shelley here and throughout his poetry says about love as our "proper Paradise" Emily Brontë consciously echoes. Being cast out of the Christian heaven, Catherine understands very well, is the direct consequence of her Shelleyan desire for oneness with her male counterpart Heathcliff. Her famous expression of this heretical faith is close indeed to what we find in the Romantic poet:

> "Surely you and everybody have a notion that there is, or should be an existence of yours beyond you. What were the use of my creation if I were entirely contained here? . . . If all else perished, and *he* remained, I should continue to be; and if all else remained, and he were annihilated, the universe would turn to a mighty stranger. . . . My love for Heathcliff resembles the eternal rocks beneath. . . . Nelly, I *am* Heathcliff—he's always, always in my mind—not as a pleasure, any more than I am always a pleasure to myself—but as my own being—so don't talk of our separation again." [*Wuthering Heights*, p. 122]

Having made this connection between Emily and Shelley, Tayler takes the further step, inspired by Winnicott and probably by Jacques Lacan as well (p. 105), of identifying this desire for oneness with another with a need to return to the mother. The Romantics' lost origin, in other words, is now gendered, and I think not just metaphorically. It is not always easy to find a clear statement of position in this book, but the following excerpts from what is meant to be an account of the common theoretical thrust of Emily's poetry and her novel will serve to indicate how Tayler is thinking.

> The principle that orders Emily's fictional world is certainly not a "rational" one . . . : it is that Catherine and Heathcliff derive from a single source that was divided long ago. [That originary principle may seem lost in the novel]. . . . But [it] is not lost in Emily's poetry. . . . [There] she renders with great poetic richness the treasured content of memory, the maternal "Being" that is the object of her faith. [pp. 74–75]

But though the maternal origin may seem lost in the novel (a point Tayler concedes in deference to J. H. Miller's deconstructive reading of *Wuthering Heights*, to which I will return), it is "in a sense"—that recurring hedge again—"not quite lost in the novel either. . . . Indeed Romantic poetry's focus on the transcendent realm was precisely what Emily carried over into Victorian fiction" (p. 75).

Varieties of Blasphemy 287

Tayler is, in fact, doing with Emily what Gilbert and Gubar were doing with her, namely, feminizing her putative Romantic rebellion, but with a difference which reflects the space between an earlier feminism bent on directly assaulting the patriarchal ideology (in robust Blakeian/Bloomian style) and a much more introspective postmodern feminism preoccupied rather less with what can be gained than with what has been (perhaps irretrievably) lost. Nowhere is the difference within the common pursuit more apparent than in Tayler's startling conclusion that *Wuthering Heights* is "a monumental suicide note" (pp. 103–04). Is this the "sense" in which Emily is the more "radical feminist" of the two sisters? It certainly is the direction in which Tayler's logic is headed, and one wonders how carefully she has considered the implications of her position.

The problem with Tayler's reading of *Wuthering Heights*—and it is a problem shared by Gilbert and Gubar, and virtually everyone who reads Emily Brontë as a belated Romantic—is an excessive identification of Catherine and/or Heathcliff with their creator. *Wuthering Heights* with its several narrators and deliberately unsettling narrative structure is a dialogic text, perhaps the most self-consciously so in early Victorian fiction. Critics have long understood this. Why, one wonders, do so many fail to consider the possibility that one of the most important things being decentered by the text is the Romantic ideology? Why does the book persistently call forth judgments such as this: "Surely the authentic Emily Brontë does not believe that real love can be exemplified by this couple [Hareton and the younger Catherine], so oblivious to the primitive forces that underlie life. The authentic Emily Brontë who wrote the masterpiece we return to is the creator of Heathcliff, vibrating with energy, and Cathy, scorning the pusillanimous Edgar to cry across the moors to her demon lover"?[8] This "classic" reading by Thomas Moser happens to be based on a simplistic (and profoundly masculinist) reading of Freud, but it is characteristic in its "monologizing" of the novel by assuming that its "authentic" voice is the one that reveals and celebrates the "primitive force," the "vibrating . . . energy" of Catherine's and Heathcliff's passion. What it discounts, in the interests of deploying its own belated Romantic ideology, is the framing and ironizing of that passion by the voices of several narrators, and, of course, the repetition and deliberate socialization of the love story in the second Catherine and Hareton (a second Heathcliff).

Another reading of the novel finds in Catherine and Heathcliff's story an exposure of the "void" (the word, we recall, is Shelley's) at the center of the Romantic ideology of love. It sees in the protagonist's all-consuming passion the narcissistic pursuit of what is ultimately an image of self ("Nelly, I *am* Heathcliff") and finds at the end of that pursuit not some ultimate peace and completeness but violence, death, and ultimately disintegration. In such a reading the "authenticity" of romantic passion is ultimately an illusion, constructed over an absence of love, and the function of the several narrators (Nelly, Isabella, Lockwood) is to ensure that the reader does not make the mistake of taking either Catherine or Heathcliff or the "ideal" of the two of them in "primal integrity" as the authoritative center of the story. Miller's deconstructive interpretation, alert as it is to the rhetorical evasions of Romanticism, helps us understand this. "The sense [in the novel] that there must at some time have been an original state of unity is generated by the state of division as a haunting insight." But, in fact, "in the unresolvable heterogeneity of the narration" we find the "clue" that our "intuition of unitary origin" is, after all, an illusion "created by figures of one sort or another."[9]

Where Miller's reading fails us is in his characteristic focus on the figuration or, as he also calls it, Nietzschean (i.e., decentered) repetition that masks the abyss. But what Emily calls upon us to do, surely, is to confront the horror of the abyss itself. If there is one thing inescapably authentic about the world of *Wuthering Heights*, it is the evocation of a moral chaos one has difficulty not naming radical evil. *Wuthering Heights* is, it seems to me, deliberately imagined as a version of *Lear,* an exploration of a world in which love is denied and distorted at the very heart of what we want to believe is our ultimate source of emotional and moral security, the family.[10] It traces that denial and distortion from the child to the adult where it issues in a "moral poison" (*Wuthering*

Varieties of Blasphemy

Heights, p. 153) of unmitigated aggression (ultimately in the very name of love) that threatens to undermine all possibility of social order. The anticipation of the late and un-Romanticizable Freud is as striking as anything one finds in Victorian fiction, and its ultimate question is that put by Isabella as she finds herself bereft of the securities of civilization in the midst of Wuthering Heights' ever-intensifying "family romance." "How," she pleads to Nelly, "did you continue to preserve the common sympathies of human nature when you resided here?" (*Wuthering Heights,* p. 173). The prospect of a world in which there is no sympathy, no common feeling between people, is for Isabella, as for Emily, the prospect of a world without hope.[11] It is the prospect, the "promis'd end," that Shakespeare contemplates in *Lear,* and it terrifies Emily no less than it does him. Her reaction is to hedge it round with the sane, if impotent, words of Nelly and, finally, to seek to correct it with, as it were, a version of *The Tempest,* as the second Catherine reclaims Hareton for civilization by way of civilization's great art of writing.

It is, as I have indicated, common for critics to trivialize so bourgeois a closure. We have seen this in Moser above; it is implicit in Miller who certainly has not liberated *Wuthering Heights* from the Romantic ideology only to deliver it to another figure of orthodoxy. From the point of view of feminism, things are much the same, whether in Gilbert and Gubar's (now) more conventional distress at the dutiful daughters who take over in the end or in Margaret Homan's avant-garde regret for the second Catherine's acquiescence in the "symbolic order," the "textuality" of the "patriliny."[12] What these several readings—Freudian, deconstructive, old and new feminist—will not acknowledge is the distinct possibility that the "defenses" Emily erects against, alternatively, the primal forces of nature or the unfigurable void may be authenticated by her decidedly unbourgeois exposure to those forces, that void. "Hold them cheap," one is inclined to quote, "May who ne'er hung there." Emily is a late, but doubtful Romantic. She shares the Romantics' skepticism over a Christian ideology that too narrowly confines our human desires and aspirations. But she, not unlike Thomas Carlyle, to whose *Sartor*

Resartus her *Wuthering Heights* bears certain significant resemblances, has also seen the potential for chaos within the Romantic revolution and sought to hem it in.

For Tayler, again, the question of Emily's Romanticism is ultimately the question of her feminism. What the novelist is doing in *Wuthering Heights,* accordingly, is "figuring" her "spirit's progress from female completeness into gender division and then (through death) back to female completeness" (p. 110). To demonstrate that Emily is essentially Romantic amounts, for Tayler, to demonstrating that she is "radically" feminist. This, of course, puts the present writer in a rather awkward position. By denying the essentially Romantic nature of Emily Brontë's masterpiece, by arguing, indeed, that the novel deliberately critiques Romantic desire, I am implicitly, it seems, denying her feminism. This, as it turns out, is an implication I have no difficulty accepting. I do not believe the novel or, for that matter, the earlier poetic work, which Tayler strains to relate back to the loss of the mother, is feminist in any important way—that is, any genuinely revolutionary sense.[13] The awkwardness of my position lies in the imputation this places me under of seeming willfully unsympathetic to the feminist presuppositions from which Tayler approaches her subjects. This, as I hope to show, is far from the case. My difficulty is not with Tayler's feminism but with what strikes me as an almost willful misapplication of it to the wrong sister. Emily has written a heretic narrative, but not, I think, the kind of heretic narrative Tayler (not to mention Gilbert and Gubar, Homans, and many others) want her to have written.

Tayler's view is that Charlotte Brontë was hopelessly disabled for the feminist revolt against the law of the father. "It was as if the sisters had divided the parents between them. If Emily's imagination was bound up with the mother, Charlotte's was equally bound up with the father. Patrick Brontë stood at the center of Charlotte's life, and her yearning toward him was the source of lifelong problems for her, both as woman and as artist" (p. 110). There is certainly truth in the notion of Charlotte's fixation on the father, literal and figurative. But it is, in my reading, precisely the effect of that fixation, the recognition of its debilitating claim

Varieties of Blasphemy

on her capacity to love and to write, that impelled her gradually towards what may well be the most powerful statement of female frustration and the need for feminist rebellion to come out of Victorian England.

We need not rehearse again here the saga of Charlotte Brontë's obsession with masterful men, whether expressed in her own life by her attraction to her father, Patrick, her employer, M. Heger, Thackeray, George Smith, or in her fiction, by her heroines' love of William Crimsworth, Edward Rochester, Robert Moore, Paul Emanuel.[14] What we do need to do is to recognize the fact that she became increasingly self-conscious about and ultimately tormented by her dependency on male love. I have elsewhere explored the religious sources of her anxiety. In that context I argued that there is ample justification for believing that in the face of Pauline injunctions against substituting worship of the creature for the creator (Romans 1:25), repeatedly alluded to in her fiction, Charlotte actually feared for her immortal soul.[15] That fear reaches a crisis in the last novel where it issues in what are perhaps best called anti-visionary experiences that punctuate the narrative—epiphanies, that is, of irremediable exclusion from the heavenly consolation she had been taught to look to as compensation for earthly deprivation. Thus after intense sexual longing, Lucy Snowe experiences an "avenging" dream: "Indescribably was I torn, racked and oppressed in mind. Amidst the horrors of that dream I think the worst lay here. Methought the well-loved dead, who had loved *me* well in life, met me elsewhere, alienated: galled was my inmost spirit with an unutterable sense of despair about the future. Motive there was none why I should recover or wish to live" (*Villette*, pp. 231–32). The condition "envisioned" here of being, in effect, excluded from the communion of spirits recalls Catherine's dream of being cast out of heaven by the angels. The cause of the casting out or exclusion is probably the same in both cases: the excessive love of man, or again, preference of the creature over the creator. If we turn to the third sister, Anne, we find that her remarkably frank (and insufficiently appreciated) portrayal of the breakdown of a Victorian marriage in *The Tenant of Wildfell Hall* turns on the same issue. " 'You don't love me with all your heart,'" complains Arthur Graham to his wife, Helen, who replies, "'I will give my whole heart and soul to my Maker if I can and not one atom more of it to you than He allows. What are *you,* sir, that you should set yourself up as a god, and presume to dispute possession of my heart with Him to whom I owe all I have and all I am.'" The consequences of the excessive love of man are no less present to this novelist's imagination than to her sisters'. Trying to keep her frustrated admirer Gilbert at bay, Helen engages with him in what amounts to a dialogue on the relation between sexual love and salvation. "'We shall meet in heaven. Let us think of that,' said she, in a tone of calm desperateness. . . . 'But if I am so changed,' [he responded], 'that I shall cease to adore you with my whole heart and soul, and love you beyond every other creature, I shall not be myself. . . . My earthly nature cannot rejoice in the anticipation of such beatitude, from which itself and its chief joy must be excluded.'"[16] The conflict of love and religion, specifically the Pauline prohibition against not simply sexual self-expression but also the far more serious sin of worshipping strange gods, preoccupies all three sisters, and in surprisingly similar terms. Clearly they debated the issue, interpreted and reinterpreted the relevant biblical texts, and designed their fiction around the temptation to idolize the creature and its consequences.

I cannot here develop properly the distinctions between the sisters' treatment of this common concern. Briefly, each is imaginatively exploring how far she can rewrite the Christian conception of the holy ghost into an *erotic* comforter sent from a more beneficent deity than Paul, for example, allows. Emily goes farthest and would have gone still farther had she lived, for conventional as the love closure of *Wuthering Heights* has seemed to modern readers, her contemporaries would hardly have failed to note how careful she was to exclude any suggestion of Christian authorization for Catherine and Hareton's love. On the contrary, Christianity insofar as it is present at all in the book is present only as a degraded or impotent belief.[17] Anne, on the other hand, is the most religiously conservative of the sisters, as the passages above suggest. Still, it is difficult not to see in Gilbert's objections to the coldness of disembodied heavenly love a rather convincing case against sexual repression—more convincing, indeed, than Helen's insistence upon it. Charlotte's position is somewhere between those of her sisters, and vastly more complex than either's. What makes it more complex is that superimposed upon the fundamental conflict between love and religion is another sort of conflict that becomes increasingly prominent as she develops as an artist. This is the struggle between love and female independence. Being mastered by a man comes to mean the threat, as it were, of two sorts of blasphemy, the one we have been discussing against god the father, and the one we now need to turn to against god the mother.

What we may call the feminist, as opposed to the religious, problematic emerges early on in Charlotte Brontë's fiction. In the Angrian tale "Mina Laury" the intelligent, imaginative, but pathologically self-effacing Mina, a prototype of Brontë's recurrent female protagonist, is the devoted mistress of the masterful, and unattainable, Duke of Zamorna. At the end of the story, enfolded in Zamorna's embrace, Mina experiences a revelation about herself. "Strong-minded beyond her sex, active, energetic, and accomplished in all other points of view, here she was weak as a child. She lost her identity. Her very way of life was swallowed up in that of another."[18] In one novel after another Charlotte will situate her heroines in just this double-bind: in the midst of enjoying the male mastery they long for (and for which they endanger their immortal souls) they find they sacrifice the "identity" of their sex. The subtext of every succeeding novel, that is, the text that underlies and continuously interferes with the love story each explicitly tells, is, essentially, how a woman can be "strong-minded" enough not simply to love beyond the bounds of Christian orthodoxy but also to preserve her gender identity within the love she risks so much to achieve.

Most of the first novel, *The Professor*, is taken up by the narrator hero's efforts to free himself from the "convenances" that inhibit his romantic, and specifically sexual, desires. The boarded-up window in his room, which prevents him from watching the demoiselles in the garden ("the unseen paradise")[19] below and which he vigorously attempts to penetrate as soon as he is left alone, nicely epitomizes the problem that preoccupies Charlotte.

But in addition to love William Crimsworth needs a vocation and financial independence. Disenfranchised and déclassé at the story's outset, he must find his own way in the world and establish his own social identity. As Taylor observes, there is a significant "gender inversion" going on here. Charlotte is letting a male protagonist enact desires and expectations she is not yet ready to attribute to a woman. Yet at the novel's close she makes a very interesting gesture in the direction of correcting the inversion. Crimsworth's wife Frances, who has always seemed to need nothing so much as male mastery, turns out to have a double nature. A hidden side of her personality emerges as she interprets the portrait of the woman loved by the most powerful and attractive man in the book (a prototype of Rochester). "'I am sure Lucia once wore chains and broke them.... I do not mean matrimonial chains ... but social chains of some sort. The face is that of one who has made an effort, and a successful and triumphant effort, to wrest some vigorous and valued faculty from insupportable constraint; and when Lucia's faculty got free, I am certain it spread wide its pinions and carried her higher than—' she hesitated" (*Professor,* p. 284). Lucia is, of course, a heroine in another story, a story Brontë does not yet have the courage to tell; but Frances's evident identification with her plight speaks volumes for her and her creator's awareness of what the convenances are suppressing besides sexual desire.

The Lucia story does not get told in the next novel. Although Adrienne Rich has found in *Jane Eyre* a "feminist manifesto" and has insisted that not marriage but sexual equality is the goal of Jane's pilgrimage, Charlotte's preoccupation with freeing her heroine from religious prohibitions on her capacity to love all but obscures the feminist plea for sexual equality.[20] The story is still essentially a romance, and it is virtually all Charlotte can do to construct the psychological conditions under which Jane and Rochester can worship Eros without offending Christ, a consummation, which she probably does not finally achieve.[21] After the "reader, I married him" and the paragraphs celebrating ideal love, she cannot help but bring St. John Rivers (and his namesake St. John the apostle) perversely back for the last word: "'even so, come, Lord Jesus!'" (*Jane Eyre,* p. 477). Why? The

Varieties of Blasphemy

obvious answer is that she has not, in fact, been able entirely to liberate herself from the Pauline strictures on love he, above all her novelistic creations, seeks to enforce. They remain leftover, unenclosable by the romantic plot. But conceivably there is more to it than this. St. John, whatever the religious implication of his closing appearance, is also the man who has dedicated himself not to love but to vocation: he is a "pioneer" who works "amidst rocks and danger." He "labours for his race; he clears their painful way to improvement; he hews down like a giant the prejudices of creed and caste" (*Jane Eyre*, p. 477). Is not Charlotte here, as with the disruptive insertion of Lucia's portrait at the end of *The Professor*, obliquely acknowledging another desire, another kind of story beyond romance, that needs telling?

Whatever the answer, the story does get told in the next novel. On the very opening page of *Shirley*, Charlotte announces that she is not writing "anything like a romance" but something "real, cool, and solid."[22] And though the story ends not just in one but two marriages, the institution of marriage is put in question in this novel as nowhere else in the Brontës' works. Is happiness in marriage possible? asks Shirley. No; affection dies, passion is a "mere fire of dry sticks," and in marriage one can no longer be one's own mistress: "terrible thought!—it suffocates me!" (*Shirley*, pp. 223–24). As others have observed, *Shirley* is Charlotte's "condition of England" novel taking us back to "the beginning of this century" (*Shirley*, p. 39), and to revolutionary class conflict between masters and men in the Yorkshire mills. But it is clearly asking us to engage another sort of social problem and revolutionary need as well. The social/political condition that comes to dominate this story is, unquestionably, the "condition of women." As she had written to her publisher when asked about the next book project after *Jane Eyre*, "I often wish to say something about the 'condition of women' question.... One can see where the evil lies, but who can point out the remedy?"[23] In her eponymous, androgynously named heroine Shirley, she tries to envision the remedy. Shirley, like St. John Rivers, "labors for [her] race," she "clears their painful way to improvement" (*Jane Eyre*, p. 477), but she is motivated by a very different religion. "'Men of England! look at your poor girls, many of them fading around you, dropping off in consumption or decline; or, what is worse, degenerating to sour old maids . . . because life is a desert to them. . . . Fathers! cannot you alter these things? Perhaps not all at once; but consider the matter well when it is brought before you, receive it as a theme worthy of thought; do not dismiss it with an idle jest or an unmanly insult'" (*Shirley*, p. 378).

Shirley comes to us liberated, ideologically ready-made. The spiritual pilgrimage that is the center of all Charlotte's plots is undergone by the novel's other heroine Caroline Helstone. Caroline is Mina, Frances, Jane, redux, but with a revised quest. Like her predecessors she has her spiritual crisis—"What was I created for . . . ? Where is my place in the world?" (*Shirley*, p. 180)—and, like them as well, her sense of selflessness is, at least initially, understood as a phallic need, a need for male love. But at the moment of her crisis the likely male fades into the background, and she finds instead the manly woman Shirley, who spends the remainder of the novel initiating her into the mysteries—a word we will need to consider further—of female self-sufficiency. But in the terms Tayler invites us to use, through Caroline's pilgrimage Charlotte (whose name, of course is a version of Caroline), displaces the eroticized holy ghost of *Jane Eyre* with a feminized one as the object of the soul's (heretical) desire.

Tayler is hardly unaware of the feminist story being told here—it would be extremely difficult to miss—but so committed is she to the formula, Romantic Emily/female principle *versus* Victorian Charlotte/male principle, that she cannot properly measure the immense step Charlotte has taken. In effect, she discounts it as inauthentic: "Even in this proto-feminist book Charlotte seems to have been prepared to attribute 'genius' rather to the male than to the female: men have it, women marry it. . . . [The two heroines] share a common fate; each achieves her goal not so much in herself as in her marriage" (p. 181). There are two responses one wants to make to such a reduction of *Shirley's* complex narratorial situation. The first and more obvious is to point out that although marriages do, in fact, close the story, they do so in ways deliberately aimed at keeping in question the value of that institution and the settled social order it is meant to stand for. Charlotte has great difficulty surrendering Shirley in particular to her future husband: she was "exquisitely provoking; putting off her marriage day by day, week by week, month by month. . . . It had needed a sort of tempest-shock to bring her to the point." And when she at last arrives, Charlotte's metaphors speak for themselves: "There she was at last, fettered to a fixed day: there she lay, conquered by love, and bound with a vow" (*Shirley*, pp. 591–92). Caroline goes more willingly to the altar, but one needs to read carefully the promises associated with her betrothal and what becomes of them. Robert will, he says, use his industrial power and capital to solve social problems, to aid the "houseless, the slaving, the unemployed" *and* to finance a school where Shirley and Caroline can teach together (always for Charlotte and Emily the one realistic possibility of female independence). But in the event, the narrator tells us several years on, Robert's prophecies were only "partially" fulfilled. What is conspicuously absent from the reformed world is Shirley and Caroline's school (*Shirley*, pp. 598–99). One goes back to Robert's closing words to Caroline upon sealing the marriage agreement—"I shall take you in" (*Shirley*, p. 598)—and notes that there is more than one way to read them.

Beyond indicating the instability of the novel's romantic closure, one must emphasize the presence and force of its feminist center, which the combined "clash" of wedding bells and the bells of national military triumph (*Shirley*, p. 598) simply cannot obscure. Julia Kristeva makes the point that it is the nature of an avant-garde text to compel us to register what is repressed even as it reinstates the repressing conditions. This is true of *Shirley*: too much has been released to contain. As Shirley herself says of her youthful "devoir" on female independence, "I never could correct that composition" (*Shirley*, p. 460). *Shirley* is, indeed, an avant-garde text and advanced in a way that Kristeva in particular would appreciate. The heart of Charlotte's feminism, in the end, is not the political case Shirley makes for equality between the sexes. It is, rather, a far more radical quest for an entirely new mythology, a quest parallel to that which, we have seen, Abrams situates at the base of European Romanticism, but in this case aimed at empowering the distinctly female imagination. Caroline's deep, secret, anxious yearning is "to discover and know her mother" (*Shirley,* pp. 200–01). This desire exceeds the missing literal mother and seeks, ultimately, a mystical originary Mother. In Kristevan terms, "The mother reemerges as the archetype of the infinitely interchangeable object of the desiring quest."[24] Caroline's guide to the mystical mother is, again, Shirley, and their intensest moment of religious transcendence occurs, at virtually the exact midpoint of the novel, in a chapter announced significantly as one "Which the Genteel Reader is Recommended to Skip." The space in which Shirley instructs Caroline is pastoral or Edenic, outside culture and specifically outside the Church with its "clash of bells" (*Shirley,* p. 313), to be repeated, as we have seen, at the novel's close. What she instructs her in is a new version of Milton's—and behind Milton, the Bible's—myth of the first woman, Eve, in which the female descends equally with the male from God and at the very least shares equally with the male in the generation of humanity: "'The first woman was heaven-born: vast was the heart whence gushed the well-spring of the blood of nations; and grand the undegenerate head where rested the consort-crown of creation'" (*Shirley,* p. 315).

The revolutionary gesture goes deeper still. If we look at the repetition of the Eve myth later in the novel in Caroline's *devoir* (embedded in chapter 27) and ask ourselves why, after all, it needed repeating, we find the likely and intriguing answer is, to bring out the difference between envisioning and writing a new mythology.[25] In its later context the *devoir* draws extraordinary attention to itself *as language* in contrast to its earlier presentation as spontaneously experienced vision—"I saw—I now see—a woman-Titan" (*Shirley,* p. 315). It is introduced by Shirley's reading of St. Pierre's text "Fragments de l'Amazon," the alien language of which presents a difficulty. The *devoir,* itself a kind of rewriting of St. Pierre's language in Shirley's own (female) language, is then not read, but declaimed from memory by Louis Moore in French which the narrator again translates in order to make it "intelligible" to her English reader. At the climactic moment in the text, the epiphanic moment when the despairing Eve calls for and receives guidance from a "Comforter," that comforter has no language but manifests itself as a "tone" beyond language: "She heard as if Silence spoke." Finally the *devoir*

Varieties of Blasphemy

ends on the problem of language: "Who shall, of these things, *write* the chronicle" (*Shirley*, pp. 458–60; my emphasis). What it seems to me Charlotte is confronting, as she closes this extraordinary novel, is the paradox of having to cast one's revolutionary vision in a received linguistic code that, in fact, functions to suppress that vision. In the Kristevan terms that Charlotte appears precociously to anticipate, the "semiotic" or pre-linguistic impulse of the "chora" presses against the resistance of and seeks to transform the "symbolic" system of the father.

> Then, the symbolic covering (constituted by acquired knowledge the discourse of others, and communal shelter) cracks, and something that I call instinctual drive . . . rides up to destroy any guarantees, any beliefs, any protection, including those comprised by the father or professor. An aimless drifting ensues that reconciles me to everything that is being shattered—rejecting what is established and opening up an infinite abyss where there are no more words. [*Desire in Language*, pp. 162–63]

If I am reading the novel correctly, if the problem of reimagining the biblical religion of the father is its pre-eminent project, and if this problem is finally thematized as a problem of language—specifically, the problem of writing a language whose origin is Evean, not Adamic—then it seems fair to conclude that Charlotte offers us an extraordinarily sophisticated exploration of the situation of women. We begin the novel with a pathetic collection of Victorian clergymen speaking like "presumptuous Babylonish masons" in their "'confusion of tongues'" (*Shirley*, p. 46). We end with the new "Levite" of industrial society, Robert Moore, having constructed a "mighty mill, and chimney ambitious as the tower of Babel" (*Shirley*, p. 599) over the green world in which Shirley and Caroline experienced their revelation of the great Mother. Framed, as it seems, by varieties of oppressive phallic babble, Charlotte's story strives to imagine a purer language.

What Tayler is doing with Charlotte Brontë's last novel *Villette* is extremely puzzling. She appears to want somehow to mitigate her hitherto pretty relentless masculinization of this novelist:

in *Villette* Charlotte "redeems" her patriarchly repressed imagination (p. 202) and "repudiates" St. John's (Tayler means St. Paul's) "injunction against female speech" in the previous novel (p. 289); in Lucy Snowe "Eve and the Virgin Mary are merged" into a triumphant resurrection "of all womankind" (p. 283). How does all this happen? It is not easy to be certain, but it appears that it comes as the result, remarkably, of a return to Christian orthodoxy. The masterful male of the novel, Paul Emanuel, is symbolically "revealed as the Lamb of God" (p. 283), and in this new form Charlotte's heroine can submit herself to him without betraying her female principle.

Whatever one may think about this way of vindicating Charlotte's claim to consideration as a feminist, one is bound to take exception to its implausible effort to make the novelist come out triumphant and transcendent in this last and most tormented of her fictions. Indeed, one is hardpressed to think of a more depressing novel in British fiction before the advent of Thomas Hardy. The novel, again, is a "heretic narrative." *Jane Eyre* had concluded in a heresy of sexual love, Rochester being unquestionably preferred to the divine father; *Shirley*, in a heresy of feminism, the divine mother, being (in my reading) preferred to both earthly and divine fathers. The heresy of *Villette* runs deeper still; it inscribes the ultimate sin of which Lockwood dreams, the sin not of re-making the holy ghost in more liberal, more humanly, womanly terms, but of denying its presence altogether.

What *Villette* is about, in a word, is despair. Writing to Ellen Nussey in the midst of composing the novel, Charlotte gives a fair indication of the impasse to which her life had come in the latter half of 1852 and which her fiction can no longer imaginatively transcend: "My life is a pale blank and often a very weary burden, and the future sometimes appalls me" (*Charlotte Brontë*, p. 508). The fundamental rhythm of *Villette* is of repeated expectation, both sexual and feminist, repeatedly frustrated. I had leisure to look at my life, says Lucy at the close of the first stage of her pilgrimage: "I found it but a hopeless desert: tawny sands, with no green field, no palm tree, no well in view. The hopes which are dear to youth, which bar it up and lead it on, I knew not and dared not know" (*Villette*, p. 228). Frances, Jane, and Caroline all look on this same desert in the course of their stories, but they get beyond it, by virtue of Charlotte's still resilient imagination. With Lucy there is no progress beyond this empty vision; it is simply repeated over and over without difference. In the second phase of the narrative there is the possibility of romance with Graham Bretton, but it issues again in a "blank": "That goodly river on whose banks I had sojourned, of whose waves a few reviving drops had trickled to my lips, was bending to another course: it was leaving my little hut and field forlorn and sand-dry, pouring its wealth or waters far away" (*Villette*, p. 378). The possibility not so much of romantic as of intellectual or spiritual fulfillment, fixed on Paul Emanuel, motivates the last third of the story. But, like his obvious prototype M. Heger, Paul Emanuel deserts the heroine at last. Far from being about the redemption of the imagination, *Villette* is about its dangers. It is the "demon" that constructs the "idol" hope, which must constantly betray Lucy (*Villette*, p. 232). And to return to the specifically feminist point, far from envisioning the resurrection of "all womankind," the novel announces the collapse of that hope and, more specifically still, of the notion of *écriture féminine* that underwrites it. The experience of acting in the school play, Charlotte's metaphor for female aesthetic self-expression in this novel, does, indeed, momentarily "reveal" a distinctively female "voice"— "my tongue . . . got free, and my voice took its true pitch." But, one needs to note, that voice sounds but once and is silenced forever: "I put . . . by [my new-found faculty], and fastened [it] in with the lock of resolution which neither Time nor Temptation has since picked" (*Villette*, p. 211).

At the "center" of Lucy's "inward conflict" finally is "silence" (*Villette*, p. 541), and it is silence that metaphorically dominates the novel's close. Hope, as Brontë well knew, lies at the very foundation of Christian faith. Paul, perhaps more than any other single biblical authority, insists upon this: "Now the God of hope fill you with all joy and peace in believing, that ye may abound in hope, through the power of the Holy Ghost" (Romans 15:13). For Lucy to conclude that "Hope is a false idol" is, as Paul's words indicate, to sin against the holy ghost, to utter, again, the unforgivable blasphemy.

At the age of eleven Emily Brontë sewed into a sampler these words from the book of Proverbs: "Every word of God is pure: he is a shield unto them that put their trust in him. Add thou not onto his words lest he reprove thee, and thou be found a liar."[26] This was a critical text for all three sisters. As the constant quoting and putting in question of biblical words throughout their fictions serves to bring home to us, each was, in one degree or another, self-consciously engaged in the rewriting of God's word, self-consciously courting and, as we have seen, committing blasphemy. Emily's "lie" (in the Proverbian sense) was undoubtedly revolutionary, but not nearly so revolutionary as Charlotte's. In Charlotte the struggle with the word of God is, by the writing of *Shirley*, radically feminist. No doubt precisely because she put such excessive faith in the "shield" of the paternal word, both human and divine, she felt so acutely and resented so deeply its unreliability. But what one needs further to recognize is that for Charlotte, even the prospect of a feminist re-writing of the word of God and the consequent liberation at once of her imagination and tongue, could not, in the end, blind her to a still more radical insight, that imagination itself was a delusion and all language a "confusion." It is an insight that marks, as decisively as anything we have in the mid-nineteenth century, the need for a new departure, at once postChristian and postRomantic.

Notes

1. Emily Brontë, *Wuthering Heights* (Harmondsworth: Penguin Books, 1963), pp. 65–66. The biblical reference is to Matthew 12:31.
2. Charlotte Brontë, *Villette* (Harmondsworth: Penguin Books, 1979), p. 235; see also my "Heretical Narration: Charlotte Brontë's Search for Endlessness," *Religion and Literature,* 16 (1984), 18–22.
3. *Holy Ghosts,* pp. 1, 6. Hereafter cited parenthetically.
4. See especially Jay Clayton, *Romantic Vision and the Novel* (Cambridge: Cambridge Univ. Press, 1987), which seems to have significantly influenced Tayler's conception of her project.

5. M. H. Abrams, *Natural Supernaturalism: Tradition and Revolution in Romantic Literature* (London: Oxford Univ. Press, 1971), p. 29.

6. Sandra M. Gilbert and Susan Gubar, *The Madwoman in the Attic: The Woman Writer and the Nineteenth-Century Literary Imagination* (New Haven: Yale Univ. Press, 1979), p. 255.

7. Percy Bysshe Shelley, *Complete Works* (London: Gordian Press, 1965), VI, 201.

8. Thomas Moser, "What Is the Matter with Emily Jane? Conflicting Impulses in *Wuthering Heights*," in *The Victorian Novel: Modern Essays in Criticism*, ed. Ian Watt (Oxford: Oxford Univ. Press, 1971), p. 197.

9. J. Hillis Miller, *Fiction and Repetition: Seven English Novels* (Cambridge: Harvard Univ. Press, 1982), p. 68.

10. Besides the name of Heathcliff, which one may argue alludes to the setting of the most famous scene in *Lear*, there is a conspicuous allusion to the play at the outset of the novel: an "indefinite depth of virulency [that] smacked of King Lear" (p. 59).

11. Charlotte's reading of *Wuthering Heights*, which is often dismissed as insensitive, echoes Isabella's yearning for "common sympathies": "The single link that connects Heathcliff with humanity is his rudely confessed regard for Hareton Earnshaw . . . ; and then his half-implied esteem for Nelly Dean. These solitary traits omitted, we should say he was . . . a man's shape animated by demon life—a Ghoul" (*Wuthering Heights*, p. 40).

12. Margaret Homans, *Bearing the Word: Language and Female Experience in Nineteenth-Century Women's Writing* (Chicago: Univ. of Chicago Press, 1986), pp. 80–83.

13. Tayler is convinced that Emily never recovered from the loss of her mother Maria. Emily's latest biographer Katherine Frank, however, writes, "It was only Charlotte who had any memory of [her mother]. . . . In later years, Emily could summon no recollection or even half dreamt-up impression of her at all." *A Chainless Soul: A Life of Emily Brontë* (Boston: Houghton Mifflin, 1990), p. 35.

14. See, e.g., Karen Chase, *Eros and Psyche: The Representation of Personality in Charlotte Brontë, Charles Dickens, and George Eliot* (London: Methuen, 1984), pp. 7–24.

15. E.g., Jane describes her love for Rochester: "He stood between me and every thought of religion. . . . I could not, in those days, see God for His creature: of whom I had made an idol" (*Jane Eyre* [Harmondsworth: Penguin Books, 1966], p. 302); or again, Mrs. Marchmont in *Villette* thinks of her dead lover "more than of God; and unless it be counted that in thus loving the creature so much, so long, and so exclusively, I have not at least blasphemed the Creator, small is my chance of salvation" (p. 101).

16. Anne Brontë, *The Tenant of Wildfell Hall* (Harmondsworth: Penguin Books, 1979), pp. 217, 409–10.

17. In chapter 30 we learn that the Established Church in Gimmerton has

evidently closed down from lack of interest, leaving parishioners only the chapel's fundamentalism, satirized by Emily in the figure of Joseph, to satisfy their religious needs (p. 326); in chapter 32 Emily gives us a memorable image of Joseph's Bible overlain by "dirty bank-notes" (p. 346).

18. *The Juvenilia of Jane Austen and Charlotte Brontë*, ed. Frances Beer (Harmondsworth: Penguin Books, 1986), p. 297.

19. Charlotte Brontë, *The Professor* (Harmondsworth: Penguin Books, 1989), p. 97.

20. Adrienne Rich, "*Jane Eyre:* The Temptations of a Motherless Woman," in *Critical Essays on Charlotte Brontë,* ed. Barbara Timm Gates (Boston: G. K. Hall, 1990), p. 148.

21. See my "Charlotte Brontë's 'Tale Half-Told': The Disruption of Narrative Structure in *Jane Eyre,*" *Modern Language Quarterly,* 47 (1986), pp. 126–29.

22. Charlotte Brontë, *Shirley* (Harmondsworth: Penguin Books, 1985), p. 39.

23. Winifred Gérin, *Charlotte Brontë: The Evolution of Genius* (Oxford: Oxford Univ. Press, 1967), p. 352.

24. Julia Kristeva, *Desire in Language: A Semiotic Approach to Literature and Art,* trans. Gora, Jardine, and Roudiez (New York: Columbia Univ. Press, 1980), p. 195.

25. Gilbert and Gubar believe the second rendering of the Eve myth "differs drastically from [the first] . . . since this alternative myth countenances female submission" (p. 394). In fact, the second rendering of the myth chronologically (if not textually) precedes the first rendering and therefore presents a problem as evidence for Charlotte's/Shirley's move *towards* conventionality after presenting the first version of the myth. But beyond this my own reading of what is happening in the *devoir* makes me skeptical of any use of it to undercut Charlotte's feminism.

26. Winifred Gérin, *Emily Brontë: A Biography* (Oxford: Clarendon Press, 1971), p. 20. The reference is to Proverbs 30:5–6.

Contributors

SUSAN ALBERTINE is Assistant Professor of English at Susquehanna University.

ELIZABETH AMMONS is Professor of English and of American Studies at Tufts University.

MILTON J. BATES is Professor of English at Marquette University.

D. S. BREWER is Emeritus Professor of English and formerly Master of Emmanuel College at the University of Cambridge.

GEORGE CORE is Editor of the *Sewanee Review*.

PETER ALLAN DALE is Professor of English at the University of California, Davis.

PHILIP C. DUST is Professor of English at Northern Illinois University.

JANET RAY EDWARDS is Faculty Associate at the Institute for Writing and Thinking, Bard College Center.

L. M. FINDLAY is Professor of English at the University of Saskatchewan.

NORMAN FRUMAN is Professor of English at the University of Minnesota, Twin Cities.

D. C. GREETHAM is Professor in the Ph.D. Program in English at CUNY Graduate Center.

JAMES M. HAULE is Professor of English at the University of Texas-Pan American.

VIRGINIA HYDE is Associate Professor of English at Washington State University.

MALCOLM KELSALL is Professor of English at the University of Wales, Cardiff.

MONA LOGARBO is Assistant Editor at the Middle English Dictionary at the University of Michigan.

BRUCE MICHELSON is Associate Professor of English at the University of Illinois at Urbana-Champaign.

JOHN R. PFEIFFER is Professor of English at Central Michigan University.

ALAN RICHARDSON is Associate Professor of English at Boston College.

ILAN STAVANS is Assistant Professor of Modern Language and Comparative Literature at Baruch College.

FREDERICK C. STERN is Professor of English at the University of Illinois at Chicago.

RONALD STRICKLAND is Assistant Professor of English at Illinois State University.

SUSAN J. WOLFSON is Professor of English at Princeton University.